RELIGIOUS OBJECTS AS PSYCHOLOGICAL STRUCTURES

MOSHE HALEVI SPERO

RELIGIOUS OBJECTS AS PSYCHOLOGICAL STRUCTURES

A Critical Integration of Object Relations Theory, Psychotherapy, and Judaism

The University of Chicago Press
Chicago and London

Moshe Halevi Spero (M.S.S.W., Case Western
Reserve University; M.A., Ph.D., University of
Michigan) is associate professor in the School
of Social Work and the Postgraduate Institue of
Psychoanalytic Psychotherapy of Bar-Ilan University
and senior clinical psychologist and Research
Scholar in Psychoanalysis and Religion at the
Department of Psychiatry, Sarah Herzog Memorial
Hospital, Jerusalem. He is a member of the Israel
Psychological Association, Israel Association of
Psychotherapists, and the American Psychological
Association, Division of Psychotherapy.

The University of Chicago Press, Chicago 60637
The University of Chicago Press, Ltd., London
© 1992 by The University of Chicago
All rights reserved. Published 1992
Printed in United States of America

00 99 98 97 96 95 94 93 92   5 4 3 2 1
ISBN (cloth): 0–226–76939–9

Library of Congress Cataloging-in-Publication Data

Spero, Moshe Halevi.
    Religious objects as psychological structures:
A critical integration of object relations theory,
psychotherapy and Judaism/Moshe Halevi Spero.
        p.   cm.
    Includes bibliographical references and index.
    1. Judaism and psychoanalysis.   2. Jewish
law—Psychological aspects.   I. Title.
    [DNLM: 1. Judaism—psychology.
2. Psychotherapy.   WM 460.5.02 S749r]
BM538.P68S63   1992
296.3'875—dc20
DNLM/DLC
for Library of Congress   91–845
                                            CIP

To my Grandmother
Belle Goldfarb Spero
(1899–1990)

Of musical notes and anecdotes;
and
wit and wisdom as antidotes

ולי מה־יקרו רעיך אל
מה עצמו ראשיהם
אספרם מחול ירבון
הקיצתי ועודי עמך
תהלים קלט:יז־יח

How weighty also are Your thoughts to
me, O God!

How great is the sum of them!

If I would count them, they are more in
number than the sand;

Were I to come to the end of them,
I would still be with You.

Psalms 139:17−18

Contents

Preface

I propose to outline a theoretical contribution to a problem recently revisited by Freud historian Peter Gay (1987): the lack of reconciliation between religion's approach to the reality of the image of God (specifically, Judaism's view), on the one hand, and psychoanalysis's (and, more generally, psychotherapy's) view of religious experience and the image of God, on the other hand. That is, I wish to examine a particular type of object representation, namely, the object representation of God (or, what in the jargon would be known as a divine "object") and its facets as a psychological and religious structure. For such an examination to aspire to any degree of success, a careful outlining of the points of view of psychoanalytic psychotherapy, Judaism, and the history of their intersection is required.

Putting aside Gay's dubious thesis that the evolution of psychoanalysis depended in great degree precisely upon Freud's atheism, his short essay usefully highlights several Jewish views on psychoanalysis—including the views of two or three "devout" Jewish psychologists. It becomes quickly apparent, unfortunately, that few have grappled directly with religion's and psychoanalysis's divergent views on the nature of the reality of the image of God. Furthermore, the literature evinces neglect, and sometimes apparent unawareness, of the fact that a completely meaningful reconciliation between psychoanalysis, psychotherapy, and religion (and Judasim in particular) requires comparison not merely of their general values, but primarily of their technical concepts, linguistic structures, and change methodologies. Thus, even congenial and otherwise sophisticated syntheses offered by the psychoanalytic community, such as the works of Ana-Maria Rizzuto (1979), the late Paul Pruyser (1974, 1983), W. W. Meissner (1984), and, most recently, Stanley Leavy (1988), leave us wanting on this account. Only if it is accepted from the start that Judaism and psychoanalysis can contribute reciprocally to each other in an efficacious and explanatory manner is there any value in seeking such reconciliation. The present text is an effort to provide a model for such dialogue.

Before leaving port, I wish to express my appreciation to a number of persons who have contributed significantly, over the years, to the sharpening of my thinking on the ideas that have taken their present form in this monograph. Chief among this group are my parents, may they live and be well. They shall always be a cherished mainstay. Yet, unquestionably, the present work could not have been undertaken, let alone completed, without the continued enabling love and support of my beloved wife, Yehudit. She alone rides closest to the eye of the hurricane—a fellow traveler at the summits and in the depths.

As in the past, Henry Charles Romberg, M.D. continues to be the first reader. Many thanks are also due to Zanvel Klein, Ph.D., a very special friend, who procured texts of great value to me. It is with unestimable sadness that I note Zanvel's untimely death during the period of this writing. His passing as if from between our tightly clasped hands came as a great shock—some of us did not clasp tightly enough; some of us, too tightly. The present text is perhaps *the* work that I'd have liked for him to have read; something with a new level of maturity, and something to argue about. May his memory be for a blessing.

Thanks are also due to the members of my in-house seminar on object relations theory (1988–90) at the Department of Psychiatry, Sarah Herzog (formerly Ezrath Nashim) Memorial Hospital, with whom some of the ideas contained herein were initially soundboarded. In this regard, I wish to acknowledge my very unique relationships in the hospital with Clinical Director of Psychiatry Ilya Averbuch, M.D., Ph.D., Chief Psychologist Gabi Shefler, Ph.D., and former Medical Director, Professor Haim Dasberg, M.D. I gladly note among this group the warm collegiality and friendship of Professor Ruben Schindler, former director of the School of Social Work at Bar-Ilan University. I am deeply grateful to Senior Editor T. David Brent of the University of Chicago Press, who since 1987 encouraged the evolution of this text, and to Ms. Kathryn Kraynik, whose important editorial suggestions persuaded and prevailed by virtue of her thorough comprehension of my argument.

I express continued gratitude to the American Friends of Sarah Herzog Memorial Hospital and an anonymous benefactor whose special endowment for this project has enabled so many kinds of fruitful exploration.

I am grateful to Bar-Ilan University Press for permission to reprint material drawn from my essay, "Current Trends in Psychotherapy, Clinical Social Work, and Religious Values: A Review an Bibliography," *Journal of Social Work and Policy in Israel* (1989), 2:81–110; to the American Psychological Association, Division 29 (Division of Psychotherapy), and Donald K. Freedheim, editor-in-chief, for permission to reprint material and figures 1, 3, and 5, which originally appeared in my essay, "Parallel Dimensions of Experience in Psychoanalytic Psychotherapy of the Religious Patient," *Psychotherapy* (1990), 27:53–71; to the Washington School of Psychiatry and David Reiss, editor, for permission to reprint material and table 2, which originally appeared in my essay, "Identity and Individuality in the Nouveau-Religious Patient," *Psychiatry: Interpersonal and Biological Processes* (1987), 50:55–71; and to Collins Fount, publisher, for permission to reprint page 169 from *Mister God, This Is Anna* by Fynn, © 1974.

Warm and deeply felt thanks are extended to the Michigan and Cleveland psychoanalytic communities within which I have found so many important teachers. I note particularly Elizabeth Daunton, psychoanalyst formerly at Cleveland's University Hospitals–Hanna Pavilion Child Psychiatry. Our formative relationship began with her sensitive discussion of my first clinical psychoanalytic presentation in 1977 of the treatment of a religiously oriented patient. And special thanks are due Donald K. Freedheim, Ph.D., a consistent patron from the first university lecture in child psychology to the last hour of psychoanalytic supervision eleven years later.

A final reflection: At similar moments throughout the ages, rabbinic scholars customarily prefaced their completed works with exquisite, multitiered poems and songs through which they expressed their gratitude to God, Creator of all things. It is distinctly possible that the entirety of this text is my vehicle. As such, it has a major shortcoming. I have attempted here to envision God through His myriad voices and awesome presences, yet I have cloaked my yearning and my awe under mechanical terms and the *legerdemain* of psychological scholarship. Just how much has remained hidden I would not venture to say, but, as Brierley warned, "The form of any hypothesis is always influenced by unconscious determinants, since we can only apprehend things in ways permitted by the specific structure of our individual minds" (1951, p. 96). Surely, my own unconscious God representations, and my relationship to these, must have found some form of expression through the particular kind of schematic structure I have constructed here. I am too inhibited to dare more and must pray that my elementary wonder might some day find more full expression and more personal form.

Introduction

Once self-reflection in the form of psychological study of the self becomes the whole atmosphere in which a person lives, there is no end to it since the person's psychic life is not yet Being itself, but only a place where Being is envisaged. There is a dangerous tendency in psychotherapy to convert the psychic actuality of an individual into an end in itself. The person who turns his psyche into a god because he has lost both world and god finds himself standing finally in the void. . . . Psychological self-reflection can never achieve that which only becomes possible through a surrender to Being.

KARL JASPERS (1963, P. 809)

The theoretical approach presented here shall regard the development of intrapsychic representations of relgious objects and beliefs and the impact of these representations on the philosophy and process of psychotherapy. The approach to be outlined seeks to enhance our understanding of the psychological development and meaning of religious experience and beliefs and to provide a new model of the *parallel dimensions* of relationship among persons and between persons and God. For ease of discussion, I will refer to interpersonal (human) relationships as *anthropocentric* and to the relationships between persons and the object of religious worship (God) as *deocentric*. These two dimensions overlap, yet they are also unique, the one not reducible to the terms of the other.

At the same time, this study is an attempt to wean clinical work with the religious patient from certain prevailing psychological ideologies or clinical assumptions. I have in mind those ideologies which tend to denude psychotherapy of its intrinsic relevance to the spiritual dimension of human experience. The proposed model is an aid to bringing forth the inherent potential of contemporary psychology and psychotherapy to address the religious dimension.

This is intended to be a hard-minded study. By this I mean that it does not purport to *replace* contemporary psychology or psychotherapy with a distinctly culture-bound portrait of human development that translates modern conventions and discoveries into idiosyncratic terms and then abandons contemporary conventions. I do not seek another homespun "Torah psychology" that priorily denounces the whole of modern psychology and its monolithic knowledge base, nor a pseudo-scientific "spiritual" psychology couched in holistic conceptions where anything goes. I am unsympathetic to earlier studies that attempted to unseat the "psyche" that only so gradually had come to be understood, or that rejected out of hand any value in the central concepts of contemporary dynamic psychiatry and psychology. With exceptionally little justification (and, occasionally, with almost paranoid vituperative), useful contemporary concepts were supplanted with constructs borrowed from didactic theological literature, such as "spirit," "heart," "evil impulse," "higher will," and so forth. If there was no risk of inadvertently overvaluing this kind of approach, I'd say it reflected an exaggerated misinterpretation of Descartes's notion, "the soul is easier to know than the body"! None of these transplantations, in addition, offered much practical insight of psychotherapeutic value.

Instead, I advocate a kind of "settling down" with the fact that psychology, psychotherapy, and basic religious beliefs represent methodologically distinct but essentially related attempts to understand and express fundamental aspects of human relationship. Yet, in order to make this assertion nontrivial, one is pressed to show how each might actually expand and enhance the other's perspectives in practical as well as theoretical ways. That is, it is critical at this point of the psychotherapy-religion dialogue to work with the empirical as well as valuational aspects of the two, despite the traditional, naive protest that religion is nonempirical and scientific psychology nonvaluational. Laor's recent reflections on the dialogue portray the logjam succinctly:

> When there is a clash between religion and science, it could be avoided by maintaining that the statements made within one of the fields are devoid of any empirical reference and that they could be endorsed as merely useful propositions . . . *Such an intellectual maneuver may cost science its informative content and religion its objects;* both lose their moral force. (1989, p. 212, emphasis added)

And if as a result the patient feels that his account of reality has not been given its just due by the therapist, the patient is not likely to acknowledge his neurosis or transference-motivated attitudes (Stone 1981, p. 720). We are in search, in other words, for more than a hermeneutic. But what could be empirical about the contents of religious belief? My own response shall become explicit below.

Chief among the areas where psychology has yet to put forth a useful contribution to religion is the conceptualization of the image of God in a manner that is compatible with the outlook of religion. By "image of God" I mean more than a static cognitive or ideational structure. Rather, one would be dealing with the nature of the important, emotionally idealized images or *object representations* that occupy human attention and interest and the process of internalization by which such images are taken in, projected outward, and related to. And inasmuch as religion views God as an *objective* (that is, real) aspect of reality, it anticipates from psychology some method for schematizing veridical object representations of God, a representation not confused with other types of representations that are modeled upon interpersonal relationships. I believe psychology can provide such a model.

In the course of interrogating the extant theories and developing our alternative model, I will need to discriminate between two sources for human representation of the image of God. The term "anthropocentric" will be used to refer to all mental representations regarding the image of God whose source is primarily (we shall no longer say "obviously") based upon the dynamics of interpersonal relations. The term "deocentric" will be used to refer to all mental representations regarding the image of God whose source we wish to construe hypothetically as drawn primarily from direct or semidirect interaction with an *objective* God or the manifestations of such an objective God. My qualifying that the source of even this *second* form of representation is only "primarily" and not wholly rooted in unique human-God interactions is not mere pedantic equivocation, but in fact relates to an important theoretical issue to be clarified in the text. In light of this distinction and as a general convention, I shall use the phrase "god representation," with "god" written in the lowercase, when referring to representations, images, or concepts of primarily anthropocentrically derived structure, and the phrase "God representation," with "God" written in the uppercase, to discriminate those singular types of representation whose structure (hypothetically) is primarily deocentrically derived. The adoption of this convention is not intended to pass any particular form of judgment upon the net theological value of the object or content of any specific religious godhead. My sole concern is to create a useful tool for speaking about the image of God that may bring psychological and religious languages closer together without doing violence to the basic tenets of either system.

Certainly, psychology tends to focus upon relationship among persons whereas religion focuses upon the relationship between humans and God. Yet their languages can be cross-applied, enabling each to contribute uniquely to the other's comprehension of its main object. Potentially, this interrelationship becomes even more intimate if one adopts the hypothesis that psychological processes have an inherently religious nature or quality. According to such a hypothesis, in its most desirable form, religious concepts would be conceived of as having a unique, specifiable psychological identity, and psychological concepts, structures, and mechanisms as having an intrinsic religious identity. I shall present a halakic metapsychology that expresses this possibility. Of course, the mere construction of a metapsychology does not in and of itself magically render our work scientific (see Edelson 1988). It is intended to help generate models through which the psychological structure of religious thinking and experience can be conceptualized and further explored. Although the model I shall use to illustrate the relationship between human and divine object representations emanates from the specifically Judaic ontology and its ethicolegal system of behavior (Halakhah), it can accommodate readily the ontologies of other faiths.

1 | Psychology and Religious Belief at the Watershed

The aboriginal religious experience, whether related to God in or beyond the world, always conceives Him from the purview of his relation to reality. The white light of divinity is always refracted through reality's "dome of many-coloured glass." No worshipper has ever isolated the idea of God from the concrete world, and placed it in some immaculate transcendental sphere. The religious experience is a composite phenomenon involving not only God but the ego and the sensuous environment of the homo religiosus. . . . *Ostensibly, religion, though flowing in the deepest subliminal ego-strata, is an eternal quest for spatialization and corporeal manifestation.*

—Joseph Dov Halevi Soloveitchik
(1944a [1986], pp. 46, 69)

The present monograph is based upon the culmination of almost two decades of clinical observation, theory building, and cautious exposition of the intricate relationship between psychoanalysis, psychotherapy, and religious belief. As in the earlier researches, this monograph has both a philosophical focus—the synthesis of psychological and religious theoretical approaches to reality—and a practical or clinical focus—the management of religious issues that emerge during psychotherapy. Of course, the theoretical approach and the attendant model to be explored have not developed within a vacuum, for they draw upon certain prior assumptions and conventions even as they challenge other prior assumptions and conventions. Nevertheless, such research, and the tentative conclusions it permits, signify, among other things, a demonstrable readiness within the field for precisely this kind of revision and complex model building. I believe a summary retrospective on the earlier work will help establish a common context.

The "Religious" Patient

Before examining the earlier research, I would clarify that the focus of this study is not merely the formally religious person who elects psychotherapy nor his or her formal religious doctrines. It is more broadly interested in any patient for whom religious feelings, behaviors, language, and metaphors are relevant in some way to the individual's relationships with the objects of his inner and external world.

According to strict definition, the term "religious patient," representative of the group from which so many of my observations are drawn, refers to individuals who become engaged in some form of psychological intervention for any type of mental health problem and who also espouse some form of ideology or practice some formal ritual related to a special set of objects known as religious objects (god, totems, special forces or influences). Continuing with the strict definition, these beliefs and rituals initially may or may not appear related to the psychological difficulties for which such persons seek treatment.

To be more specific, one can further distinguish four subgroups of religious patients:

1. Devotees of the major religious or ethical value systems who, coincidental to their beliefs, happen to suffer from some mental disorder allegedly not enmeshed in the individual's overall religious lifestyle.
2. Individuals whose idiosyncratic religious beliefs and practices are,

on the main, the outgrowths of psychotic or otherwise disturbed psychological developmental processes.

3. Individuals whose mental disorder (for example, dissociative states) appears to be the direct result of pathological modes of attitudinal manipulation practiced by some figure or group, wherein the manipulative techniques and message are ensconced in religious terminology or lifestyle (see Clark 1979; Halperin 1983; M. T. Singer 1979; Spero 1982a).

4. Individuals who undergo for the first time in their lives a form of situational crisis, or who experience the resurgence of earlier symptoms as a result of mid-course changes in legitimate religious beliefs or lifestyles, and those adjusting to such changes; for example, converts, nouveau-religionists (*hozrim be-teshuvah* or *baʿalei teshuvah* in Hebrew; see Shaffir 1983; Spero 1987b; Witztum, Greenberg, and Dasberg 1990; Yogev and El-Dor 1987), and defectors from faith (Shaffir and Rockaway 1987).

These distinctions are useful in psychiatric and psychological practice and can be legitimized readily on a variety of phenomenological and dynamic grounds. And it is certainly the case that each group presents its own special treatment and ethical complications. However, careful consideration suggests that the relationship between psychological development, psychopathology, and religious belief is even more complex. Factors in addition to the mere advent of "mixture" play a much more significant role in assessing the quality of religious belief. These factors include, for example, the nature and quality of psychodynamic pathways of expression, cognitive-structural representations, and the level of internalization of emotional relationships surrounding the *objects* of faith. Each of these factors results from special processes of development, which may have special kinds of trajectories that depend not only upon the dynamics of these processes but also upon the way in which one defines the nature and qualities of their objects.

Nevertheless, the task remains challenging. The quality of an individual's religiosity may not be apparent at the early stages of psychological intervention. On the other hand, there are patients whose religious ideologies and metaphors are boldly expressed early on, even on psychodiagnostic protocols (Kehoe and Gutheil 1984; Lovinger 1984; Peteet 1981, 1985; Pruyser 1971; Spero 1987a, chap. 11; Wikler 1979). Even with such individuals, however, it is not immediately clear to what extent this "religious" material, and the inferences which may be drawn from it, reflect pathological or adaptive processes. From which kind or quality of religious material, one may rightly wonder, is the clinician and theory builder to draw in attempting to conceptualize the nature of the development of the image of God? Paul Pruyser expresses this dilemma well with the following question:

> Which data of experience are *religious* experience? Could it be that patients are giving us religious responses without our knowing it? And perhaps without their own conscious knowledge? There was a time when sexual references in language, action, and fantasy went unrecognized because the power of sexuality and the role of symbolism were not yet understood! (1960, p. 122)

Moreover, given the admixture of anthropocentric and deocentric kinds of imagery and metaphors from virtually the earliest moment of observation available to the objective researcher, how can the relative weights of these two dimensions be accurately assessed? Is it beyond the realm of possibility that the religious experiences and imagery of infanthood play a role in the maturation of the relationship between the human and an *objective* God and do not necessarily point to that which must be regarded as *essentially* ludic, immature, and transitional, and *never* objective? Is it not possible, therefore, that one errs fundamentally in assuming that infanthood feelings of oceanic wonder or oedipal awe, given the *relational* context in which these are customarily first encountered, cannot point to the existence of an objective God with whom humans enter into a relationship?

This text shall struggle with these questions throughout, but even at this point it is evident that the key issues cannot be resolved satisfactorily on objective grounds alone. Rather, a practitioner's ideology—for example, is God a subjective object or an objective object?—unavoidably frames the initial givens from which all further research extends. And such ideology exerts its influence no less upon the exquisitely sensitive process of psychotherapy.

In view of the above, I consider the concept of the "religious patient" to be of relatively little utility, even though everyone understands intuitively, more or less, what is intended by this term. The above clarification has now extended our interest to what, for convention's sake, I shall term "religious phenomena." Religious phenomena, including certain very specific structures known as religious objects, emerge or are experienced at various moments in an individual's life; they play a very special kind of psychological role and fill a special sort of psychological space, whether or not the individuals in whom such phenomena emerge conceive of themselves (or are conceived of by others) as adherents of formal religious doctrines or practices.

The subsumptive term "religious phenomena," in the strict sense, refers to any fantasy, belief, idiom, or practice that has as its object a representation (whether actively representable or not) known as God or is related to such an object representation. The strict sense includes so-called mature religious states featuring very abstract, depersonified god representations, but also includes states of extremely concrete, ritualistic, obsessive obedience to godlike presences or their totemlike physical representatives, where pathological emotion and behavior rule and the image of the particular deity object is practically imperceptible. For, although a god representation of some kind is barely evident in the latter, even its primordial form or presence is of special importance insofar as such representations produce states and ideologies which, overall, point to some object that may, in fact, have objective existence and other objective qualities independent of the level of representation it has been fated to achieve in the individual case. Furthermore, and contrary to philosophical custom, I believe it is not necessary to posit a specific kind of emotional or affective attitude toward this kind of object, such as awe, reverence, or worship, since, in fact, the entire gamut of emotions have been directed toward this object at one time or another. Of course, when the discussion turns toward the emotional relationship between humans and God, then the affective component of a divine object representation would be germane.

The value of a term with a broader sweep is brought forward by the clinical discovery of what Ahlskog (1985) terms "latent theologies" and what I have called "precursor religious objects" (Spero 1989, 1990a, 1990b), following the rationale of Anna Freud (1936, p. 80) and Hartmann, Kris, and Loewenstein (1946, p. 33). Both terms underscore the disposing nature of certain early childhood experiences and representations toward what may later take the form of adult theology or religious practices. Ahlskog highlights the return of childlike qualities in all forms of adult religiosity. My concept emphasizes that certain early, precursor objects may not adopt their "formal" religious character until much later in life, although they may wield an implicit and dynamic influence until then.

Rizutto (1974, 1976, 1979, 1982; cf. McDargh 1983) also argues that certain particularly suitable inner representations may, in some persons, develop further into what are recognized as explicitly "religious" objects, whereas the same representations, in other persons, may not so develop. To animate the point, whatever psychological mechanism "creates" or disposes toward the sense of God's beneficent paternalism in religionist A, or God's infanticidal nature for religionist B, may also create, in apparently nonreligious persons, a sense of divinelike omniscience concerning a naturally benevolent father, or a sense of an engulfing, ubiquitously hovering presence regarding a malevolent father. Thus, regardless of whether these latent or precursive psychological qualities ever succeed in achieving formal religious identity, their *religiouslike* influence endures. The clinical-empirical discovery of such phenomena adds to the inadmissibility of continued efforts to discriminate unilaterally between "religious patients," for whom religiously sensitive psychotherapy might be warranted and religiously relevant issues sought, *versus* "nonreligious patients," who might be treated without such sensitivity.

The above has direct implications for the parallel issue of "religious" versus "nonreligious" psychotherapists, including the often alleged need for "religious" practitioners to offer psychotherapy to religious patients. I have dealt with this topic in considerable detail elsewhere (1990a, 1990b) as part of the larger question of identification between religious patients and their therapists. In general, I have yet to encounter any satisfactory defense of this special need. Other than allowing, initially, for some ease of communication and comprehension of religious metaphors and ideas, I am impressed, with Pruyser (1971), that this special preference can as easily be a hindrance and complication (see Kahn 1985; Kehoe and Gutheil 1984). In fact, both the areas of alleged cultural or religious similarity between patient and therapist, as well as the subtle, unconscious biases of the nonreligious and the religious psychotherapist, represent vast danger zones.

The "Religious" Therapist

Following the above, I do not consider "religious" therapists to be a special class of practitioners. I would rather emphasize the fact that the same developmental factors and object-relational needs that underwrite the religious *process* and result in religious *phenomena* in the case of the patient exist in the therapist as well. Therefore, the therapist's cultural or religious beliefs are relevant to psychotherapeutic work because, after all is said and done, the therapist is a quantitative factor in the therapeutic process. This is so for several reasons.

First and most obviously, the therapist manipulates certain interventive skills which have a demonstrated influence on the patient's behavior. Second, the therapist's listening activities, including the manner in which he imposes linguistically coherent schema upon the patient's associations, reflect to some degree the therapist's world and not simply the patient's (Kris 1982; Lacan 1964, 1966; Spence 1982). Third, the psychotherapist operates out of explicit and implicit professional values that constantly influence the way he or she comprehends the patient's material and which occasionally put the therapist in opposition to the patient's beliefs at the deepest level of their abstraction and internalization. These values are perhaps least well understood and monitored when they are multiplied and intricately interwoven into the major themes of life, death, sexuality, love, power, play, trust, and hope (Bolgar 1960; Buhler 1962; Hoehn-Saric 1974; Leitman 1982; Lytton 1984; Levy 1976; Wile 1977).

As a fourth consideration, there has been, as an outgrowth of the important discoveries of the object relations school, an increase in the number of psychotherapies which emphasize the role of certain elements of the therapist's own personality as curative factors. An earlier version of this idea was expressed by Alexander's and French's (1946) notion of the "corrective emotional experience" and continues to be the philosophy of the existential schools (Boss and Condrau 1967; Bergman 1953; Krill 1974; May 1961; Sinsheimer 1969). Thus, whether the image of, or experience with, the therapist cures via the provision of an advanced form of friendship or is taken in by the patient as a "good" object or introject, whether the therapist must simply "understand" the patient or attempt somehow to contain the patient within the therapist's psychic structure, these avenues would seem certainly to increase the opportunities for the influence of the therapist's ideologies (Epstein and Feiner 1979; Fairbairn 1955; Guntrip 1961; Searles 1979).[1]

The above approach seemingly contradicts the tradition of "therapist incognito" and the role of professional neutrality, which were intended, among other things, precisely to block the clandestine influence of personal ideologies (Freud 1912). It is evident, however, that the incognito mask is more permeable than originally imagined.

To clarify matters, it must be acknowledged that even the offering to the patient of aspects of the therapist's personality is not modeled upon pure self-disclosure and sympathy. For it is not the therapist's personal beliefs and naive, idiosyncratic characteristics which operate as a treatment force, but rather his *analytically forged* and professionally calibrated personal characteristics. Tarachow (1963), following Buber, early on emphasized the therapist's very natural "basic object need" to take the patient as person, which the therapist must stifle in order to enable the patient to grow. The therapist's personality traits can only be utilized in therapy if they have completed a very rigorous smelting process.

Therefore, the psychotherapist undertakes a maximal and thoroughgoing self-analytical process, as similar as possible to the one to be implemented with one's patients. Ideally, this increases the likelihood that the therapist will be able to recognize and comprehend the manifest and deeper meanings of the patient's material. On the subjective level, it assures a more harmonious resonance of the patient's experiences within the therapist. It is problematic, however, that therapists' religious views and beliefs—or the lack of them—are typically *not* subjected to such analysis. In the absence of such analysis, in the case of therapists of similar cultural backgrounds as their patients, the dimension of putative cultural similarity occludes to the point of uselessness. Moreover, using the broad definition adopted in this text, whatever dimension of the therapist's "religious" dispositions escapes analytic scrutiny remains relatively unrestrained against taking direct and indirect expression during psychotherapy.

It is also the case that special forces unique to the psychotherapeutic process itself influence the religious beliefs of patient and therapist simultaneously. Whatever the nature and quality of the patient's or therapist's religious beliefs upon entering psychotherapy, these—or, more importantly, their underlying dynamic and object-relational structures—will be subjected to the impact of reshuffling psychic energies and other factors. Values that were relatively constant or dormant prior to electing psychotherapy now come under the creative sway of narcissistic reinvestments in the self, resistance, and the awakening of aggressive feelings in its wake, or the reassignment of feelings (including devotional feelings) following the development of transference. Some values will survive this activity while others will undergo minor to major modification. This will be the case especially when the patient's crises preceding psychotherapy have already initiated seismic activity in the areas of personality upon which religious feelings are predicated. Finally, to the degree that the therapist is not aware of the dynamic qualities of his or her own religious attitudes, subtle changes in the patient's beliefs are more likely to exert unmonitored influence upon the therapist's objectivity and freedom of movement in these domains.

During psychotherapy, then, religious values and practices are not merely incidental objects tossed about passively during a psychic storm, nor ought one to presume that these objects will settle where they may in the due course of the analytic process. *Religious objects and values are variously determined and plurivalent, such that neither therapist nor patient can artificially cordon them from the therapeutic process nor assume their constancy.* They cannot be expected to appear or remain solely in announced "religious" contexts. Nor, by the same token, ought religious material to be anticipated only among formally religious patients. Religious meanings and objects can be activated tangential to related issues, by association, by displacement, or by the alignment of unsuspected parallel plates of psychic structure.

This basic notion can be illustrated as in figure 1—which is intended only as a graphic schematization, satisfactory for the while, of

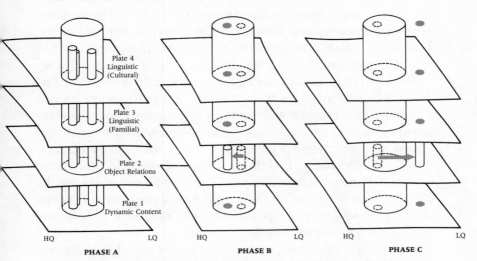

Figure 1   Cross-structural Change in a Religious Object Representation

the relationship among properties of any given religious representation, and not as a structural rendition of what a religious representation *is* like. For purposes of illustration, we will imagine a specific religious object representation (denoted by the cylinder in the figure), such as a paternally oriented god representation, heavily influenced or "corrupted" by the sadistic traits of an individual's actual (objective) father. Phase A in the figure illustrates a probable state anterior to the application of psychotherapy (or, for that matter, the advent of some crisis).

Like all representations, this representation in its fictive restive state is characterized by a certain dynamic content (plate 1), such as ideational or pictorial imagery related to one of the psychosexual/psychosocial developmental stages, weighted by some positive or negative valence of libidinal or aggressive affective tone or other relevant valence of the regnant drive states (for example, active/passive). Since the levels per se are not under consideration here, I have arbitrarily indicated the right-hand side of the plate as the lower quality (LQ) of the dimension in question and the left-hand side as the higher quality (HQ).

Such representations will also be characterized by a measurable, overall level of internalization and other object-relational qualities (plate 2), which bear upon such qualities as the degree of subjectivity/objectivity, externality/internality, and level of differentiation between representation of self and other that is achieved by the given religious representation. Furthermore, the very addition of a new plate reminds us that there will be an interaction between these two sets of factors and that this interaction will itself influence the net quality of the religious representation in some fashion. One may further imagine the influence of linguistic and expressive patterns drawn from the family circle (plate 3) and larger, cultural-linguistic configurations (plate 4), which include the important register of myth and legend. Of course, some of these plates may be subdivided for clinical purposes (for example, to distinguish the cognitive and connotative aspects of dynamic thematic material), and additional plates may be added. Moreover, in reality, these hypothetical plates do not overlap *strictu sensu* but are contemporaneous, and interdigitate functionally and, to a certain degree, structurally as well.

Once a significant change takes place within one of the relatively stable psychic structures schematized here by the four-tiered cylinder, at least two kinds of shift may occur. In the first (Phase B)—illustrated by the movement of the little cylinder within the larger cylinder—a subcomponent of the larger representation may undergo change, leading to related seismic changes at the level of other plates without, however, necessarily causing *major* change in the other plates. For example, when the focus of psychotherapy has activated an atmosphere that conduces the patient to discuss shameful feelings in a less inhibited way, which succeeds in reducing some of the dynamic conflict surrounding, say, the themes of exposure, looking, and being seen (plate 1), there may follow, in turn, an improvement in the level of internalization (plate 2) of some of the imagery hitherto associated with these dynamic themes. Specifically, the introject-level experience of an all-powerful, all-seeing, personified "eye of God" that almost literally follows the individual may submit to modifications taking place in other domains, slowly maturing into a more abstract, depersonified sense of divine providence or—I think it not fair to say "ultimately"—a sense of heightened moral self-awareness and conscience.

Another kind of change may take place (Phase C) when a subcomponent of the religious representation is in some way ablated, repressed, or otherwise dislodged in a major way from within the overall representation. Admittedly, this does not transpire readily, but it does occur frequently and takes expression in some of the more uproarious varieties of religious conversion, cultic religiosity, and in the sudden abandonment of religious ideas or belief in God. The reader should also observe that in the cases of Phases B and C, one could look downward from plates 4 *through* 1 as if they were transparent filters and imagine detecting an unaligned subcomponent that formerly occupied a specific lateral position on a given plate and, relative to that position, a specific position along the vertical axis among the other plates. By adopting this viewpoint, it would be possible to conceive of the different forms of transference-type overlay that might be cast upon unaligned or misaligned religious images or representations. This will be discussed more thoroughly in chapters 5 and 6.

Thus the pictogram in Phase C does not merely illustrate the collapse of a religious representation. It lends to our conceptualizing that, during such episodes, the broken-off or relinquished subcomponents of the original representation—be they the imagery, ideational, memory, or affective subcomponents—become free and, due to unbending principles of psychic economy, tend to seek out or become attached to other energy pools, memory configurations, and representational structures. Under some conditions during this kind of anaclisis, the new adopting structure may lend to the freed subcomponent some of the characteristics of the host structure (such as its level of internalization) or, under other conditions, the newly adopting structure may acquire characteristics of the former subcomponent. *From this small set of permutations alone it becomes clear how it is that so-called religious material*—and even a large quantity of unexpected material misidentified as *non*religious!—*may appear in contexts and time-phases that might not ordinarily predict or anticipate such appearances.* These conceptualizations expand considerably our understanding of what it means to say that as change occurs among the instinctual drives and human interpersonal object representations upon which religious values rest, or are modeled upon, some amount of change, often directly proportionate, can be expected in the kind or quality of religious values and in their level of internalization.

At junctures (which are next to innumerable) during psychotherapy where beliefs, meanings, values, and their attendant levels of internalization begin to change, the participants may begin to experience each other *subjectively* as less or more similar than initially supposed. After all, the patient's projections and displacements are, in the main, responsible for how the patient perceives the therapist, regardless of the therapist's true characteristics. These misperceptions encourage the development of transference upon which the bulk of therapeutic cure or change is based. Among such misperceptions will be various impressions regarding the therapist's ideology or belief. A therapist thus has no valid reason to ignore the study of how the patient apperceives the lack or presence, or the kind and quality, of religious feelings and attributes in the therapist and must conceive of ways to incorporate these themes into the therapeutic scope. For such perceptions on the patient's part, as I have labored to show, are neither extraneous nor erroneous in the simple sense, but reflect prevailing transference tendencies and other aspects of the patient's object relationships. As such, they will inform the therapist of the quality of the patient's inner experiences with religious and other objects. Furthermore, as will be discussed below, the patient's slowly increasing acuity for disentangling projections from more realistically based impressions and knowledge is itself a central tool for similar kinds of work with perceptions of God.

God-Oriented Religiosity

As I have chosen to speak in terms of "religious phenomena," a less strict sense of the term "religious" must also be noted. It is encountered in relation to experiences described variously as "spiritual," "cosmic," or "eminently other," from which, at the same time, the specific experience of a personalized god is excluded. This less strict sense includes extremely general, diffuse, nondescript, apparently objectless "spiritual" states, no matter how advanced or abstract their attendant philosophies. Speaking of the roots of religiosity in infantile psychological experiences, Freud himself commented, "One may rightly call oneself religious on the grounds of this oceanic feeling alone, even if one rejects every belief and every illusion . . ." (1930, pp. 64–65). The type of highly abstract, numinous spiritualities discussed by Erik H. Erikson (1959, pp. 64–65; 1982), Erich Fromm (1960), and Ira Progoff (1956), for example, specifically highlight the independence of these "mature" forms of religiosity from discrete concepts or images of God.

As shall be discussed further in the following chapters, I take the view that linguistic signifiers, terms, beliefs, idioms, or practices that are *not* related to an internalized God representation, no matter how "spiritual," oceaniclike, value-inducing, or humanistic their quality, ought to be regarded as *distinct* from beliefs that do embrace some form of God representation (although they are certainly related phenomena). McDargh (1991), therefore, wisely distinguishes between "God relational perspectives" and "faith relational perspectives," just as do Fowler (1981) and Kegan (1982). Faiths without God representations are sometimes considered more advanced than God-oriented religiosities, based, I think, on a mistaken understanding of the concept of internalization. That is, some writers presume that the higher the level of internalization of a perceptual object, such as the "image" of the object known as God, the more abstract will be the concept of God, up to the point where ideally *all* image-bound representation of God vanishes. But along with this may vanish certain important and valuable qualities of relationship, demand, commitment, affection, and so forth that are entailed by this object. I shall show that this portrait by no means indicates a necessarily higher achievement. In fact, one may contend that forms of religiosity *without* a God representation are only an aboriginal or precursor phenomenon and may indicate the failure to record or further utilize the kind of experiences or "registrations" (Laor 1989) that create that special space where God images are discovered, created, and rediscovered. In the light of this possibility, imageless religiosity ought not to be confused with forms of religious belief that revolve around some form of internalized God representation.

There is a philosophical and a practical reason for adopting this qualification, and, somewhat ironically, my own views force me to put aside the philosophical arguments in favor of the practical ones. Philosophically, there are those who believe that religious belief and feelings, simply by definition, require an internalized object known as God (McDargh 1983; Pruyser 1974; Spiro 1966). William James stated trenchantly that religious belief ought to be characterized by a certain "thickness," by which he meant the apperception of something "there" behind the belief (1897, p. 211), and something "more" than just consciousness of so-called religious experience (1902). At the other extreme, the ultimate object of the "numinous" kinds of religiosity promulgated by humanistic or existentialistic philosophies tends to be not God, but man. As Hans Küng criticized, "The question raised [by humanists Fromm and Adler] is about the function of *belief in* God, not about the *reality of* God. . . . What is important [for them] is not so much the affirmation or denial of God, of whom we know nothing, but the affirmation or rejection of certain human values" (1979, p. 115, emphasis added).

Nonetheless, even while cleaving to a God-oriented religiosity, one can accept the possibility that the *absence* of God from a person's "religious" worldview may be only apparent; that is, an extant God concept may be denied, repressed, or displaced. Second, even where a God representation does not exist at any level of personality, it remains of interest from the psychological and religious point of view to discover what impeded the development of a God representation. More than occasionally, this issue is of direct clinical relevance, such as when a suffering person who seems to crave a relationship with God is stymied in this area by the very factors that impair his or her interpersonal relationships. If, for the sake of argument, there is no such thing as God, then acquiring an interpersonally designed god image may or may not be of sustaining value and might, in principle, be entirely substituted for by other kinds of catharsis, relationship, objects, or abstractions. In principle, such a god ultimately might be jettisoned entirely, leaving no trace, and to no ill effect. However, if

God in fact exists, and if it is God that a person really seeks, then there can never be durable satisfaction through misidentifying God with substitutes—primitively totemistic or intellectualized and abstract.

Indeed, the very focus of this text is a prevailing psychologistic view which posits that even multidimensional, discrete god representations are a "function of a belief in God and not the reality of God." God representations themselves, according to this school, are attributed to psychic manufacture rather than to any actual form of interchange between a human and a veridically existing divinity. The fact that religionists believe in God, and have somehow built up psychic representations of this God, would not dent the psychologistic conviction that, in the final analysis, the religionists do not possess what they believe they possess (save the belief itself!). There is, evidently, no easy philosophical way to dismiss objectless spiritual systems from our purview.

Instead, I have adopted a practical consideration for concentrating primarily upon characterizable god representations: There are empirically demonstrable qualitative differences between god-oriented and god-less religious belief systems, including the different kinds of overlap each of these kinds of religious systems may have with general styles of interpersonal living. Insofar as these differences are often of clinical importance, we need a language for conceptualizing them.

I should like to bypass the thorny issue of whether religious phenomena strictly defined—namely, those related to a specific object representation of God—indicate greater or lesser emotional maturity and psychological achievement than the diffuse, abstract "spiritual" or "noetic" states of consciousness. Such analysis tends quickly to become bogged in faith assertions. On one hand, if an object such as God does not exist but rather is germinated out of remnant childhood perceptions and unsatisfied wishes, as Freud supposed, then no matter how sharply one chisels God's features, the final representation is a deus ex machina. In this point of view, God and the enterprise related to this image informs us only about man, as Küng declared. The religious phenomena bearing upon such an object might be considered, according to this view, creative sublimatory activities ensconced within an atavistic fantasy. One might sympathetically underscore the normal need for a special, unchallenged realm of illusion, but this leaves the uncomfortable feeling that a great deal of weight and responsibility is being shouldered by a mere illusion (this is exactly what troubled Freud). At any rate, it is often argued that one might expect the concrete imageries of this realm to eventually achieve more depersonified form because their fate ought to be no different than the representations of human objects in general upon whom such imageries are based. As earthly parents are eventually abstracted into depersonified influences, aspirations, and identifications, this argument holds, so, too, must the gods of psychological dawn be replaced by a fully rational understanding of the causal forces and laws of the universe, by brave acceptance of something akin to Freud's twin ideals: *Logos* (Reason) and *Ananke* (Necessity).

On the other hand, if an object such as God does in fact exist, then knowing or somehow representing this being clearly would seem to be a more mature achievement than the opposite. Unless, of course, one holds, in addition, the particular theological point of view that argues that God wishes to remain unknown, to be experienced only vaguely, and perhaps to be best encountered as an amorphous, inchoate, diffusely experienced "presence." Yet even according to this particular theological view, it might not be considered a waste of religious and psychological energy to attempt to conceptualize or represent such a god since this view admits, after all, that *some* kind of god exists "out there." Conceptualizing such a god, even if fated to eternal incompleteness, would simply fall into line with myriad other endeavors throughout a lifetime to fully know and comprehend objects, similarly beyond our total grasp, that are of special importance to us.

Once again it is clear that qua psychologist, the writer cannot easily forward *evaluative* judgments about the differences among the objective contents of human beliefs about God. However, the psychologist may attempt to conceptualize that which the believer believes, to schematize the believer's internal and external relationships with the objects of his or her belief, and to evaluate the nature of the balance between those religious objects whose genesis or current status is steeped in intrapsychic conflict and those which are not. Regarding representation-oriented religious beliefs, one may state that although all psychological reality—the known world—depends upon some kind and quality of object representation and early emotional experience, including reverential, helpless, oceanic, catastrophic, and omniscient experiences, not in every case will the object of such experiences be identified with an object called god.

But this datum may warrant varying conclusions. If one assumes *a priori* that an objective God cannot be evidenced, then one concludes perforce that the development of discrete "God" representations is a matter of endopsychic fabrication, based upon tradition, education, or cultural experience. For those who subscribe to this assumption, it is equally possible to imagine alternative lines of development wherein the so-called godlike qualities of experience, such as contained in early oceanic experiences or oedipal awesomeness, are retained *without* the individual developing a god representation. If, however, one is committed *a priori* to the existence of God, then one would conclude differently from the earlier pool of observations: Some persons achieve more descript or clear representations of God, aided perhaps by culture and tradition. Other persons, for a variety of reasons, perceive God only dimly, through trace experiences that could, however, under better conditions—or, as is often the case, under *later* conditions— promote a more sensate representation and relationship with God. The qualitative distinctions in the level of God representation will need to depend in large degree upon the criteria generally used for evaluating interpersonal object representations and relationships, *assuming* some evidence that God "chooses" to be known through such pathways. When such evidence is available, the parallel pathways of deocentric and anthropocentric representation can be at least hypothesized. Absent such evidence, much less can be said.

It will suffice for our purposes to say that there are more mature and less mature versions of *both* the objectless (god-less) "spiritual" states as well as the strictly defined religious phenomena that revolve around a structured god-object representation. Our practical interest is the ability to work clinically with these varying levels of maturity and quality of internalization of primary experiences and to be able to conceptualize *from the patient's point of view* the god object that lies behind them.

The task remains to delineate briefly the two key terms of discussion—psychotherapy and religion. Simply put, I practice psychoanalytic psychotherapy and am a religious Jew, and this is central to my leaning toward specific and technical as opposed to general and philosophical forms of reconciliation between the two domains. Of course, much more will need to be said in order to clarify the two lines of intersection. There is also a need for background on the earlier literature from which my ideas are drawn and new ones developed. In the course of this retrospective, I shall linger upon one of the chief contributions of my earlier work: the halakhic metapsychology. The hala-khic metapsychology is a unique conceptual product derived from the Judaic ethicomoral system known as Halakhah, the practical value of which will add much to the present discussion (the strictly clinical applications transcend our interests in this text and can only be touched upon). The halakhic metapsychology merits description since it embodies a particular model of synthesis between psychological science and religion. Specifically, it rests upon particularly Judaic assumptions regarding how God is to be known, and through what categories conceptualized, in a way that encompasses psychological as well as theological doctrines in a single set of structural categories.

The First Term of Discussion: Psychoanalytic Psychotherapy

The psychological aspects of the present work tend to focus specifi-cally upon psychoanalysis and psychoanalytic psychotherapy. As often as possible, I will speak in terms of general psychological con-cepts and principles that are fairly widely recognized and which dovetail easily with the more specific psychoanalytic terms and con-cepts to be referred to. However, not *all* of the psychoanalytic con-cepts I work with, and in terms of which I think, are familiar or acceptable to all psychotherapists. Sometimes, this will be the case re-garding precisely those psychoanalytic concepts, such as transference or the notion of unconscious drives, that are basic to this specific kind of psychotherapeutic work. Understandably, some readers not sym-pathetic to clinical psychoanalysis may therefore prejudge this entire effort as needlessly encumbered by its complex and sometimes ab-struse metapsychology and may wonder why I do not simply leave it all aside for clearer waters.

A full reply, of course, on either the personal or professional level, will lead us far afield. Yet, three points bear mention by way of response.

First, psychoanalysis's clinical and theoretical views represent a le-gitimate psychological enterprise that submits itself routinely to nu-merous forms of external and internal criticism and evaluation (cf. Edelson 1983a and 1983b; Fisher and Greenberg 1977; Grünbaum 1979; Hook 1959; Masling 1983 and 1986; Rachman 1963; Von Eckardt 1982). The general outcome of this evaluation suggests little grounds for abandoning psychoanalysis out of hand or vilifying its scientific status (see Dahl, Küchale, and Thomä 1988). Clinically and heuristically, much is to be gleaned by toiling in psychoanalysis's expansive, multicontoured boundaries and comparing it creatively with the varied conceptual worlds it borders (such as, linguistics, sociology, and religion). At the very least, therefore, psychoanalysis is a viable doctrine with an enormous scope and range of clinical applications. And insofar as psychoanalysis maintains specific points of view regarding religion in general, and Judaism in particular (see Bakan 1958; Gay 1987; Ostow 1982; Zilboorg 1967), it merits research in terms of its own language and values.

Second, psychoanalysis as a therapy remains the treatment of choice for a significant cluster of psychiatric disorders, such as the neuroses and severe character disorders. The domain of its usefulness increases exponentially when one considers the thousands of psychiatrists, clinical psychologists, clinical social workers, and religious counselors who, even while applying nonpsychoanalytic treatment modalities to their patients, nevertheless guide themselves diagnostically and philosophically, and even gauge the course of treatment, according to select psychoanalytic or psychodynamic doctrines. Perhaps one of the most widely distributed of the eclectically adopted psychodynamic doctrines is, in fact, the principle of the childhood origin of the psychopathologies as well as the constructive, health-inducing sublimations. Thus, somewhat ironically, inasmuch as religious belief tends to be subsumed under one or the other of the latter two categories, the psychogenic model of religious belief has managed to survive even among many nonanalytic schools.

This point, too, has an even more profound dimension. Throughout the course of psychotherapy, the psychoanalytic point of view is *active*. That is, it governs the therapist's expectations, the kind of predictions generated, the formulation of an inner representation of the patient, and ultimately the course and achievements of the psychotherapy. During the thousands of hours of psychotherapy in which a psychotherapist participates, he or she must constantly monitor whether observations confirm or disconfirm the immediate hypotheses being evolved in order to work with the patient at hand. Simultaneously, he or she is monitoring whether such observations of the patient at hand confirm or disconfirm the *general* theoretical structures with which he or she works. Contiguously, the ratio of these general and specific ideational structures interact synergistically to form additional structures and links necessary, for example, for producing linguistically appropriate interpretations that the patient can understand. Consequently, if religious patients are encountered even in alternative therapies that are informed in more than minor ways by psychoanalytic theory, psychoanalysis's structural and linguistic categories regarding religious belief and its objects, once again, become important and subtly influential.

Finally, psychoanalytic treatment is the kind of psychotherapy I provide my patients and represents the set of assumptions, norms, and symbolic framework within which I and my patients encounter each other and seek understanding. My professional work, fortunately, has introduced no occasion for general dissatisfaction with the overall theory. Happily, many of the kinds of patients (for example, narcissistic, borderline, and schizoid personality disorders) whose intense psychopathology might indeed have challenged seriously my faith in basic psychoanalytic theory and therapy, had actually begun to challenge psychoanalytic clinicians in the decades preceding my entry into the field. In fact, it was precisely this kind of treatment population that engendered the development of new ways in psychoanalysis which so broadened its applicability (following the doldrums inaugurated by the neo-Freudian culturalist school).

This revitalization, as it were, took place through at least three great developments. First, the persistence of the then-experimental treatment of seriously disturbed patients slowly honed psychoanalysts' technique and expanded their insights into the patient and also into the therapist treating such patients. Second, by adapting itself to advances in theories of perception, cognition, and linguistics—for example, the work of Jean Piaget (1937, 1945), George S. Klein (1956, 1967), Ferdinand de Saussure (1916), Lèvi-Strauss (1949), and David Rapaport (1951, 1967)—psychoanalysis's applicability was broadened to the so-called conflict-free spheres of ego functioning, although this trend ignored the complexities of the internal relations between self and object. This oversight was corrected, however, by the third development: the insights provided by object relations theory—beginning with the work of Melanie Klein (1942, 1975), W. R. D. Fairbairn (1952), and D. W. Winnicott (1953, 1958). These three adjustments resulted in the eventual metamorphosis of an outmoded ego psychology into what currently is called psychoanalytic developmental psychology (see Blanck and Blanck 1974, 1979, 1986; Guntrip 1969; Mendez and Fine 1976).

Accordingly, the psychoanalytic theory one encountered in the early 1970s was quite sophisticated clinically and mature theoretically. Its classic texts and foundational case studies now rippled with new meanings derived from the heightened focus provided by semantic, symbolic, semiotic, and structural analysis. It was readily perceived as more suitable than ever for exploring with sensitivity the inner workings of the religious self and its objects. Serendipitously, at about the same time that I began studying Freud, I read the excellent and still unparalleled reappraisal by Harry Guntrip (1961), a Protestant minister and nonmedical psychoanalyst of the object relations school, and the refreshingly unphilistine critique by Father Joseph Nuttin (1962), a Jesuit priest and psychoanalyst (being myself a yeshivah seminarian at the time, living under the specter of chastisement and ban for studying psychoanalysis at all, I fully appreciated the fact that Nuttin's book appeared bearing the *imprimatur* of the archbishop of Chicago and the *nihil obstat* of the Censor Librorum. Needless to say, these approbations would have brought little relief to *my* mentors!). Their focus in these early works was not primarily religion, and yet there emerged a refreshing capacity to incorporate the religious aspiration and the psychoanalytic prism in a sophisticated way. These, in addition to the later discovered works of Paul Pruyser and W. W. Meissner, which dealt directly with the religious patient, cemented the conclusion that psychoanalysis, in principle, was neither as antipathetic to or unsynthesizable with religion as was often held (cf. also Appel, Higgins, Ostow, and Von Domarus 1959). And it is psychoanalysis alone that appeared to offer the maximally appropriate environment for cataloging and understanding the psychological nuances of religious metaphor.

The Second Term of Discussion: Halakhah

By far the most galvanizing force in my coming to regard psychoanalysis and psychoanalytic psychotherapy as inherently appropriate to the religious worldview was the in-depth study of Halakhah, the system of Jewish law which governs Jewish life. For it was precisely within the plurivalent rabbinic interpretations embodied in halakhic reasoning, law, and lore that I sensed a compatriot interest in a "depth" approach to human psychology, the sexual and aggressive drives, the role of language and imagery, the tension between conscious and nonconscious forces, and so forth. Here and there, to be sure, one found anticipations of behavioral, gestalt, and other principles and doctrines. Taken on the whole, however, a psychodynamic approach predominated.

Of direct relevance to the present work are only those central definitions and tenets of Halakhah that document the assumption in Jewish belief that God is to be perceived from within a life lived in accordance with Halakhah (general descriptions can be found in Chajes [1849/1960], Levi [1981], Schechter [1909], and Urbach [1984]). This is necessary in order to establish that the halakhic framework, as studied and lived, represents an analogic structure of the relationship between God and the human personality. Once conceptualized and internalized, and depending on the quality of conceptualization and internalization, halakhic structures themselves become a living component of the psychic representation known as God.

To begin, the Bible itself does not speak explicitly of a formal system of Halakhah per se—more typically referring to the notion of "Torah" (Hebrew for "instruction")—yet the functional identity of the halakhic system is referred to frequently. Literally, Halakhah denotes "going" (Hebrew: *holekh, la-lekhet*) in God's ways (Ex. 18:20), laws (Ezek. 37:24), statutes (Lev. 26:3), and teachings (Ex. 16:20). According to Orthodox Jewish doctrine, Halakhah actually includes two inseparable components: the so-called Written Law (namely, the Five Books of Moses) and the Oral Law, whose transmitted teachings were eventually partially transcribed in the form of the Mishnah and the Jerusalemite and Babylonian Talmuds. The two great talmuds were formally closed by about 500 C.E., terminating the formal hermeneutic exposition of mishnaic tradition. This did not mean, however, an end to the exposition of new *halakhot* (laws). The organic halakhic process continued in the form of glossification, the redaction of major codices and, to the present, the adaptation of contemporary problems and changes to halakhic norms (the responsa literature).

The so-called practical halakhic literature is interlaced with discursive homiletic material, known as the *Aggadah*, which conveys broader structures in the law, such as humanistic or personal elements, Masoretic (that is, Sinaitic) ethical traditions, and rabbinic teachings on contemporary sciences, arts, and philosophies. In contrast to the stylistically "lean" halakhic literature (and despite its massiveness), Aggadah exceeds in its particularly rich ethical instruction pertaining to interpersonal behavior. Many of the so-called gray areas of ethical decision making and other supererogatory obligations are worked through precisely via the pithy stories and aphorisms contained in the Aggadah. As Kadushin has clarified (1977, p. 221), social interaction alone is insufficient for transmitting "concepts." There is needed, additionally, a system of communication that will make values concepts as vivid as objective cognitive concepts, and the rabbis developed this through the literary quality of aggadic exegesis. The rabbis apparently considered the aggadic literature more suitable for expounding the idiosyncratic, subjective, and culture-bound elements of human behavior (see *Maggid Mishnah* to *M.T.*, *Hil. Shekheinim* 14 : 5; Commentary of Vilna Gaon to Prov. 14 : 2).

Taken together, the specific laws (Halakhot) and specific homilies (Aggadot) can be viewed as "categories of significance" reflecting the organismic character of relatively normative value concepts (Kadushin 1972, 1977). However, since Aggadah, unlike the halakhic material, was never codified, it is difficult at times to decide whether a given aggadic axiom or belief represents consensual opinion. This introduces a need for caution. For our purposes, I have followed the convention of working with aggadic statements that appear frequently in the Talmud, or that are appended to clearly halakhic decisions, based on a Masoretic tradition or even *post hoc* (see Levine 1987). At the same time, Judaism tends to be liberal in utilizing aggadic citations for supporting homiletic and ethical instruction. This fact has always posed an interesting dilemma for the study of psychology and Judaism. For, on one hand, there are sufficient difficulties involved in yoking psychological or psychotherapeutic practice to formal halakhic (legal) specifications, given the technical complexity of Jewish law and the diversity of opinion in which it is enveloped (for example, abortion counseling, the management of erotic transferences, etc.). The difficulties treble when one attempts to work with key concepts where the sole or primary rabbinic considerations of the topic take place in aggadic material (such as human nature, the soul, the limits of freedom, the relationship between humans and God, etc.). Fortunately, the student of psychology has yet to exhaust the numerous aggadically based traditions which, over the centuries, have come to benefit from conferred consensuality.

When referring to practical Halakhah applied to daily life, it is customary to speak of a corpus of 613 basic religious obligations that apply to all of the major areas of belief, family life, ritual behavior, damages, jurisprudence, and commerce. In fact, the true practical scope of Halakhah extends through thousands of rabbinically instituted "fences" or bylaws, injunctions, and customs. The purview of Halakhah is essentially boundless in that there is no behavior that is not to be subsumed under one or another of Halakhah's general or specific forms (what Urbach [1984] terms the "principle of external contemporaneity"). The same can be said, therefore, for the *conceptualizing* potential of Halakhah.

As described, Halakhah would appear to be a form of governance beginning at a specific point in history; namely, the Sinaitic Revelation. In fact, Jewish philosophy maintains that halakhic observance emerged on a voluntary basis already during the Patriarchal era (Talmud, *Kid.* 82a, *Yoma* 28b; Gen. R. 49:3, 64:4; Ex. R. 23). This tradition, taken literally, suggests that the Patriarchs, aided by prophecy, practiced Halakhah to the full extent of its eventual post-Sinaitic form—"down to the rabbinic enactment of the intermingling of prepared foods" (*Yoma* 28b). However, the far more significant emphasis appears to be on their intuitive appreciation of the underlying philosophical or moral rationale of the Law. From a sociological and psychological point of view, in fact, this tradition is quite valuable, for it allows some sense of commonality between the formal universalisms of Halakhah and the social and individual mentalities to whom the Law was intended to appeal across the centuries.

A priori Aspects of Halakhah

There is another tradition that emphasizes the ahistoric element of Halakhah. According to doctrine, the Halakhah, inasmuch as it is the expression of God's desire, transcends time and is immutable. Its basic structures, therefore, are not coterminal with reality as we know it and must be considered in some sense contiguous with the initial will of God to initiate those creative processes we identify with creation. Commenting on "And you shall keep my statutes" (Lev. 19:19), the Talmud states, "These are the statutes with which I set up my world" (Jer. Talmud, *Kel.* 1:7). Echoing this, the rabbis state that the Torah and Halakhah served as a blueprint for the creation of the world and human nature (Talmud, *Pes.* 54a to Prov. 8:32; Gen. R. 1:2). This ideology was given additional weight by emphasizing (in a way impressively similar to psychoanalytic concepts, especially those of Jacques Lacan) that halakhic categories already influence the human prior to birth, inducing some sort of structure even when a human is in what one would consider a prementational state—for example, "Before I created you, in the womb I knew you; and before you left the womb, I sanctified you" (Jer. 1:4; also Gen. 18:18; used as the basis for the sacredness of the firstborn, Talmud, *Ar.* 29a, *Ned.* 13b).

Positing Halakhah prior to empirical or historic reality apparently conflicts with the axiom that Halakhah is given to human province (Deut. 30:11–15; Ps. 115:16), is intimately bound to time (Jer. Talmud, *R.H.* 1:3 to Lev. 23:3), and enables and adapts itself to change. Indeed, this major problem has its own place. Note, however, that from the standpoint of moral philosophy, the aforementioned tradition helps substantiate the important idea that basic morality is logically and chronologically prior to the historic event of Revelation. This is as things should be, since one would like to assume the constancy of the basic psychological structures addressed by an event such as Revelation. If basic moral—and, we would like to emphasize, psychological—structures and systems were not available to man prior to the moment of Revelation, the Torah could not obligate itself upon man (see Shubert Spero [1983] citing Malbim to Ps. 24:4).

A relevant teaching on this point is that of R. Simlai (Talmud, *Sot.* 30b) who states:

> To what can the fetus in its mother's womb be compared? . . . A candle is lit over its head and it looks and observes from one end of the world to the other. [They] teach the fetus the entire Torah, as it is written, "Let your heart hold fast my words, keep my commandments, and live" (Prov. 4:4). As soon as the fetus reaches the outside air, an angel comes and strikes its mouth [thereby creating the philtrum], causing the fetus to forget all the Torah it learned.

This tradition has customarily been interpreted as implying a special divine kindness that enables all subsequent learning in the real world to be, that is, essentially, a matter of *re*learning. We could amplify this to mean as well that morality could not have been made incumbent upon humans if a prior state of basic cognitive and emotional structures, which house moral sensitivity and judgment, had not existed. This possibility was further discussed at length in the nineteenth century by R. Meir Simhah of Dvinsk (*Meshekh Ḥakhmah* to Deut. 30:11–14), who speaks of human intelligence as a "book" or an instrument preset to intuit basic morality (for example, the Seven Noahide Laws) and other ethical imperatives.

It is by now apparent that in addition to the all-encompassing quality of Halakhah as applied to the extended, historical world, its *a priori* structural quality is an equally essential characteristic. This has been expressed felicitously by one of Halakhah's greatest contemporary expositors, Rabbi Joseph Dov Halevi Soloveitchik: "The essence of the Halakhah . . . is the creation of an ideal world and the perception of the relationship that exists between it and reality, in all of its manifestations. There is no phenomenon, event, creature for which *a prioristic* Halakhah does not have an idealistic standard of judgment" (1944b, chap. 2:6). Now, if according to Jewish philosophy there exist *a priori* moral categories, in some sense predating Creation, then it is consistent to imagine that the psychological means by which these categories are to be perceived may also have been "fitted" or disposed in some *a prioristic* way. It was, indeed, axiomatic for the rabbinic expositors that Halakhah addressed human nature in a most sophisticated way—"Torah plumbed the depths of human nature" (Talmud, *Kid.* 21b; see Rashi to Deut. 21:11). In still other references, the Torah is described as having been created side by side with the very personality traits it is designed to curtail or modify—"Said the Lord, 'I created the evil inclination; I created the Torah as an antidote'" (Talmud, *Kid.* 30b). Through citations such as these, we begin to conceive of the possibility of speaking of *a priori* halakhic forms not only for moral values but also for the psychological structures that subtend and apprehend moral values. Since the Torah was viewed as timeless, the aforementioned axiom implies that at least some of the fundamentals of human psychology must also be considered *a priori* and constant structures, even though the actual vicissitudes of specific personalities in the real world submit (at least primarily) to the fluxes and forces of human, social, and environmental dynamics.

For present purposes, I will differentiate between the revealed, plastic, time-bound, and linguistically encapsulated extensions and applications of Halakhah, which are drawn *in each single instance* from complex processes rooted at Sinai, and the unrevealed, timeless and immutable, *a prior* categories of Halakhah, which predate history and could, indeed, serve as a veritable blueprint for reality. The former shares an *a posteriori* but nonarbitrary relationship to the latter, similar, if not identical, to the relation between the specific language, beliefs, and symbols of the individual and the larger unconscious structural laws and categories of language and symbolification as propounded by Lèvi-Strauss (1949). This point is important because it initiates the possibility that halakhic categories qua ordered structures operate along the same lines as what we generally recognize as psychological, sociological, or anthropological categories.

The *a priori* halakhic categories are, of course, unknowable to us directly and exhaustively, but are to be inferred from two chief sources. First, from practical Halakhah, inasmuch as it hints to God's own ways. This is expressed by the rabbis repeatedly (Talmud, *Shab.* 133b, *Sot.* 14a, *Ḥag.* 7a, *Bek.* 29a, *Ned.* 37a; see *Maharshah*, s.v. *sheloshah simanim* to *Yeb.* 79a; Ex. R. 26:2, 31:19; see also *M.T., Hil. De'ot* 1:6, *Hil. Avadim* 9:8):

> Said R. Ḥama ben R. Ḥanina: "How is one to understand the passage, 'You shall walk after the ways of God' (Deut. 13:5)? Can a man walk with the Holy Providence, for is it not also written: 'For God, your Lord, is a consuming fire' (Deut. 4:24)? However, as He clothes the naked, so shall you clothe the naked; as He visits the sick, so shall you visit the sick; as He consoles the mourner, so shall you console the mourner; as He buries the dead, so shall you bury the dead . . . As He is compassionate and merciful, so shall you be compassionate and merciful . . . Just as I repay good for bad, so shall you repay good for bad . . . Just as I am benevolent with no expectation of reward, so shall you be benevolent with no expectation of reward; just as I lend without interest, so shall you lend without interest."

Interestingly enough for our purposes, the rabbis emphasized that these qualities of God take on special clarity—we will say "representability"—through the Aggadah as well as the practical Halakhah (Sifri, *Ekev,* Psik. 13):

> The interpreters of the masoretic symbols [*dor'shei reshumot*] taught: Is it your desire to recognize the One who brought the world into existence? Study the *aggadah,* for through it you will recognize the Holy One and cleave to His ways.

The second link to the *a priori* Halakhah is via nature; not as casually and unsystematically encountered, but rather from careful study of its lawful configurations (such as science) as secondary elaborations of *a priori* halakhic processes. Maimonides declares the last point emphatically (*M.T., Hil. Yesodei Torah* 2:2, 4:12):

> And what is the pathway to loving and fearing Him? When man *comprehends* His actions and His wondrous, great creations, and he sees in

them His immeasurable wisdom, he at once loves, praises, and desires mightily to know the Great Name.

And again in the Laws of Repentance (*M.T., Hil. Teshuvah* 10:6), commenting on "And you shall love the Lord, thy God" (Deut. 6:15), Maimonides states:

> According to the knowledge will be the love. If the former be little, the latter will be little; if the former be much, the latter will be much. Therefore, a person must devote himself to the understanding and comprehension of the sciences and studies which will inform him concerning his Master, as far as is the power of man to understand.

Halakhah, then, as a body of literature, comprises traditions, derivations, arguments, symbols, precedents, and decisions of legal nature. Halakhah is also a metaphysical concept, a religious category uniting divine and temporal spheres by hypothesizing ethically relevant qualities for every element of known reality. At its farthest extensions— what I have called practical Halakhah—it tends toward maximum particularity, specificity, and immobility. At its core, it tends toward maximum generalizability, universality, and cross-applicability, reaching back to *a priori* halakhic categories. At its farthest reach, using medicine as an example, Halakhah yields a technically and ethically correct way to transplant the heart from donor A to recipient B under conditions C. Closer to the core, Halakhah is concerned with the theoretical and applied bioethical values of the definition of death, allotment of healthy organs, transplantation and human identity, and so forth. At the point closest to ultimate categories, in other words, Halakhah stamps moral value upon the underwriting biophysical phenomena such as *substitution, compensation, exchange, transfer,* and *growth*—regardless of whether such phenomena are subsequently applied to molecular activity, cellular motion and metamorphosis, intrapsychic dynamics, external behavior, or the complexities of interpersonal, family, and group interaction.

Once one begins to expand the significance of the original, narrow meaning of Halakhah to include the complex interaction between conceptual and relational structures and the real world, it becomes possible to speak of a Halakhah broad enough to expand the area of parallel between psychology and religion. In this broader sense, one is no longer speaking simply of the architectonics of law, or even of a system of symbols (cf. Finkelstein 1977; Heschel 1977), but of a complex dialogue between humans and God, using the formal structures of halakhic mechanics as one of its representational frameworks. Through the linguistic and higher conceptual properties of Jewish law and lore, God speaks, loves, creates, destroys, recompenses, strikes down, builds up, punishes, regrets, and forgives. Humanity is enjoined to do the same, guided by halakhic structures which define the degree to which, in so behaving, humans are likened to God. If it must be said that the above characterizations of God are anthropomorphisms, it may also be said that similar characterizations of humans are deocentrisms!

It is difficult to say whether halakhic practice makes one *Godlike*, simply put, because we have no idea what God, indeed, *is* like. On the other hand, Jewish tradition holds that God has made known his wish that humans behave in accordance with Halakhah, precisely to enhance the sense of relationship (Talmud, *Avot* 3:18):

> [Said R. Akiba]: Beloved is man, for he was created in the image of God. It is by special divine love that he is *informed* that he was created in the image of God, as it is said: "For God fashioned man in His own image" [Gen. 9:6]. Beloved are Israel, for they were called the Children of God. It is by special divine love that they are informed that they were called the Children of God, as it is said: "You are the children of the Lord your God" [Deut. 14:1]. Beloved are Israel, for to them was given a precious instrument [the Torah]. It is by special divine love that they are informed that to them was given the precious instrument through which the world was created, as it is said: "For I give you good doctrine; forsake not my Torah" [Prov. 4:2].

Through ethically appropriate behavior, one recognizes that both oneself and one's neighbor are "selves" created in the image of God, thereby moving oneself into an especially close if limited proximity with God's instrumentality of relationship with humanity. In rabbinic literature, this reciprocity is enhanced, as Solomon Schechter once observed (1909), by portraying God as describing himself in apparent *imitatio hominis* (for example, "I am partner to their anguish . . . ," Talmud, *Meg.* 29a, Ex. R. 2; see Ps. 91:15, Is. 63:9; see also Shubert Spero [1973, 1980, 1983, p. 91] *contra* Samuelson [1969]). Through this medium, the idea of an empathic relationship between the human being and God becomes conceivable (Katz 1959, 1975). Practical halakhot which embody this presumption, in turn, lend the empathic relationship a structural, psychological internalizable identity. And around the precipitate of this relationship, an image of the divine object takes form.

Concluding Comments

In view of the above, one might paraphrase in a new light the rabbinic doctrine of *imitatio Dei* as originally formulated by Maimonides (*supra*, p. 27):

> Just as He addresses man through psychological structures within which He has planted His image, seeing as man is, after all, a psychological, object-seeking being; so, too, shall you address Him through psychological structures, seeing as He wishes to make Himself available as object!

A provocative expectation follows from the above, which, in my opinion, is one of the unique contributions of psychology to religion. If one adopts the idea that the processes and structures of psychological development have some kind of recognizable halakhic identity— which shall be delineated in the following chapters—then, theoretically, it is no longer admissible to discard many of the things that have been said about religious belief by psychologists and psychotherapists *simply on the grounds that psychological language is antithetical to halakhic (or religious) language.* For, in fact, many allegedly problematic psychological interpretations—indeed, the entire enterprise of outlining the "psychological" underpinnings of religious experience—may actually provide relatively accurate perspectives on what is *in essence* a halakhic reality. Psychological assertions are therefore *quite* relevant and elemental to religious experience, and not as if from without but from within.

We may now direct our attention to traditional and novel approaches to the sense in which God can be spoken of as a psychological object.

2 | Developments in the Psychology-Judaism Literature

Schizophrenia is a way of man's self-alienation to cry itself out. It is therefore that the process involved in [therapists who are] awakened to a degree to it is bound to contain not only an ethical but also a religious element. I mean "religious" here in the sense that the response has to do with the roots of existence, with trust, hope, solidarity, and with distrust, despair, helplessness, and hatred . . . No wonder, then, that where the narrow self-consciousness of contemporary science is not perceived by therapists, their theories are bound to contain hidden religions *which sometimes and somewheres remain fruitful and open.* In other instances, they will lead to unnoticed, shifting dogmatisms fatal for the task!

—AARNE SIIRALA, CITED IN OTTO A. WILL, JR.
(1979, P. 573)

The creative tensions and special strains within the two great languages of psychology (psychotherapy) and religion (Halakhah) have slowly begun to reveal symphonic qualities. Sometimes, these qualities are glimpsed momentarily during the therapist's attentive reverie in the consulting room, as some patient's religious metaphors and deeper psychological structures become meaningfully interwoven. Other times the linkage comes to mind during unrestrained dashes at the drawing board of theory. What has emerged from my own interpretation of the melody, I believe, is a defensible theoretical approach to the relationship between psychological and religious process, of how their objects of interest might be perceived and conceptualized. The current challenge of generating a new, and I hope significant, theoretical component for this body of knowledge must be viewed in the context of earlier endeavors so that the reader might better understand the characteristics of the field. A retrospective such as this has never before been undertaken, and it will help establish a common entry point.

Foray into the Psychology-Religion Literature

There could be no beginning, of course, without first extracting the subtopic of *psychotherapy* and religion—in particular, the Jewish religion—from the existing literature on general psychology and religion and organizing this material critically.

The psychology-religion literature, which began to mature during the late 1940s and 1950s, fixated on the allegedly nearsighted classical psychoanalytic doctrine on the development of religious belief and, alternatively, on the budding but equally astigmatic humanistic (neo-Freudian) psychological point of view. In most instances, psychological philosophy tended to be applied or compared to sociologically oriented theories of the development of religious belief, with very little appreciation of the intrapsychic developmental and dynamic qualities of religious behavior, disordered or healthy. The infrequent clinically oriented studies were confessional, theoretically superficial, and technically unimaginative, even if superb in their phenomenological descriptiveness (for example, Boisen 1952). Indeed, Pierre Janet's classic studies of psychotic and hysterical religious personalities (1890, 1926), while rich in detail and valuable theoretical speculation, only further contributed to the pathology-oriented approach to religious belief. Accounts of religious conversion, chocked full of phenomena that might attract the neurologist as well as the minister, were a major interest (for example, James 1902; Salzman 1953; cf., much later, Kobler 1964). As a rule, the overall image of the religious personality emerging from this period was either that of the idiosyncratic madman (mystic, at best) or of the rather dry if healthy-minded follower of conventional, humanistic religion, featuring structurally well-demarcated religious "roles" and "mature," nondramatic rituals (Clark 1958; Doniger 1962; Ostow and Scharfstein 1954; Reik 1951; James 1902).

If during this period there was only a small literature addressing psychotherapy and religion in general, an even smaller literature attended psychotherapy and Judaism. The initial searches uncovered several papers and texts dealing with psychology generally and Judaism, and much nonacademic, pastorally oriented polemic regarding the philosophy of psychoanalysis and Judaism (see Gay 1987). Even this writing seemed to halt around the late 1950s until the mid-1970s (see Bulka and Spero 1983; Spero 1976, 1977a, 1977b, 1978). The primarily historical, educational, or pastoral focus in these early papers was of relatively little practical or clinical psychiatric value (for example, Gold 1971; Gross 1959). Moreover, the Jewish content in these essays typically was quite meager—the loristic, talmudic citations too sporadic and the grounding in Jewish law, when provided, too flat and simplistic—to sustain the occasional glimmers of true insight.

There was another important development taking place just prior to the war and during the post–World War II period, although it was initially marginal to psychotherapy and closer to the domain of religious counseling and theology. The thinking of exegetes such as Karl Barth, Friedrich D. E. Schleiermacher, Rudolf Bultmann, and Dietrich Bonhoeffer emerged within Christianity and offered new approaches to the relationship between the transcendent God and the mundane world. In general, these represented efforts to narrow the existential gap between the word of God and the lived experience of God's presence in the world. Although properly of theological interest (see Berger 1979), this new work is germane to the present study insofar as it focuses on singular qualities of *psychological* experience (anxious longing, awe, love, dependence) that have always been viewed as integral to God's relationship with humanity.

The contribution of this new emphasis to a potential synthesis between religion and psychotherapy was best formulated by Thomas

Oden (1967). His theses merit brief review below, due to their relevance for the psychotherapy-Judaism dialogue. Over and beyond the
areas of agreement between my and Oden's theorizing, I shall later
develop the special role played by Halakhah in providing the kind of
"link" Oden so keenly felt necessary for spanning the psychotherapy-
theology gap.

Progress in the Psychotherapy-Christianity Dialogue

In the course of the pursuit of any lettered attempts at dialogue, it
quickly became apparent that much of the dialogue toward the end of
1950 between psychotherapy and Christianity (for example, Appel,
Higgins, Ostow, and Von Domarus 1959; Browning 1966; Ducker
1964; Guntrip 1949, 1957; Pattison 1969; Tillich 1958) held significant, creative potential for being integrated with specifically Jewish
doctrine and the dilemmas its adherents encountered in psychotherapy. The key realization was that if God is to be found within
creation, and especially within human interpersonal experience (as is
implicit in the Christian doctrine of grace and in the eucharistic rite,
and, although in slightly different form, in certain aspects of the Jewish philosophy of Halakhah), then this could be expected particularly
to be so within the interpersonal nexus of the psychotherapeutic experience! On the other hand, it was observed that when counselors or
psychotherapists utilize this same assumption as license to preach or
"pronounce," the risk is incurred of obviating the special functions of
psychotherapy, prematurely replacing these with the apodictic functions of religion.

The latter observation, in fact, encouraged many writers to retreat
to a more conservative position. It was emphasized repeatedly that
psychotherapy cannot replace the *rite* of the Eucharist, despite the
significant similarity between the rite and the fact that psychotherapy
patients also *internalize* the therapist in one fashion or another (and
some patients even more concretely "incorporate" the felt presence of
the therapist, perhaps rendering more uncomfortable the comparison
between "taking in" the therapist and the transubstantiation of the
ingested eucharistic wafer). Similarly, despite the sensibility of the
claim that repentance-type experiences occur throughout psychotherapy, it was reasserted strongly that psychotherapy even at its fullest cannot supplant the direct confrontation and reconciliation with
God on Yom Kippur via the ritual of *viduy* (confession). The sentiment

was that religious rituals or mechanisms, in their sacred contexts and formal, ritualistic boundedness, could not really be considered *identical* to psychotherapeutic "rituals" and mechanisms, given their clinical context and teleological boundedness.

Christian thinkers slowly began to abandon what was viewed as a merely mechanical "pairing" of psychotherapeutic and theological concepts (for example, confession = catharsis = psychotherapy). Unhappily, however, virtually all movement toward reconciliation seemed to come to an abrupt halt. Each effort to strike comparison was offset by a counterweight drawn from this or that particularity of either psychotherapy or religion: psychotherapy is a secular, technical enterprise—religion a sacred, salvific encounter; psychotherapy is an artificial, functional, one-sided relationship—religion a uniquely intense, mutual, and reciprocal dialogue. Chief among such antinomies—and yet to be adequately resolved (I shall tackle it later)—is that psychotherapy views God and religious experience as illusory objects, even if socially useful ones, whereas religion must possess God as an objective phenomenon which, paradoxically, transcends external objectivity (Leavy 1990, p. 50).

Oden expressed, at one point, an awareness of the paradoxical depth as well as the limits of the psychotherapy-theology relationship:

> The authenticity that can at least partially be *conceptualized* by existential analysis, and at least partially *actualized* by effective psychotherapy, can never be *fully* actualized and, therefore, never *fully* conceptualized except in response to a relationship in which one is loved, known, and understood by one in whom mistrust is impossible. (1967, p. 119)

Such a relationship, for the sake of argument, cannot be provided by a human. Yet such a profound indictment of psychotherapy, I must point out, ought to have tendered an absolutely mortal blow to the psychotherapy-religion dialogue. Far more contemptuous attacks, in fact, were expressed by some Jewish theologians. Interestingly enough, while the latters' incriminations were accepted on the popular level, none ever achieved a level of sophistication comparable, say, to the kind of critique raised by Oden.

Nevertheless, there were always a handful of psychologists who persisted toward dialogue, apparently driven by resilient intuitions and perhaps by the need to discover a very specific, very special kind of object whose satisfactory conceptualization would match some deeply nurtured *a priori* response. But this alone would not be sufficient. Clearly, some kind of language transformation or other kind of adaptation was necessary before further interlocution could occur between the two systems. A traditional solution was to seek intrinsically psychotherapeutic aspects of religious ritual and experience, thereby "interpreting" religious ritual and custom in scientific terms. A typical illustration of this within Judaism was the anthropological and psychological interpretation of the bar mitzvah rite or the laws of mourning. To be sure, these were illuminating analyses as far as they went (e.g., Ostow 1982). A far more useful expedient, however, would be to postulate intrinsically religious characteristics to the psychotherapeutic process. If a given theology can sustain the belief *that psychotherapy is an intrinsically religious phenomenon*—which it will be incumbent upon that theology to assert—then special religious values can be discovered *within* the mechanisms and workings of psychotherapy, removing these mechanisms as phenomena and processes from the domain of the "secular." If this much can be secured, it may further be the case that psychotherapy's *religious* values will be found to unfold precisely in its uniquely *therapeutic* functions and *not* in imitating the *formal* functions of religion.

Oden, in fact, acknowledged as much: "There are implicit ontological assumptions in all effective psychotherapy that are made explicit in religion; and by means of the analogy of faith, the process of psychotherapy can be understood as an arena of God's self-disclosure" (1967, p. 12). But now a new question looms. Shall this dialogue begin with the ontological assumptions of theology or of psychology? Shall we expect religious practice (and theology) to illuminate "godly" or "sacred" aspects of the psychotherapeutic process, or shall the psychotherapeutic endeavor (and psychological science) be allowed to reveal the fullest ontic depths of religious encounter? And to what degree ought the therapist be concentrating on God's self-disclosure in psychotherapy, and to what degree concentrating on the patient's self-disclosure in religiously meaningful terms? It will be my thesis that both of these goals, while salient, are to a large degree secondary to three clinically more practical and theologically more useful goals: first, the disclosure during psychotherapy of the latent ordered structures and object-relational frameworks implicit in the patient's religious discourse; second, the unjoining, to the greatest extent possible, of occlusive, interpersonally based structures and dynamics from whatever seems to be the most rudimentary ("pure") forms of religious experiences; and, third, creating or refurbishing a potential space for the representation of what may be considered the objective divine object.

Paul Tillich (1953; 1958), for one, opined that human culture will always initiate the questions for religion to address. In his view, theology must await humanity's existential awakening—which he believed happened to occur most fully during psychotherapy—and then must "correlate" its response to the terms of human psychological need. But this approach conflicted sharply with the mainstream Christian (Bonhoeffer 1955, p. 325) and Jewish (Heschel 1955) position that religion begins with God's word to human beings. Tillich's approach allows contemporary culture inordinate dominion over the questions for revelation to answer. Moreover, as a potential model for dialogue (on the theoretical level, at least, since his brand of existential psychoanalysis never quite panned out as a practical cure of severe mental disorder) Tillich's "principle of correlation" seems to insist that the search for God begins within the psyche, without conceptualizing some kind of *a priori* presence of God in the therapy room. In other words, Tillich sought to accommodate an idiosyncratic God, discovered by the patient accidentally, rather than a specific God that the patient has been "guided" to discover.

The overall acceptability of Tillich's point of view depends on the reader's theology. Clinically, Tillich's approach, on one hand, is favorable—even though it wasn't for Oden—precisely because it avoids the objectionable presumption that "good" psychotherapy must necessarily result in the discovery of the therapist's God or any other specific form of God. And, as previously noted, when God's presence in the therapy room becomes *over*emphasized, the result tends to be concrete religious counseling or catechization. On the other hand—and here I agree with Oden—it ought to be possible to conceptualize the *a priori* presence of God in the therapeutic process and also to conceptualize those subsequent stages in psychotherapy when, perhaps, very specific, nonidiosyncratic images of God begin to form. Tillich certainly lacked such a model and, therefore, could only conceive of psychotherapy as an ultimately artificial or, at least, adopted hoist toward religious discovery. Thus, he prematurely ceased exploration of the structural analogies between religious and psychotherapeutic experiences. As for the "dangers" inherent in God's very presence in the therapy room, the model I am looking for ought additionally to be able to conceptualize a kind of divine self-limitation parallel to the kind of self-limitation practiced by the psychotherapist.

Such an intriguing possibility leaves only the question of how is one simultaneously to detheologize and desecularize psychotherapy? How, conceptually, can therapy be a religious artifact, ultimately of the relationship with God, at the same time as it is considered to be a mediate, mortal, limited, technical, neutral, and (as is most unkindly put) "purchased" friendship?

The solution emanates from the aforementioned hypothesis that psychotherapy is itself an inherently religious encounter, capable of nurturing toward theology's propositions and demands. That is, psychotherapy—obviously in its most efficacious and complex forms—can be enjoined by theology to function precisely in terms of its own self-directed methods of operation because the phenomena of psychotherapy are divinely designed to enable, among other things, the coming to surface of innately God-oriented strivings and other developments which may be of religious value, *and only in psychotherapeutic ways and pace*. That is to say, this approach insists that the much-valued psychotherapeutic developments can take place only when psychotherapy operates as *psychotherapy* and not prematurely as a religious rite. Further exposition of this approach awaits the unfolding of the halakhic metapsychology in chapter 4.

New Rapprochement between Psychotherapy and Judaism

During the same period, unfortunately, few Jewish authors attempted comparable integration at any level beyond that of conflating the most general values of psychiatry and Judaism (Appel, Higgins, Ostow, and Von Domarus 1959; Gross 1959; Noveck 1956; Ostow 1982; see Gay 1987). More than a decade later, Abraham Amsel's twin undisciplined texts, *Judaism and Psychology* (1969) and *Rational Irrational Man* (1976), and Joseph Abraham Wulff's primer *Torat ha-Nefesh* ["Doctrines of the Soul"] (1971) were promulgating that integration was anathema. All that seemed acceptable was the incorporation of randomly selected Maslowian-type aphorisms for counseling purposes (cf. Ahren 1970) or the forced induction of a smattering of behavioral techniques for use in treating behavioral anomalies with which Jewish patients were "somehow" afflicted.[1] Joel Klein's *Psy-*

chology Encounters Judaism (1979a; see also 1979b) completed this genre with an attempt to deracinate psychoanalysis and many other forms of psychotherapy by attacking earlier attempts at creative synthesis by myself and Reuven P. Bulka (1976).[2]

There was the hope in some quarters that an indigenously religious (Jewish) psychotherapy could be extracted from the pithy, heavily introspective *Musar* ("ethical perfectionism") literature, which flourished during the early nineteenth century (see D. Katz 1974). To be sure, this much-vaunted literature evinces a certain inward-looking, self-tortured, castigative, and iconoclastic tenor laypeople associate with devotees and recipients of psychoanalysis. More important, it includes a great deal of intuitive, psychologically oriented, therapeutic*like* insight (Goldberg 1982). Conspicuous in this last regard are the writings of Rabbis Israel Lipkin-Salanter (1819–83), Eliyahu Eliezer Dessler (1890–1953), and Abraham Issac ha-Cohen Kook (1865–1935). In his own manner, each author recognized the role of a psyche with independent operational tendencies (not limited to the traditional *yezer ha-ra* as the single, preemptory "evil" motive), delineated "dark," unconscious realms and impulses, and appreciated the constructive and destructive role of anxiety (Don 1985). Pachter (1972; 1985) made a largely successful effort to prove that Salanter's doctrine, in particular, contains multitiered psychological postulates and methodology, and Gottlieb (1975) and Rachlis (1974) attempted to show that Salanter's work contains insights compatible with contemporary psychotherapeutic wisdom (see also Goldberg 1976).

Overall, however, this hope faded since the so-called *Musar* methodology must be judged as essentially educational or orthopractic, with its major therapeutic technique being a kind of didactic drill. *Musar* analyzes the petitioner's emotional despair in terms that fail to move much beyond counsel to conscious motives and their ethical implications. The *Musar* literature is not organized around a central body of psychological theory and it does not contain an outline or schematic of the development of normal and abnormal behavior. *Musar* methodology, such as it is, is bereft of any well-articulated and practicable method for reaching the other-than-conscious byways and roots of the kinds of deep-seated, pervasive pathologies which may manifest as, among other things, moral poverty and flawed character.

Despite these doldrums, there did emerge a separate group of essays that demonstrated greater facility with the overlap of psychological and rabbinic language and metaphor and that sought to develop an area of potential mutuality unnaturally relinquished over the centuries. These authors defined the task, at first, as being more historical and sociological in orientation, namely, to elucidate Judaic religious aphorisms and halakhico-legal doctrines in terms of contemporary psychological concepts and perspectives, and vice versa. This elementary approach yielded some informative documents (such as, Hirsch 1947; Gold 1971; Gorlin 1970; Gross 1959; Levi 1970; R. Rubenstein 1968). These essays, overall, tended to highlight select rabbinic-aggadic aphorisms and principles while excluding the vast and far more significant corpus of Jewish legal doctrine. Detailed, even encyclopedic, limnations of the halakhic criteria of insanity continue to appear (Brayer 1990), yet rarely struggle with the many subtle psychometric and diagnostic issues that surround this issue (cf. Spero 1986, appendix II). And, as before, true clinical, therapeutic dilemmas lay fallow.

What I would consider the newer work expanded from the above direction into sophisticated comparison of Judaic and contemporary psychological views on such topics as psychological instincts and motivation, free will and determinism, sin and neurosis, sexuality, and substance abuse, focusing wherever possible on the conceptual intersection between Halakhah and psychotherapy. The essays tended to highlight the respective praxes as well as the philosophical models of man in psychological literature. Reuven P. Bulka's work is especially noteworthy in this regard for his persistent integration of Viktor Frankl's Logotherapeutic doctrines with various aspects of Jewish lore and ethics (see Bulka and Spero 1983). Bindler's studies (1976, 1980) provide excellent examples of the synthesis of cognitive psychology and the concept of *kavannah* (meditational intentionality) as illustrated in the intricate structures of the laws of prayer. The novel achievement was a familiarization via inquiry, not only with the common language and values of psychology and Judaism at a higher level of complexity, but also with their operational methods and practices for influencing and modifying behavior.

It became paramount to begin work on a very sharply defined and religion-specific dialogue or "synthesis" between Judaism, psychology, and psychotherapy, for it was clear by now that there could be no further progress until such time as one deduced fully the psychological mode of language inherent in Halakhah and the halakhic mode of language inherent in psychology (Spero 1977). This next step, however, had to await a few additional qualitative developments in the field.

Values in the Clinical Practice Domain

Whatever its limitations, the early research resulted in an apprenticeship with two vast language systems and ideologies: psychology—particularly, psychoanalytic psychology and its particular form of psychotherapy—and religion—particularly Judaism and its unique praxis, Halakhah. This explorative work enabled an intelligent response to the major question: Why should values and ideological material be at all relevant to the technical, scientific work of psychotherapy conducted, after all, as Freud repeatedly admonished, with surgical detachment and neutrality?

The early research makes plain, in fact, that both of these languages express, implicitly and explicitly, unique ways of framing the relationship between exoteric, immediately knowable, and directly observable aspects of existence versus those aspects which are esoteric, only mediately knowable, and whose existence and action must be inferred rather than observed in a simple sense. Each attempts to straddle the transition from subjective to objective perception and experience, only to postulate that most of life transpires in a quasi-illusory, quasi-real, representational, and therefore intermediate zone of experience. In addition to their specific common and contrasting values and beliefs, each posits representational structures that imply the internalization of certain kinds of experiences and objects with whom certain kinds and qualities of relationship are possible. To keep things manageable, psychotherapy expresses the above through technical concepts, methodologies, and professional values; religion does so through theological tenets, rituals, and ethicomoral values.

A certain danger lurks precisely in this attempted transformation of what is transitional and quasi-illusory—the world of values—into "theories," "facts," and "technics." Otto Rank was particularly sensitive to this and warned, earlier than anyone else:

> Facts are no more explained by re-evaluating them ideologically than ideologies are explained by labelling them as psychological facts! The materials of psychology are not facts, but ideologies, such as spiritual beliefs, which again are not simply facts related to a definite reality, but ideologies related to a definite mentality. (1950, p. 56)

True to his vision, Rank feared that psychotherapists more than occasionally achieved cure by substituting psychotherapy or therapeutic values for faith and the authentic realizations gained by grappling with reality head-on (Rank 1941; see Becker 1973; Progoff 1956; Rieff 1966). One must acknowledge, argued Rank, that psychotherapy's "demands" and rules, no less than religion's, are actually laden with special signifiers and other clues allowing relatively easy inference of the value system implicit in such demands. Hence, ideology, values, and metapsychological tenets immediately become inseparable from clinical work.

The above must be taken a step further. In the course of actual work with patients, the attention of sensitive therapists has been drawn to the frequency with which religious themes and related material appear during therapeutic sessions, among formally and not-formally religious persons alike. For some therapists, these themes and related material become "issues" (to use the terms encountered in the literature) that result in "professional conflicts," "dilemmas," and irresolvable "paradoxes." However, as is the case in general with professional training in this field, most clinical impasses or moments of noncomprehension in therapy are resolved not by rushed application of a welter of strategies, maneuvers, or other technical tricks. A therapist's professional development comes about more subtly, through the accretion of intellectual and emotional insights concerning the patient that take place within the therapist's own conceptual and emotional apparatus. Working with silent hypotheses and slowly-transforming mental representations of the patient (including the therapist's internalization of the patient's perception of the therapist!), the psychotherapist attempts to share, contain, and resolve that which has arrested or destroyed the patient's growth.

As the therapist's capacity for containing, holding, and comprehending the patient increases, something akin to healthy developmental conditions for growth become reestablished. This includes a detoxification of many of the types of feelings which the patient hitherto experienced as detrimental to his or her existence. It is these kinds of awarenesses, in addition to traditional intellectual "insight," which the psychotherapist eventually transmits to the patient. Many of these modifications take place precisely in the special domain of abstracted and conceptualized emotions and perceptions known as values (see London 1964; Saari 1986). Yet, such developments transpire smoothly and reliably only when the therapist has previously explored the role of similar phenomena and their psychological underpinnings in his or her own life. Accordingly, having recognized the role of values in normal and pathological development, and in the fabric of psychotherapy, it would appear necessary that the therapist include in his or her own self-analytic work a great deal of ideological material (see Bolgar 1960). From a new direction, then, values and attitudes become relevant to the psychotherapeutic process.

Acknowledging this fact, the great ego psychologist Heinz Hartmann wondered whether psychotherapists might keep their personal values in abeyance, except for the domain he termed "health values," that is, the therapist's professional values (1960, p. 72). His thought was that in this manner the therapist might steer clear of "moral issues" in actual psychotherapy. But whose moral issues? If he meant the patient's, Hartmann had himself declared that the patient's moral issues would *necessarily* arise during therapy and that these would be dealt with "in their relatedness to the total personality of the patient" (p. 89). Harry Guntrip, in his earliest work (1949), similarly counseled that psychotherapy and religion avoid collision, although in his mature, fully psychoanalytic studies (1961) he, too, had become fully aware that moral structure is an inextricable and dynamic element of human personality and its presence in, and relevance to, psychotherapy, therefore, well-nigh unavoidable.

Perhaps Hartmann sought to bracket out the *therapist's* moral issues? Here, again, it was Hartmann himself who noted (1960, pp. 55, 57) that values tend to "irradiate" other elements of personality, making it difficult on the practical or theoretical level to separate moral, personal values from professional values. Moreover, as I established above, the therapist's ability to work with valuational (moral) material depends in large part precisely on understanding one's own personal moral or ideological development. This means that such values and understandings ought to be "available" (in the therapist's mind) for use during therapy!

Thus, while therapists are well-advised in any case to refrain from direct moral debate or arbitrage with their patients, my concern is with the deeper dynamic underpinnings of the therapist's morality which can and do easily work their way into his or her perceptions of the patient's dilemmas or become involved in subtle transference-countertransference reactions to the patient's moral material. This is especially apposite to the contemporary view advocating the constructive use in psychotherapy of the therapist's countertransference reactions to the patient. Taken as a whole, then, the contemporary clinical perspective must acknowledge in the deepest of ways that values and ideology are unavoidable presences in the therapist's working province (see also Gartner et al. 1990; Hoehn-Saric 1974; Meehl 1959; Schafranske and Malony 1990; Wile 1977).

Unfortunately, little clinical work operated in view of such perspectives. Some of the efforts that came close to grappling with the emergence of religious valuational material during psychotherapy (for example, Farrell 1955; Meehl 1959; Rubins 1955) were theoretical, although inevitably the psychoanalytic papers were the most clinically descriptive (namely, Bergman 1953; Bronner 1964; Ekstein 1956; Novey 1957). Lovinger (1984) has recently attempted to reexamine the need for specific and detailed knowledge of the patient's religious values and myths. The sister fields of social casework and clinical social work evidenced an even greater dearth in such literature, a state of affairs that has changed only most recently (Breitman 1983; Krasner 1981–82; Loewenberg 1988; Rockowitz, Korpela, and Hunter 1981; Schindler 1987; see also Canda 1988a, 1988b, 1989; cf. the bibliography in Spero 1989, pp. 101–10). Most troubling, in addition, was that until late 1970 there are no worthy analyses by Jewish writers of the additionally complex values dilemmas or limits posed by Halakhah to the practice of psychotherapy or social casework (cf. Ostrov 1976).[3]

In order to respond to this lack, two additional tasks remained. It was prudent, first, to absorb any existing, general theoretical discussion which did justice both to psychoanalytic therapy and to the complex and mature forms as well as pathological varieties of religiosity. Practically, it was important to coordinate in some rhythmic, natural way the "standard" pathways of treatment and the additional domains of potential exploration provided by religious material. Sophisticated work within the realm of psychology and religion must involve more than the proferring of superficial mechanical techniques for "avoiding" or resolving willy-nilly the "complications" presented by the religious patient in treatment. Yet, this meant more than simply labeling emergent religious material during therapy as "resistance" or isolating it artificially from the treatment. At the same time, it required an advance beyond interpreting such material in an indigenous or symbolic way only, that is, within the terms of the patient's religious worldview, as pastorally oriented therapists tended to do. For, having labored so long to attain the levels of meaning made comprehensible by dynamic psychology, it would be a step backward to *supplant* analytic interpretations with exegetical overinterpretations claiming to reveal ultimate religious meanings (see Freud's critique of Silberer's [1912] "anagogic" interpretations [1900, p. 524ff]). Optionally, one might wish to harness exegetical-type interpretations, which presume the terms and symbols of the patient's meaning frameworks, onto the overall psychodynamic treatment interpretations, yet some criteria must be established for determining the developmental priorities of these different levels of interpretation and the relationships among them.

Developmental priorities, indeed, do emerge more lucidly by considering the particular ways religion and psychology each internalize and abstract the aforementioned aspects of reality—or, the way each system explains how external things or objects, perceived as "out there," find their way into the mind. That is, beyond even the traditional psychodynamic (oedipal) interpretations of religious symbolisms, the professional is interested simultaneously in the characteristic forms of inner psychic representation such abstraction results in, the object it yields, and the kinds object relationships it enables. With our interests expressed in this manner, we are allowing that the basic techniques of psychotherapy remain essentially the same, but may now become attuned to new frequencies of discourse and levels of comprehension, thereby drawing into the therapy entirely new dimensions of the patient's experience.

At first, this work was conducted largely in an intuitive way. Once the literature had been properly organized, however, pertinent and useful opinions were located in the handful of texts written by clinically sophisticated ministers and religiously devout psychoanalysts (such as, Boisen 1952; Nuttin 1962; Oden 1967; Guntrip 1957, 1969; Meissner 1984). Particularly inspiring where the painstaking semiotic analyses of clinical material with religious patients provided by Greene (1969) and Harley Shands (1970). Earlier, ideologically tinged negative attitudes toward religious material could now be abandoned since the possibility had emerged of reframing the relevant issues and of exploring not only the pathological but also the healthy, adaptive aspects of religiosity. With these advances, it would be fair to state, Freud's own ironical premonition was realized:

> If the application of psycho-analytic methods makes it possible to find a new argument against the truths of religion, *tant pis* for religion, but defenders of religion will by the same right make use of psycho-analysis in order to give full value to the affective significance of religious doctrines. (1927, pp. 36–37)

The Clinical Literature and Its Essential Bias

To conclude the assessment of the extant literature, I return to examine a final point. After considering the literature as a whole, including the psychoanalytic writings, an irksome feeling persisted that the most adverse clinical dilemma had somehow slipped by, that the meta-clinical issue of the difference between the therapist's and patient's attitudes toward the objects of religious belief had absconded. It was not clear just how psychotherapists were to enable religious patients to tease apart the neurotic from non-neurotic aspects of their religious beliefs, or how one was to discriminate a "religious" defense mechanism from autonomous religiosity. It was vexing that, in the long run, one was not learning precisely how fellow clinicians actually *worked* with their patients' entrenchment behind religious prohibitions and limits, beyond how they conceptualized this entrenchment. And this, even though it was by now evident that the allegedly problematic religious material (some were already terming it "religious resistance") was likely to appear numerous times throughout a psychotherapy of any considerable duration, not lending to simplistic or once-and-for-all kinds of intervention at the outset of therapy.

By any account, the major quandary, philosophically and clinically, was the legacy of Freud's original psychological interpretation of the image of and belief in God as a projected intrapsychic fantasy evolving from infantile wishes. In fact, this particular psychological model of the development of religious belief, which I shall grapple with presently, remains a central assumption for most schools. Yet it hews straight into the basic worldview of the religious believer—a worldview the believer considers to be not only fundamentally non-pathological, but also in no way diminished by the impoverished psychological, sociological, or philosophical descriptors scientists must perforce utilize in evaluating its dimensions.

As noted, most psychological approaches to religiosity and the objects of religious belief, including many approaches proclaiming sympathy to religiosity, advertently or inadvertently maintain a central psychological bias handed down from earlier epochs. This subtle but evidentally essential bias permeates psychological theorizing about God and religious beliefs and practices. This bias certainly has been qualified here and there—its proponents admitting that religion is not *merely* fantastical, illusory, transitional, or playful (see Laor 1989; Leavy 1988, 1989; Loewald 1953; Meissner 1984: Zilboorg 1967)— yet, over the years, it has managed to retain its basic form.

The bias—which, in fact, many regard as a proper scientific hypothesis—presumes that neurological and psychological factors precede religious structures, further implying that the latter is in principle reducible to the former. From this pan-psychological view, quite simply, godlike fathers and fatherlike gods both emanate from the earliest (infantile) psychic experiences, or from subsequent superego dynamics, whose ultimate boundaries lie deep within some unknown terminus where brain fiber and mind coalesce. The psychological point of view, of course, admits to the prior existence of certain objects (mothers, fathers, language, societal and cultural values) which the budding psychic structure of the newborn child "finds" in the world and with whom it interacts. However, the existence of *these* objects can be granted veridical status since they are directly and empirically demonstrable. The existence of gods is not. Gods, at best, point to human parents whose image gods parallel in striking ways, and upon whom is apparently predicated the image and quality of and the sense of relationship with God.

Freud, Melanie Klein, and others felt they had uncovered the bedrock of religious experience by linking it, for example, to the infant's "oceanic" experience of the world, the experience of oneself as "the beginning of everything," the projected attribution of omnipotence to the objects the infant finds in the surround, and the deeply ambivalent dependence upon these objects. And there can be no denying the great importance of such descriptions for comprehending religious experience. Yet such descriptions could be viewed as *complete* or *adequate* only by those who have priorly adopted a psychologistic worldview. For only on this assumption does it appear logically necessary to conclude from the aforementioned clinical observations that religious objects are *nothing but* modified psychological artifacts. But if that is to be viewed as the case, then Attfield's critique must be applied:

> There is nothing necessarily in the association of alleged experiences of God with certain conditions found in infancy or in brain chemistry or in social need to require necessarily the conclusion that the latter *produce* or *generate* the religious experiences. To assume that such an interpretation is preferable to saying simply that certain psychological conditions *accompany* the spiritual dimension, may be to take for granted the dogma of metaphysical materialism [what I have termed "psychologism"—MHS] . . . Unless the domain of spiritual awareness has been rejected at the outset as an interpretive category—for which rejection there does not seem to be sufficient ground—and by a drastic conceptual revision, this said domain is replaced by psychopathology or whatever other natural substitute, there is no necessity to speak of various causes producing all illusions of God. (1975, p. 340)

Alternatively, it is entirely plausible that Freud's psychoanalytic observations are actually accurate descriptions of a special kind of experience that is not only essentially psychological—that is, an experience that transpires in the mind/brain—but also *essentially* religious because it is taking place, in fact, on some level between a human and a veridical object, somehow perceived, called God. This alternative view would allow that, contemporaneous with the interpersonally based, humanly distorted perceptions of God (the dimension Freud underscored as terminal), there are also, hypothetically *veridical* perceptions or intuitions of God (the dimension Freud disavowed). The religionist demands a conceptualization of this sort. The religionist wants the essential objects of his or her belief to be recognized as primary in the full sense of the term. That is, he or she may acknowledge the secondary or derived nature of many of the descriptive accretions that have become part and parcel of the God representations (for example, the Michelangelo-inspired "hand" or "face" of God). Up to this point, patients can readily accommodate psychoanalytic refractions of their God images. In the final analysis, however, believers seek to view the object of their representations and beliefs as an existential given, not further reducible to this or that psychological instinct, endopsychic need, or transitional phenomenon.

For such a revised conceptualization to work, of course, it would need to be compatible with the metaphors of contemporary psychology, allowing these to continue to illuminate old and new facets of religious behavior, elucidating the inner, private, phenomenological or "felt" aspects of the religious experience. In this regard, our understanding of religion is enriched even by comparison to the *psychotic* as well as the neurotic processes; namely, splitting, projective identification, and incorporation (see Boisen 1952; Bradford 1984; Eigen 1975, 1986; Fauteux 1982; Freud 1911; Greene 1969; Milner 1969; Ostow 1986; Perez 1977; cf. Grotstein 1980), for there are dimensions of *God's* infiniteness, timelessness, unboundedness, omniscience, and ubiquitousness that are perhaps best portrayed through psychotic perception.

In the end, the religionist requires a model that depicts the structures, mechanisms, and dynamics of psychological development in such a way that incorporates not only empirically evident human objects (mother, father), but also the not empirically evident *divine* object![4] To date, the professional literature contains no theoretically sound *and* clinically sophisticated model for distinguishing between the religious patient's view of God as an objective reality and the psychological view of the image of God as a product of representational dynamics (cf. Laor 1989, Leavy 1988, 1990; Spero 1985).

At this juncture, we need to consider in greater detail the point of view I have characterized as the psychologistic model of religious belief and its pervasive influence. Following this, I will return to the unique contribution of the halakhic metapsychology, as background to the specific religious worldview of halakhic Judaism, as one particular way to address the dichotomy between religious and psychotherapeutic values.

3 | The Psychologistic Approach to the Image of God

Whosoever says he has religion must derive a faith from it which is transmitted to infants in the form of basic trust; whoever claims that he does not need religion must derive such basic faith from elsewhere.

—ERIK H. ERIKSON (1959, P. 65)

In the following survey, I shall consider the traditional psychological account of the development of religious objects and the quality of reality it extends to the image of God.

Much of the dilemma begins with the theories of Sigmund Freud. Anyone with even tangential interest in the fields of psychology and religion will admit familiarity with what was intended to be for all time the psychoanalytic demolition of the foundations of religious belief. This was based on the great Freudian equation of religion with infantile magical thinking and obsessional neurosis. Representative citations are legion, such as the following remarks in his chapter on determinism and superstition in *The Psychopathology of Everyday Life:*

> In point of fact I believe that a large part of the mythological view of the world, which extends a long way into the most modern religions, is nothing but psychology projected into the external world . . . [it is the] construction of a supernatural reality, which is destined to be changed back once more by science into the psychology of the unconscious. One could venture to explain in this way the myths of paradise and the fall of man, of God, of good and evil, of immortality, and so on, and to transform metaphysics into metapsychology. (1901, p. 26)

By depicting the image of God as a projected fantasy, Freud meant specifically to portray God as an endopsychic product, something fabricated entirely of psychological cloth. The concept of endopsychic fantasy was, in fact, one of Freud's earliest scientific interests. Writing to Fleiss on 12 December 1887, Freud had already enthused (emphasis added):

> Can you imagine what *'endopsychic'* myths are? . . . The dim inner perception of one's own psychical apparatus stimulates illusions of thought, which are naturally projected outwards and characteristically into the future and the world beyond. Immortality, [divine] retribution, life after death, are all reflections of the inner psyche; a psychomythology! (Letter 28, Freud 1954, p. 237)

Freud is only too consistent when he reiterates his views in the *New Introductory Lectures on Psycho-Analysis:*

> Religion is an attempt to master the sensory world in which we are situated by means of the wishful world [i.e., *wish-fulfilling fantasies*] which we have developed within us as a result of biological and psychological necessities. But religion cannot achieve this. Its doctrines bear the imprint of the times in which they arose, the ignorant times of the childhood of humanity. Its consolations deserve no trust. Expe-

rience teaches us that the world is no nursery. The ethical demands on which religion seeks to lay stress need, rather, to be given another basis; for they are indispensable to human society and it is dangerous to link obedience to them with religious faith. If we attempt to assign the place of religion in the evolution of mankind, it appears not as a permanent acquisition but as a counterpart to the neurosis which individual civilized men have to go through in their passage from childhood to maturity. (1933, p. 168)

In these citations, which are considered to comprise the anathematic equation of religiosity with pathology, Freud unquestionably identifies the processes of neurotogenesis with the genesis of religious belief, and the object of religious belief with projected wish-fulfilling ideas. These conceptions remain essentially unchanged throughout Freud's writing.

The Critique of Freud

An ample literature has outlined, criticized, and defended Freud's conceptualization of religion, the lion's share of which is devoted to teasing apart what Freud said from what he is interpreted to have meant, including much psychobiographical analysis of the dynamic motives for his particular ideas on the subject (see DeLuca 1977; Gay 1987; Zilboorg 1967). Meissner (1984, chaps. 2–3) offers an excellent summary of the dialogue between Freud and his student, the Protestant minister Reverend Oskar Pfister (himself later a lay analyst), regarding Freud's approach to religion. Whereas Pfister sought rapprochement, Freud leaned inexorably toward his neurotogenetic theory, probably externalizing through such debate a certain degree of his own latent ambivalences toward Judaism, religion, and perhaps even his own theory. In any event, this body of scholarship is not our main concern here. What is of concern clinically is that, give or take this or that aspect of his theoretical outline, Freud had propounded a psychologically positivistic explanation of religion (Küng 1979; Ricoeur 1970; Rieff 1966), or what can be termed the psychologistic hypothesis.

By using the term positivism, rather than the more traditional term "psychological materialism," I wish to emphasize that Freud did not reject outright the meaning or value of nonmaterial or "soft" structures—although his biological framework may cast this image upon him (see Fodor 1968). On one hand, although Freud repudiated his original neurobiological model by 1896, strains of the original mentalistic model can be detected even in his final writings (for example, 1940, pp. 163–64). On the other hand, as the object relations theorists were first to appreciate (Guntrip 1961), Freud's major impulsion was toward a completely psychological, nonmaterial theory of self. In fact, it is probably more correct to state, as Robert Solomon demonstrated (1974), that Freud generally viewed the "psychic apparatus" as an overall system subserved by a specific set of characteristics that are *simultaneously* neurological *and* psychological. It would be obviously incorrect simply to label such a theory materialism.

Rather, as a positivist, Freud's approach aimed at reducing complex structures to simplex forms and to admit the priority only of the simplex forms. And the basic simplex form for psychoanalysis is the endopsychic fantasy or representational version of so-called objective reality, inner or outer. To hedge our bets on the materialism issue, we may concede that, sometimes, the reductive direction of psychoanalysis is toward linguistic-symbolic forms; other times, even further to instinctual quanta and psychosexual discharge pathways. Of course, Freud fully grasped that complex structures have independent value and a "right" to endure (such as sublimations and larger character configurations), but only when these are operating efficiently, economically, and adaptively, or "maturely." Neurotic structures, Freud concluded from these premises and from his select clinical evidence, merited dissolution—and he included religious beliefs in this group. Tracing backwards the developmental trajectory of any religious belief, in other words, one would discover ineluctable frustration by human caretakers of the child's wishes, neurotogenic conflicts, endopsychic fantasy formations, and nothing more.

Sophisticated post-Freudian students of religion, therefore, have realized that the key problem is not whether or not to view religion as illusory (DeLuca 1977; Küng 1979; Meissner 1984; Pruyser 1983; 1985). *Much of reality is illusory* and *no less "real" therefore* (Khan 1973; Winnicott 1953). In fact, on the level of everyday, conscious experience, God perhaps need not be experienced as any more or less tangible than other transitional phenomena (such as the "reality" behind the beloved teddy bear). Rather, the illusory quality of religious beliefs and objects may be one of their most precious and "redeeming" qualitative aspects. As I understand Rizzuto's lucid contributions on this point (1979), the illusory quality highlights that dimension of the god representation by virtue of which it can be put aside, for long periods of time if necessary, and then be drawn out from hibernation during periods of need or interest without having sustained any appreciable change. Yet even when acknowledging this much, most authors shy away from the question of what degree of reality to attribute to the thing-that-lies-behind the god representation. Instead, the post-Freudian approach has concentrated for the most part on highlighting the efficient and adaptive aspects of religiosity (for example, Allport 1950; Fromm 1950; Guntrip 1969; Meissner 1984), so as to differentiate religious structures per se from wholly neurotic structures.[1]

Stated in concrete form, when the psychologistic hypothesis acknowledges a distinction between godlike father images and fatherlike god images, it is to admit only that godlike father or mother images allow some hope of pointing back ultimately to a real interaction with an objectively experienced *human* being. *Fatherlike god* images, however, are not expected to reveal objective gods at the end of the experience. It will be admitted, in other words, that "gods" point to what are known as *perceptual* objects and to their psychic-representational forms which, insofar as these produce effects in the real world, may be viewed as *psychologically* real (see James 1902, p. 506). This hypothesis has been consistently reiterated (compare Ostow and Scharfstein 1954; Loewald 1953) and only occasionally challenged (Laor 1989; Leavy 1990; Pruyser 1971 and 1977; Spero 1985).

Reconsidering Freud

Regardless of whether Freud may be justly accused of pathologizing or even merely of psychologizing religious belief, the clinical by-product of his theorizing remains its staggering illuminatory power, albeit after making certain necessary adjustments. For the sensitized researcher, psychoanalytic observation continues to reveal new ways of appreciating the adaptive and developmental aspects of religious belief. Freud, in fact, envisaged—sometimes ruefully, other times in what seems like farsighted resignation—a reversal of roles whereby the study of religion might ultimately elucidate psychological processes (see Meissner 1984, chap. 2; Meng and Freud 1963). I cited above one such statement which appears squarely in the middle of *The Future of an Illusion* (1927, pp. 36–37).

Freud, himself, demonstrated such kinds of elucidation, in didactic prose shorn of all rhetoric, when, for example, he recapitulates the ways in which the Wolf Man's religious beliefs were complicated by his infantile neurosis (1918). After describing the general adaptive potential of religion, Freud considers three impediments in the Wolf Man that "opposed" the development of what Freud is willing to call mature or non-neurotic religiosity: (1) a constitutional tendency to not pick up new sublimations over his existing obsessions; (2) the Wolf Man's hypersensitivity to ambivalence, due to which he over-exaggerated the healthy ambivalent aspects of religious belief; (3) the emergence of repressed homosexuality, which interfered with a "healthy" oedipal identification with Jesus Christ. Now this kind of analysis—which one may consider typical of the psychoanalytic school—need not be viewed as absolutely reductionistic. For, by reverse inference, it is from Freud's very analysis that one also deduces that *creative* or "mature" religiosity will be characterized by mobile rather than fixed instinctual energy, the ability to tolerate ambivalence, and the primacy of sublimation over repression in the formation of ritual. Obviously, the problem is primarily not the psychodynamic principles themselves, but the larger, possibly independent issue: the empirical status and representability of the object of religious psychodynamics.

Regardless of one's view on the matter, classical psychoanalytic formulations of the dynamic meaning of religion still enjoy a great deal of heuristic vitality and clinical utility (Fromm 1950; Küng 1979; Nuttin 1962; Zilboorg 1967). Yet this tends to encourage a selection process which is itself problematic. Some writers wish to leave aside altogether Freud's observations on religion, throwing out the good science along with the ideologically tinged bathwater. The majority, however, argue for selectivity (DeLuca 1977; Moxon 1931). By extracting select insights from the body of Freud's work, for example, some observers restate more conservatively that Freud appreciated and formulated the fundamental characteristics of only *certain kinds* or qualities of religious belief, leaving open the possibility that psychoanalytic-type explanations aimed at overly compulsive, ritualistic religion might not apply to other "higher," or in some way more mature forms of religion (see, for example, Fromm 1950; Nuttin 1962).

Matters have not cleared up considerably via this distinction. The question remains, precisely for those in agreement with the classical Freudian and, by most accounts, the contemporary psychoanalytically oriented view: How far are Freud's watershed clinical intuitions to be legitimately extended into the heartland of religious feeling and belief? There is a blatant failure to grasp that the problem with the Freudian approach is not that it is erroneous, but rather that it is incomplete. In fact, psychoanalysis's fundamental contributions to the understanding of religion ought to be expanded, not overhauled, so that it *will* apply to "higher" as well as "primitive" forms of religion. It is largely the theory's incompleteness, as opposed to rank invalidity, which accounts for the real frustration with Freud. For example, Freud claims to be unprepared to explain the development of the *idea* of God (1927), and yet all the critically important fieldwork for such theorizing already exists in his writings on the formative role of the early "imago" or psychic representation of the father in the development of the first protoimages of God. Could not the religious believer carry these ideas forward, adding as a given, from the religious point of view, the possibility of a real God whose image or ideational representation it is that takes form in early childhood? These contributions need to be retained and carefully studied.

A different version of this problematic catches up with those who espouse no particular allegiance to the psychoanalytic doctrine. It is popularly thought that nonpsychoanalytic theoreticians, by rejecting Freud's overall theory, have managed to steer clear of a "reductionist" approach to the development of religious belief. In fact, while such theoreticians may successfully avoid the pathomorphic or infantilizing element in Freud's theory, few of the alternative approaches escape the maw of the psychologistic worldview. While they may no longer speak in Freud's tone of voice, as it were, they do not veer significantly from his psychological positivism. Few dare to posit an objective, nonhuman being behind the god representation and to attempt to formulate in psychological terms the properties of the relationship with this presence.

After all the analyses to date, as I noted in 1985 and as Stanley Leavy reiterates in a recent paper (1990) and text (1988), the psychological approach has still not given us access to the transcendental entity that is to be found *beyond* the early mother-child matrix or oedipal triangle. Rather, as Leavy concludes (1990, p. 56), "We are still left with the religious claim that while man may variously discover God and variously identify Him, he does not invent God. What psychoanalytic view have we with respect to *this* reality?" The result, clinically, is a very real skew in the impact of our hopefully ameliorative interpretations and a fateful misjudgment of the real object of our interventions. To this I would add Leo Stone's comment in full, referred to obliquely at the outset, "I have not yet seen a patient who wholeheartedly accepted the significance of his neurosis or trans-ference-motivated attitudes or behavior if he felt his 'reality' was not given just due" (1981, p. 720). Thus, even of the nonpsychoanalyti-cally oriented theorist, one must demand: How is a *real* divine object to enter into the therapeutic process?

The Influence of the Psychologistic Bias

The influence of the psychologistic bias is evident wherever theoreti-cal or clinical examination adopts the *psychological* validity of religious beliefs and objects as the sole or ultimate unit of analysis. I shall try to illustrate subtle and less than subtle varieties of this influence.

The most obvious illustrations of this bias come from actual clinical analysis. Here, one would refer to instances where an analysis or psy-chotherapy is terminated at a stage that is defined as satisfactory from the point of view of symptomatology and salubrious character change, but leaves the deeper connections of faith and character untouched (assuming this was possible). The presence of the psychologistic bias will be inferred from the rationale for termination. One rationale might be that work has been broken off since further analysis of the neurotic or defensive substructures threatens to unhinge or deplete some other important character traits or cultural investment, such as the patient's religious beliefs. The underwriting assumption is that re-ligious beliefs and so forth are *merely* psychological structures, neu-rotic or substitutive in nature, which upon dynamic analysis will evaporate into early, primitive object impressions.

There is a second approach, somewhat different in outlook and permitting a broader holding capacity for the religious objects. Here, the decision to break off work, following similarly acceptable clinical accomplishments, is in deference to the inaccessibility of the deo-centric dimension of experience to the therapy rather than to any thought that religious objects are simply a neurotic extension of the presenting clinical symptoms. This is admittedly a most elementary way to illustrate the bias, since I believe that one does not *have* to stop therapy at even this point. As shall become clear below, one ought not to suspend therapy at this point since so-called religious issues are of-a-piece with allegedly nonreligious issues. For now, however, the point is that the second approach acknowledges, or at least acquiesces to the possibility, that the final nature of the objects of religious experience is not reducible to the general terms of anthropocentrically derived models of development or conflict.

It is worth remarking that, as a matter of fact, the analysis of other creative interests, such as painting or writing, generally does *not* result in their outright obliteration. Religious beliefs, readily analogous to other creative sublimations and "interests," retain their form and some of their other values for personality even after their "psychogenic" roots have been exposed (Eagel 1983; Friedman 1982). This discovery is, in part, what drew the attention of post-Freudian thinkers to the fact that religious belief is nutured also by non-neurotic factors, including the so-called conflict-free aspects and the object-relational, transitional aspects (Kris 1952 and 1956, note 8). Thus, it has often been argued that the complex nature of religious belief may itself assure that the elimination of religiosity ought not to be considered a likely negative consequence of psychotherapy. There are, however, instances when this is *exactly* what happens, in which case the problem is reinstated in full. Slawson's (1973) psychotherapy of a celibate priest suffering from anxiety neurosis, for example, resulted in relief from illness and also abandonment of celibacy and priesthood. Thus, it is insufficient to redress our dilemma merely by pointing to the complexity of religious belief, since even this contemporary view leaves the patient's perception of God, in the final analysis, in a state of locked belongingness to the objective properties of the world and their intrapsychic variants. Thus, even if thoroughgoing analysis does not result in the brute disappearance of religious belief, a purely psychologistic approach to religious objects introduces a skew into the analyst's comprehension of an entire dimension of the patient's psychological experience of religion.

The first approach is illustrated by Knight's (1937) concern that psychotherapy might in certain circumstances capsize the patient's religious beliefs. Specifically, I am underscoring the fact that, despite his successful twelve-month treatment of a seriously disturbed Protestant minister without jarring the patient's beliefs, Knight hinted that further analysis would probably bring about the abandonment of belief or psychotic regression in the process. Knight's therapy succeeded, in a sense, precisely by avoiding deeper work with religious issues, leaving one with the sense that these issues were problematic essentially because they were religious! Cohen and Smith (1976), on the other hand, did not halt their behavioral intervention to eliminate the compulsive symptoms of their Christian Science patient. Among other communications to her therapist at a relatively later stage in treatment, the patient admitted doubts about her religious commitments, but discussion of such topics, or even viewing such a communication as somehow relevant for understanding the presenting symptom, was presumably not a factor in this avowedly behavioral, symptom-oriented intervention. By the end of the treatment regimen, the patient was no longer obsessive compulsive and no longer a Christian Scientist. Cohen and Smith concede that the first ethico-moral dilemma was accepting this patient into treatment in the first place, knowing that both parties were, by so doing, violating Christian Science teachings (Cohen and Smith 1976; Cohen 1977). (In fact, the patient's religious doubts predated the therapy, yet the technical question remains to what degree ought therapists to inquire into cultural issues during the initial anamnesis.) Primarily, however, Cohen and Smith took the defense, subsequently supported by London (1964, 1976), that psychotherapy is directed at conflicts or disorder and not at patients' beliefs.

In the introduction I discussed the fallacies inherent in this view and, in particular, its erroneous assumption that religion- or God-related "issues" and related material can be separated from the totality of personality structure and not focused upon during therapy. Given this, I have gradually become uncertain even about the technical recommendation to "balance" the focus upon religious versus nonreligious issues (see Peteet 1981; Sevensky 1984), *since it is by no means clear that any religious metaphor that emerges during therapy is without relevance to the dynamic process.* Be that as it may, the larger problem by far is the influence of an implicit psychologistic bias upon Cohen's and Smith's delineation of the clinical task. That is, despite the patient's expressed religious doubts (albeit late in the therapy), and aside from the fact that the patient herself delimited the "main" problem as a discrete behavioral one, perhaps the therapist errs in not exploring whether such religious doubts are in some fashion linked to the manifest or presenting behavioral problem. Granted that the patient suffers from a psychoneurosis, is her "main" problem to be viewed as wholly based on interpersonal conflicts or maladaptive learning, or should the "main" problem be viewed as truly between the patient and an objective God—and involving some inadequacy in their relationship—subsequently transferred into the interpersonal plane?

For example, might not this patient's overall phobic and compulsive preoccupations represent, say, the displacement of deocentric-related doubt and insecurity onto the compulsive ritual or flight to dogma? If, for the sake of argument, the patient's interest in Christian Science was originally the outcome of a search for inner peace and surcease from nagging existential doubts, expressed symptomatically in compulsivity, one could approach the symptom in one of three ways. One might opt to exclude all "belief" material from the treatment focus, leaving it for pastoral intervention. Such a decision, I have shown, tends to be arbitrarily reached and is, in essence, indefensible clinically (see also Bollinger 1985). Second, one could reduce both the symptomatic compulsion and the deeper existential doubts to interpersonally based psychodynamics. Alternatively, one might maintain the link between the belief-related areas of conflict and the allegedly behavioral symptoms, yet distinguish between their interpersonally related dimensions and their deocentrically related dimensions. Through the latter approach, both the healthy and immature sides of the religious belief and the behavioral compulsion come to light.

In yet another example, Galper (1983, p. 359) observes of his work with cult indoctrinees:

> Needless to say, the code of ethics of the major mental health professions explicitly states that the therapist cannot tamper with the religious practices and beliefs held by his patient. At the same time, successful treatment of active cult members in great majority of the cases results in that person's voluntary departure from the cult.

Without responding to the ethical quandary he has posed, Galper continues as if therapists are merely passive participants in an unavoidable cause-and-effect nexus: "Therapeutic release from the dissociative disorder [in cultic faith] is almost invariably accompanied by rejection of the cult belief system which the patient had previously internalized." Now it may appear relatively easy to justify influencing such developments in the case of the cultic religious personality since it is almost unanimously agreed that cultic religiosity is essentially pathological (see Halperin 1983). But is it beyond the realm of possibility that latent in bizarre, even apparently destructive, religious behavior is a special kind of striving that, despite its pathological turnings, has an objective God as its ultimate goal? If so, is it acceptable for therapists to reduce this search to the terms of endopsychic psychogenesis or psychopathology?

In fact, one senses a slippery slope here. Wolberg, for instance, declares:

> The general consensus is that good psychotherapy will not alter an individual's faith *unless* such faith has been employed not as a genuine means of searching for meaning but as a neurotic defense, *in which case* faith will loosen itself from destructive anchors toward a more wholesome mooring. (1977, p. 328, emphasis added)

By sleight of hand, the focus has been shifted from the capacity of psychotherapy to deal with religious beliefs to the intrinsic strength of "good" faith. For Wolberg, such faith is apparently defined retroactively, by its resilience during "good" psychotherapy. (I, for one, would not wish for my candidacy for neurosurgery to be determined *post facto* from whether or not I survived the surgery!) Faith that dissolves during therapy will necessarily be viewed by Wolberg as "bad," as having been uncomplex, more akin to neurosis than to healthy sublimation (see also Bronner 1964). One slides, as it were, right back to a situation where it becomes legitimate to ask, as did Knight (1937), Helene Deutsch (1951, p. 189), and Novey (1957), whether psychoanalytic treatment could be deemed complete if a patient at the close of therapy still maintained religious beliefs. Novey's opinion was that, in fact, the analysis could be considered complete, yet his rationale is revealing (1957, p. 90): "If we suggest that religion represents a reasonable reaching out on man's part for a socially acceptable and integrative solution for his oedipal dilemma and his dependency needs, consistent with the current stage of human development, than no issue would be taken with [the patient's] religious participation."

In effect, Novey, Wolberg, and others have maintained the traditional dichotomization of neurotic, "ingenuine" versus non-neurotic, "genuine" faith, oblivious to the possibility of neurotic, defensive needs for an objective God and neurotic, conflict-ridden needs to reject an objective God. The key question is begged: Does every neurotic structure terminate in interpersonally based psychological mechanics? Is the persistence of oedipal dynamics sufficient to prove that religious structures are predicated upon interpersonal (human) objects, or may similar dynamics indicate the existence of a unique kind of interaction with a nonearthly father? More important, Wolberg ignores the fact that psychotherapy may subtly alter an individual's faith simply by ignoring it. That is, under the sway of the dichotomizing approach, the therapist fails to enable significant characterological developments that may have been initially heralded by neurotic symptoms and were only apparently unrelated to religious belief: the religious significance of such will go unnoticed.

Psychologistic Bias in Outlines of the Development of Religious Beliefs

The psychologistic bias persists as well in some of the theoretical approaches to the development of religious beliefs and God concepts. For purposes of comparison, I have summarized some of the relevant schedules in table 1, lining up the diverse approaches as cross-consistently as possible. I have utilized Freud's psychosexual stages as one main anchor, representing the psychoanalytic approach. Although Freud did not outline a developmental sequence for religious beliefs, his analyses of the religious dimensions in certain milestone case histories allow one to outline the key fixation points of different forms of religious pathology. I have also noted the qualitative steps in self-other differentiation as another anchor, representing the object-relations approach.

In attending to table 1, four points bear mentioning. First, each column highlights particular aspects of the process of development of God concepts, and these should be viewed as overleafing and interacting components. Second, each of the developmental outlines, whether or not their authors so state, probably conforms to Erikson's notion of *epigenetic phasing* (1937, 1959)—namely, that successive stages are qualitatively dependent upon and influenced by the nature of developments in prior stages—and also to Piaget's notion of *horizontal décalage* (Piaget and Inhelder 1948)—that is, that pockets of earlier levels of functioning may persist for a time simultaneous with ongoing development within a stage.

Third, it is in principle likely that many of the specific stages can be further subdivided whenever there is supporting evidence from general developmental theory. When this is the case, it is useful to further subdivide the correlative developments in religious belief or level of

Table 1
Stages and Levels of Faith Development

Self-Other Differentiation	Psychosexual Stage (Freud)	Psychosocial Stage (Erikson)	Faith Cognitions[1] (Meissner
no self-other differentiation; omnipotence	oral	trust vs. mistrust	prelinguistic internalization of "good-enough" life conditions
narcissism	(early)		merger of self/God experience: mystical self (unio mystico): fusion experiences
grandiose self, idealized parental imago: splitting	(late)		dependence upon terrifying god image: submission; animism, magic
masochistic submission: differentiation of inner/outer world solidifying: initial integration of cohesive self	anal	autonomy vs. shame, doubt	ambivalence: one-dimensional protosymbols: law and order morality; use of myth; paternal orientation
internalization of pre-adult superego; complex psychosocial representations	phallic (Oedipus)	initiative vs. guilt	true moral anxiety: multidimensional images/laws; spiritual vs. nonspiritual distinguished
	latency	industry vs. inferiority	less projection and compartmentalization
	genital	identity vs. identity diffusion	
internalization & synthesis continue ↓			increased realism; embraces tension; mixtures of abstract and concrete
	adulthood	intimacy vs. isolation	relativity; partiality
		generativity vs. stagnation	mature love and faith
		integrity vs. despair	

God concept so as to refine the usable theoretical frameworks. Thus, the first two years of life, which are treated relatively globally by most of the outlines in table 1, can, in fact, be further subdivided in accordance with the substages of separation-individuation outlined by Margaret S. Mahler (1971) and her co-workers (Mahler, Pine, and Bergmann 1975). Rizzuto (1979, pp. 206–7) examines some of these

Table 1
(*continued*)

vel of ligion reud's cases)	Basic Strength vs. Basic Pathology (Erikson)	Binding Ritualization vs. Deadening Ritualism (Erikson[10])	Levels of Faith[11] (Fowler)	Legend
e-animism Schreber[2] American Physician[3] (Haizmann?)[4]	hope vs. withdrawal	numinous vs. idolism		*Legend* [1] Meissner 1984 [2] Freud 1911 [3] Freud 1928a
imism cases			intuitive-projective (4–7 yrs.)	[4] Freud 1923 [5] Freud 1909a [6] Freud 1918
session and boo Ratman[5] Wolfman[6]	will vs. compulsion	judicious vs. legalism		[7] Freud 1909b [8] Freud 1928b [9] Freud 1906 [10] Erikson 1982 [11] Fowler 1976
	purpose vs. inhibition	dramatic (play) vs. moralism	mythical-literal (6–7 yrs.)	
ds, Totems d Surrogates Hans[7] Dostoevsky[8] Haizmann onotheism	competence vs. inertia	formality vs. formalism	synthetic-conventional (12–adult)	
	fidelity vs. repudiation	ideology vs. totalism	individuating-reflexive (18–adult)	
ience Leonardo da-Vinci[9]	love vs. exclusivity	affiliation vs. elitism	paradoxical-consolidating (min. 30 yrs.)	
	care vs. rejection	generationalism vs. authoritarianism	universalizing (min. 40 yrs.)	
	wisdom vs. disdain	philosophy vs. dogmatism		

possibilities in her correlation of self-concepts, God representations, and Eriksonian stages of psychosocial development. These further refinements can be most usefully linked to more subtle changes in religious belief.

My own approach of this kind is outlined below in table 2 (Spero 1987b). It offers a phenomenological description of two key aspects

Table 2

Separation-Individuation Subphases
and Correlative Aspects of Religious Transformation

Separation-Individuation Subphase	Quality of Relationship with Religious Community	Quality of God Concept
Symbiosis:		
State of psychic undifferentiation; pervaded by sense of "omnipotent fusion."	Attempts to achieve state of "oneness" with history and identity of new social group; introjection of other as a self-object, suffused with sense of goodness, well-being, and omnipotence.	Protective, all-good God concept, largely made up of intrapsychically derived object representations or grandiose self-object representations, fueled by narcissism.
Coenesthetic sense of mother as part of self ("oneness" as opposed to the objectless state during the earlier autistic stage).	Expectation of being magically understood—words unnecessary; profound sense of joy during group or shared religious experiences.	Profound sense of union with God ("I needn't speak or even pray; God understands my thoughts."); perception of having sinned gives rise to intense feelings of self-annihilation.
Sense of "we" invested with narcissism; confident expectation of total need fulfillment; transformation of objectless state of tension into a state of longing for the object that reduces tension.	Sense (i.e., arrived at without psychological work) that group membership will solve all problems and curb all troubling impulses.	
Role of mother: (a) provide nurture, (b) social symbiosis, (c) protect infant against excessive stimulus, (d) provide optimal closeness.	Expects/demands that group will provide same four elements.	God as "experience" rather than an entity.
Danger: too abrupt individuation can lead to sense of radical abandonment!	Sense of absence of past and/or continuous failure of group to provide in a "good enough" way during this stage can lead to a catastrophic sense of failure, dislocation, and marginality, in some cases leading to	

Subject turns to define "other than mother"; interested in outside world so long as mother is present.	Becomes increasingly aware of religious traditions and knowledge but also begins to sense differences between himself and the group (absence of past); also wants, as compensation, increasingly greater self-expression and to be identified as "religious." Or, may be afraid of learning new material.	Begins to think *about* God and to recognize the fact that God is not an aspect of self. At this stage, the religionist may alter between fusion with God so as to experience greater independence from community and vice versa.
Relates to others with curiosity and interest and not just stranger anxiety.		
Dangers: premature differentiation (e.g., too sudden awareness of self-mother differences, unpredictable mother, too intense pull of symbiotic mother) which may lead to narcissistic preoccupation or development of false self, fighting continuously against object loss.	Begins to exchange fantasies based in symbiotic stage for hard work of *study*. Begins to become more sensitive to the needs and desires of the religious community, giving rise either to empathic, cooperative relations or resentment and feelings of loss. This may be masked behind a premature religious identity, based in idealizations, or in more global disaffection, or hypomanic religiosity.	Begins to experience God less as "all good" or "all bad," and less as fantastical, but still as mysterious.
		God as an iconic image, of introject quality.
Practicing:		
(Early) great interest in things belonging to mother, but as long as mother is at safe distance (age of transitional objects).	Searches for symbolisms expressing possibility of connection with past; interest in religious symbolism in general.	Heightened interest in the symbolic aspects or explanations of God.
(Late) exuberant exploration of other-than-mother world. Mother accepts child's movement away, leading to self-esteem; mother's admiration leads to healthy self-love.	Increased knowledge and increased familiarity with religious community lead to lessened pain of absence of past and more self-confidence.	Tends to fantasize God's acceptance and approval, expressed in notions of divine providence guiding his religious odyssey.

Table 2
(Continued)

Separation-Individuation Subphase	Quality of Relationship with Religious Community	Quality of God Concept
Practicing: (Continued)		
Every step forward, and the anxiety of separating, is reinforced by an experience of "elation at escaping engulfment" (Edward, Ruskin and Turrini 1981, p. 19).	Conflict over memories of "freedom" prior to religious transformation; entertains thoughts of deviant religious doctrine as a means to maintain distance.	Religious doctrine and God's influence seen as potentially enslaving, yet there is fear of attempting to escape. Such feelings used to be transformed into a more mature sense of commitment.
Needs feeling of "blessing at end of road" (Anthony 1971) in order to continue to move forward.	Searches for tangible evidence of reward or becomes preoccupied with eschatological doctrine.	God experienced as benevolent, ever-present father figure, a less threatening image than would be provided by maternal God concepts at this stage.
Dangers: "lowkeyedness akin to depression" regarding the now more palpable experience of mother's separateness.	A precocious nouveau-religionist may "differentiate" too soon due to his or her own innate oversensitivity, rather than to fault in the individual-community relationship.	
	Mourning over loss of early religious feelings related to symbiotic sense of oneness and omnipotence. May lead to depression. Alternatively, the individual may build up and internalize more stable and realistic self- and community- and God representations, but also more realistic, less noxious representations of parents, former friends, and earlier self-images.	Revises God representations along lines more in accord with a distinct self-other relationship; begins to sense responsibility to God.
Rapprochement:		
Wishes to regain sense of omnipotent union, and will "woo" mother to achieve this, yet fear of engulfment and newfound skills and pleasures derived from indepen-	Fear of being unique reappears, manifested in increased intolerance for diversity of opinion or nonmainstream ideology or practices. Also wants sense of religious	Return to conception of God as mysterious, all-encompassing, and understanding force.

Rapprochement: (Continued)

Learns to depend increasingly on complex, reciprocal relationships and modes of communication	Relationships deepen and become less need-dominated, and slowly less orientated toward the task of striking differentiation between himself and the community; like the rapprochement child, may still expect magical help and sustenance from outside sources, but does not wish to perceive such help as coming from outside (may lead temporarily to a sense of aloneness).	Same as in middle column. Conceptions of God become almost completely internalized, and relationships based more and more on a model of reciprocal relations. Expectations of magical help become more entrenched in complex ideology or theological mechanics, with greater emphasis on the role of the individual's behavior.
Fear of object loss formerly dealt with by introjection and idealization now giving way to fear of loss of object's love, dealt with by identification.	Abandons early introjections and idealizations of religious leaders, mentors, and heroes, moving toward more stable and complete identifications (guilt and shame regarding religious issues may become central now).	Increasing sense of self-worth which the individual is more capable of separating from imagined "divine judgments."
Needs to have more accurate sense of self-esteem in order to rely less on infantile narcissism. The above transformations are encouraged by advances in language development, use of fantasy, quality of internalization of object, and reality testing.	Religious growth vis-à-vis relationships with religious community may be arrested at this point by intrinsic problems in self-other differentiation; leading to development of false "religious" self, splitting in moral perspectives or between religious/nonreligious aspects of life, or pathological internalized relationships with "bad" religious community.	Danger of splitting between "good" and "bad" God introjects, and pathological internalized relationships with "bad" God concepts or narcissistic mirroring before "good" God self-objects, etc.
Dangers; succumbs to symbiotic attraction or, in defense, develops false self; blurred self-other boundaries; splitting; identity diffusion and sense of worthlessness; pathological internalized relationships with "bad" objects.	In best situation, has by now begun to resolve autonomy and individuation issues (including sense of historical location) vis-à-vis religious self-other relations.	Individual is on the road to experiencing a relationship with God not based wholly in anthropocentric experiences.

of religious experience—quality of God concept and quality of relationship with one's religious community—in terms of Mahler's
subphases of self-other differentiation. This format clarifies (1) the
normative aspects of religious development, (2) pinpoints areas of
possible fixation and arrest in such development, and (3) illuminates
dimensions of experience that undergo adaptive or pathological regression when religious change takes place later in life (such as repentance or conversion). Another intriguing example would be
Likierman's (1989) recent analysis of aesthetic experiences, such as
"hope" and "restoration," which he roots in the successful negotia-
tion of the schizoid phase and the recovery of the sense of "goodness." This sense of "goodness" must be not only restored but also
reformed as the aesthetic aspect of so-called "good" objects. Such an
approach has great potential for elucidating the aesthetic aspects of
the experience of God and, clinically, the experiences of loss and recovery of faith.[2]

The final point is perhaps most crucial. On one hand, despite the
evidence of bias one may wish to discern in these models, their contributions remain valuable even for the religionist and the professional seeking an alternative model of religious development. This is
so because most of these outlines do not view god representations as
pathological developments in principle and, with minor adjustments,
may be perceived as descriptive of deocentric relationships as well as
interpersonal ones and as applying to the internalization of an objective God as well as a purely endopsychic one.

On the other hand, they are incomplete in another way. Under ideal
circumstances, it might be supposed, the developmental phases or trajectory of the god representation can now (or will inevitably) be traced
with an exceptional degree of detail, bringing the genesis of the god
concept into the epicenter of all other psychological developments,
while throughout the author may choose to remain uncommitted as
regards the actual objectivity of the god behind the representation.
One clear expression of the hesitancy to commit to an objective God
object can be found in David Elkind's sophisticated research (1971).
Elkind approaches God concepts from a cognitive perspective and
posits four major elements of contemporary religion that provide
ready-made solutions to the specific adaptational problems engendered by cognitive development. Explicating these elements, Elkind
states that *God concepts* address the search for conservation (in the

Piagetian sense); *scripture*, the need for representation; *worship*, the search for symbols of relationship; and *theology*, a means of linguistic comprehension. All four adaptations arise out of confrontations with psychological needs, according to Elkind, yet he views their ultimate form *sui generis* and as not reducible to these needs. This is a very favorable attitude. At the same time, however, Elkind states explicitly that he is not positing the existence of specifically religious psychic elements or drives which can at any point be said to exist independent of psychological dynamics, and he certainly takes no stand on whether the objective object of religious cognitive structures exists. But by the end of the day, the question remains: If God exists, and assuming that this entity participates objectively, together with the human self and other, in the process of the development of religious representations, then all extant models are missing a full one-third input from a major shareholder, regardless of whether or not we can yet fathom in what ways our models would change were we to immediately supply them with this additional input!

The Contributions of the Object Relations School

The psychologistic bias is modified considerably by the object relations contribution to the development of religious belief. Due to the sharper descriptive resolution of the object relations approach, its formulations enable a better sense of the experience-near aspects of the parallels between interpersonal relations and deocentric or God-and-human relations. The object relations school in no way denies the special importance of psychosexual and psychosocial conflicts in religious experience and the usefulness of this focus in therapy. It recognizes that the psychodynamic concept of the superego bears a special relation to values by virtue of being a major repository of early and subsequent object representations at various levels of internalization (see Post 1972). Yet, whereas in the past the emphasis has traditionally been on the drive valences, structural (id-ego) conflicts, and signal anxiety (shame/guilt) aspects of values, contemporary object relations writers highlight aspects of psychological experience, including religious experience, from the novel perspective that values are themselves object-relational structures (Compton 1987; Eagel 1983; Meissner 1978, 1981; Plaut 1986). The psychodynamic school did not yet emphasize, as did the object relations school, the role of the self in its developing relation to objects, including religious objects.

The special emphasis on stages of separation-individuation, self-other differentiation, transitional qualities, autonomy, mutuality, empathy, and loss and the so-called schizoid and depressive techniques of dealing with loss, make it possible to portray with greater depth and range the quality of human relationship with god images, concepts, and representations.

Several authors from this school outline the development of religious experience and god representations or concepts in terms of object relations theory and transitional phenomena (McDargh 1983; Meissner 1984; Randour and Bondanza 1987; Rizzuto 1974, 1976, 1979, 1982; Spero 1987). The proposed "stages" and "modes" in these outlines utilize classically positivistic language, yet evidently a special attempt is being made to not reduce God or god representations to a pathological endopsychic product. The key object relational contribution lies in its perspective that an "object"—in our case, the personal god concept or representation—is not merely a *product* of psychological development, but also *enters into relationship* with and promotes the development of the self. The consensus among these authors is that whether or not one adopts a highly structured, formal religion, some intrapsychic paradigm (what I term a "precursor") for a deity concept must form early in life as a result of natural developmental processes. This precursor religious object—which may debut as a teddy bear, a mythic hero, or the hazy image of a grandfatherly face behind the clouds—will tend to be healthy if one's concurrent and overall object relational functioning is healthy; destructive if otherwise. The formation of the religious paradigm or precursor, in other words, is as inevitable as the creation of the first transitional object, though it is not inevitable that it will eventually take the form of God.

An excellent example of this approach is W. W. Meissner's (1984) recent reformulation of the psychoanalytic perspective on the development of religious beliefs, paying close attention to some of the object-relational aspects of the evolving god concept. As can be seen from the summary in table 1, Meissner's schematic follows the developments in self-other differentiation and the role of transitional phenomena during these stages (see also Pruyser 1985). Expanding on classical psychosexual and psychosocial developmental schemata, he profiles five developmental aspects of religious experience:

> 1. A primary or profoundly regressive state dominated by conditions of primary narcissism and practically nonexistent self-other dif-

ferentiation (in this state, it is most difficult to differentiate "mystical" experiences and bona fide psychosis);

2. a state following differentiation of the grandiose self and an idealized parental imago, featuring an animistic and magical God;

3. an intermediary mode featuring a highly cohesive self struggling with the remnants of separation-individuation issues via preoccupation with "law and order";

4. a superego-oriented, complex, multidimensional religious experience much more sensitive to differences between subjective and objective aspects of faith (in which stage Meissner supposes are found the majority of adult religionists);

5. the highest level of integration of illusion and reality, featuring the least amount of primitive regression.

Meissner's outline clearly moves beyond the classic projected fantasy model. And yet, at no point does he state distinctly whether or not his outline is an effort to flesh out, so to speak, the real or objective God behind the psychically represented god. He summarizes in a rather traditional fashion:

> The burden of the preceding argument has been that human religious experience, like many other parameters of human involvement and expression, reflects the underlying dynamics of the human personality and derives from critical developmental experiences and achievements. The developmental course, with its attainments, resolutions of crises, deviations, distortions, and developmental defects, sets the frame within which human experience is articulated and evolved . . . Religious traditions are expressions of human need and potentiality. They arise out of specific cultural and social matrices and cannot be satisfactorily assessed in isolation from these contexts. (1984, pp. 158–60)

This type of conclusion does not advance much beyond Guntrip's earlier conclusion that, in the end, "religious experience is the same kind of 'stuff' as 'personal relations experience.' They differ in range but not in 'type,' and both promote personal integration or 'wholeness' of personality in which a human being feels 'at home' in both the human and universal milieu, experiencing a feeling of kinship and belonging" (1969, p. 328). To be sure, we may accept that there is a single mind/brain entity within which God as well as interpersonal relationships are represented and, as research and clinical experience have demonstrated repeatedly, that the quality of these representations often overlap. But do we know enough about the way these representations point to their respective objects to permit full and exhaustive assessment of their "range" and "type"?

Erik H. Erikson's modification of his life cycle theory (1982) provides an eloquent approach to the numerous tensions or polarities implicit in the transformation of childhood to adult god concepts and related religious representations (see table 1). Though not couched in object relations language, Erikson adds depth to the concept of religious precursors by indicating that the fundamental aspects of what eventually will be called religious experience are taking form already in the earliest months of life. He proposes that coeval with his eight well-known epigenetic steps in psychosocial development, each with its polar modes of resolution, individuals also advance stepwise though the polarity between fructifying and binding *ritualizations* (from the "numinous" to the "philosophical") versus *ritualisms* (from "idolism" to "dogmatism"). Each of the eight ritualization-ritualism polarities is complementary to the ongoing psychosocial developments.

Ritualizations are special patterns of mutual recognition that capture both the separateness and the distinctiveness of the "other" as experienced during different stages of development, whereas ritualisms tend to be stereotyped, repetitive, and illusory pretenses that obliterate the value of social organization (such as truncating the "numinous" into sheer idolatry). Psychosocial development from ritualism to ritualization is especially receptive to what is called religious experience and plays a role in determining the final form and structure of the "God" the individual experiences as real, in a way that will be commensurate with the parallel epigenetic developments in identity and self.

Erikson's approach still bases itself upon the uniqueness of self-other differentiation in the mother-child relationship and subsequent oedipal and larger communal relations. The aura of the hallowed presence, whether it is experienced in art, music, or religion, derives from the emergence of an "I" in the presence of an "Other." The first such discovery, in the context of mother and child, is basic to all subsequent experiences of the numinous. Erikson characteristically explains that special sense often attributed to the experience of God: "The numinous assures us, ever again, of *separateness transcended* and yet also of *distinctiveness confirmed*, and thus of the very basis of a sense of 'I'" (1982, p. 45). However, when he concludes that

> a charismatic or divine image, in the context of the ideological search
> of adolescence or the generative communality of adulthood, is not
> "nothing but" a reminder of the first "Other." It is an "epigenetic
> recapitulation" on a higher developmental level (1982, p. 40),

he is, on one hand, reasserting Freud's classic discovery:

> The trait of overvaluing the loved one, and regarding her as unique
> and irreplaceable, can be seen to fall just as naturally into the context
> of the child's experience, for no one possesses more than one mother,
> and the relation to her is based on an event that is not open to any
> doubt and cannot be repeated. (Freud 1910, p. 169)

Erikson seeks to delete the sense of "fixation" that trails Freudian religious beliefs and objects and to emphasize instead the newness of
mature religious forms. This is handy for, as I noted above, recent advances enable us to highlight, in fact, many special kinds of early
experiences having to do with the subtle aspects of self-other differentiation and self-discovery that work their way into higher aesthetic
and religious experiences (such as Likierman 1989). On the other
hand, Erikson's theory also allows a step beyond. It allows for the
startling existential possibility that a human needs a relationship with
God at each stage, no less than with his or her earthly parents, in
order further to define the self and the "reality" in which they meet.[3]

Ana-Maria Rizzuto's comprehensive work (1974, 1979, 1982) specifically accommodates the possibility of the god representation as
not simply a *product* of developmental processes, but also as an active
influence upon healthy or pathological psychological development.
Rizzuto has done a considerable amount of clinical investigation of
the correlation between god representations and maternal, paternal,
as well as triadic representations. In this, she continues the tradition
of researchers, such as Beit-Hallahmi and Argyle (1975) and Mc-
Keowan (1976), who studied the complexity of identifications and
projections involved in the formation of god representations, and is
supported by Roberts (1989), who recently augments the model by
demonstrating the role played by self-representations in the formation of god concepts.

Although Rizzuto's specific developmental outline does not differ
much in sequence from those already reviewed here, her conceptualizations adhere rather tightly to and clarify extant psychodynamic,

object-relational, and Eriksonian schedules. Yet, despite the unparalleled contribution her work lends to clarifying the phenomenological experience of interaction with varying god representations, her basic starting position is the now familiar one:

> Having no sensory experience of God, children are forced to create the representational characteristics of their God out of the most extraordinary beings they know: their parents. Subjectively, God may remain even in the context of a militantly atheist family because the young believer needs the psychic services God provides privately to the child. (1982, p. 358)

Her *psychological* point is, of course, well taken. That is, much of what is attributed to God indeed comes indirectly through identifications with special attributes of and relations with humans; much the same, I would add, by contrast, as children build representations of absent parents based upon "transitive identification" with available persons whom they associate with the former (see Lewis and Brooks 1975). But it must remain open as to whether such representations as, for example, "the hand of God," even if anthropomorphic *linguistically*, point to a sensory experience that is wholly human-interpersonal in source (that is, endopsychic), as Rizzuto would seem inclined to believe, or somehow deocentric, expressing something actually constituent of the experience of God's helpfulness.

Although Rizzuto's schema reaches back to even earlier than the oedipal stage, it still fishes God out of an inherently interpersonal perceptual pond. Thus, God is portrayed as a reflection of maternal mirroring during the critical symbiotic stage of self-object relations (1979, pp. 178–79; cf. the recent challenge from the research of Kirkpatrick and Shaver 1990). Actually, Rizzuto ventures back one step further yet, positing that both God *and the child* begin as preconceptions in the parental mind (p. 183). In the final analysis, however, the God of Rizzuto's schema is mortal:

> In summary, then, throughout life God remains a transitional object at the service of gaining leverage with oneself, with others, and with life itself. This is so, not because God is God, but because, like the teddy bear, he has obtained a good half of his stuffing from the primary objects the child has "found" in his life. The other half of God's stuffing comes from the child's capacity to "create" a God according to his needs. (p. 179)

Perhaps Rizzuto does not have in mind a literal fifty-fifty split, but one cannot overlook the fact that both clumps of dimensional stuffing allotted to God come from the child or from the empirical world. Nothing is provided by God himself.

Let us face squarely the dilemma that should by now be evident. For all of her differentiating between tangible transitional objects and the senses in which God could be a transitional phenomenon, Rizzuto seems unwilling to extend further backward beyond what our positivistic training—and perhaps "good *sense"*—has taught us to acknowledge as factual or as "existing." Rizzuto is not going back to an objective God; she is going back either to (a) an objective *psychological process* that bears upon religiouslike objects and feelings, or (b) to empirically demonstrable objects that predate so-called religious experience. Thus, Rizzuto simply *must* conclude: "God is a special transitional object because unlike teddy bears, dolls, or blankets made out of plushy fabrics, he is created from representational material whose sources are the representations of primary objects" (p. 178). God is therefore indefinitely, and quite ironically, chained to being a representation—albeit a very special one—of preexisting representations.

The difficulty I find throughout Rizzuto's analysis can be usefully amplified by considering at this point the identical blindspot in a recent essay by Nathaniel Laor (1989)—and it is, unwashed, the result of being so close and yet so far away. Laor, like Rizzuto, is searching for some earliest kind or quantum of fundamental psychological perception that might be viewed as kicking-off the process of representing God and might be characterized as preconflictual or nonconflictual in nature to contrast the terms of Freud's pathogenetic thesis. Rizzuto, as we saw, grounded matters in the subtle interaction between the parents' wishful image of the infant, their own identities, and their own (or their culture's) preformed god representations, melding in the crucible of the early mirroring self-object experience (pp. 178–84). Laor coins the notion of a "religious register," which he conceives of as not *itself* the aboriginal religious experience per se, but rather as "logically prior to the empirical religious experience and thus constitutes its meta-level" (p. 227). Laor intends that a religious register must be first activated by something other than itself in order for it to subsequently enable productive or nonproductive metaphoric exchange and interpretation of the kind we call religious. And he selects as the minimum priming affective experience (my terms) for this the state of limitless *wonderment* and the capacity for *wondering*. (In fact, the state of wondering is most apposite to the kind of mirroring experiences that Rizzuto considers formative in this phase, as well as to the classic notion of early oceanic feelings.)

Is Laor saying that humans have a built-in capacity for detecting the experience of God and for formulating a relationship with God? Not yet. Actually, we are obligated to pay careful attention to the way Laor puts his idea forward: "It may well be that the minimum requirement for the religious register at large could be defined by the position of wondering vis-à-vis a *concept* of God who ought not to be what we think or imagine a Deity to be" (p. 227). What is the "concept of God" in Laor's purview? He immediately clarifies: "Although such a concept of the Deity has neither unconscious nor empirical correlatives, although such a concept is abstract with a mere negative content, it is constitutive of a whole register of universal human experience" (p. 227). In fact, Laor includes even this very tenuousness of the God concept thus defined as another one of those universal human religious experiences. But if there already exists an entity, however tenous, that may be referred to as a "God concept," *awaiting to be known*, then in what sense is the religious register primary? I surmise that Laor is referring to God concepts in the sense of preformed or *a priori* "concepts" which persist at all times within the overall set of a cultural group's linguistic structures, awaiting discovery or rejection by the expedient of each individual's register. Of *these* types of concepts it can surely be said that they tend "not to be what we think or imagine a Deity to be."

All of this is actually quite agreeable. But what keeps just out of sight—by now irritatingly so—is the issue of whether one might ever be able (or be allowed) to speak in terms of *other* concepts of God that are *not* bereft of "empirical correlatives" or are filled only with "negative content." Otherwise, all that awaits the believer at the end of Laor's line is the same that awaits at the end of Rizzuto's line: a representation of primary objects and, to include Laor's Lacanian allusion, a representation of the *negatives* that are part and parcel of these primary objects (such as crises born of absence). If this essentially tautological conception is all that can be garnered from even these patrons of the gods, then it is entirely unobvious how their otherwise brilliant theorizing should dent perceptibly the existing templates psychotherapists cast upon their patients' religious metaphors.

A final, discerning expository study of an object-relations approach to religious belief is provided by McDargh (1983). Following the earlier outline of Fowler (1976a, 1976b), McDargh posits six stages from intuitive-projective faith (ages 4–7) to what he terms "universalizing" faith. McDargh's contribution inheres in several essential hypotheses regarding object representations of God:

> 1. The "raw material" for god representations is early aspects of self-other differentiation, family interactions, and progressive reworkings and revisions of such material. Oedipal foundations are relevant here as well as other interpersonal experiences. Linguistic structure is perhaps an even more fundamental but, as of yet, unexplored underpinning.
>
> 2. Healthy god representations ultimately promote more healthy self-development ("self-becoming," in his Maslowian jargon) and may also work in reverse. At best, god representations evolve and grow simultaneously with the self-representation—a point of considerable diagnostic significance.
>
> 3. God representations originally emerge during the transitional phase, lending to them that particular durability characteristic of transitional objects.
>
> 4. God representations are unique in that parents within religious cultures do not systematically attempt to convince the child of the unreality of this particular representation, or at least not entirely.

Against this background, McDargh concludes, with Rizzuto, that there is probably no human being without a rudimentary god representation, and this god representation may be compatible with healthy faith and support psychological maturation, or it may support the opposite. As before, however, there is no evidence in McDargh's approach of the role of an objective object called God.

By way of slight digression, in related work regarding religious returnees, I schematized the stages of self-other differentiation (following Mahler), emphasizing at each stage parallel qualities of the God concept and qualities of relationship with the religious community (Spero 1987b). This can be further refined by elucidating the ways in which religious rituals and beliefs, in normal and patient populations, incorporate and extend what Mahler (1971, p. 171) termed the "substantive issues" of early separation-individuation. Four functions appear salient: (1) "bridging," similar to the transitional function, or the way in which religious ritual, including religious memories, relate the individual to familiar surroundings; (2) "conduction" (my term), or the response to the warmth and "feel" of the human body; (3) the sense of "confident expectation," or the ability to establish basic trust with god objects or through religious beliefs; and (4) the appearance of a "basic mood," as another way of dealing with separation and as the earliest indication of true "longing," whether for parents or ultimately for God.

A final source is somewhat peripheral to formal object-relational outlines. This material comes from contemporary discussions of psychotic religious imagery, but I have included it because it features considerable reflection on the development of god images, often articulated within an object relations focus.

For example, Eigen's (1986) and Bradford's (1984) recent, intensive work with psychotic personalities provides a particularly riveting and multifaceted portrait of their patients' gods. Their vantage point is furbished precisely by extensive clinical apprenticeship in the anfractuous depths of the psychotic mind, with patients whose hypertrophized imageries and warped indices of internality-externality readily grant a special form of aliveness to their "inner" representations of God and related objects. One must bear in mind, therefore, that psychotics may thus vivify many kinds of objects of significance to them. Such animation does not grant objective status to their perceptions, no matter how "real" they come across. On the other hand, the psychotic's unique visions result partly from the fact that he or she momentarily sees through the fictional distinction between "inner" and "external" space and the limits of spatiotemporal categories. More so perhaps than any other human, the psychotic truly *perceives,* unaided, or unrestrained by the "consensual" interpretations of reality provided from birth in the form of language, myth, and morality.

Culling from such perceptions, Eigen concludes that it is precisely the psychotic's vision that teaches that "God is not a blank hodgepodge or a collapsed morass, but, whatever else, *a relational being in the depths of His own nature,* a dynamic movement that supports our openness to revelation and response, and requires us to live on the cutting edge of faith" (p. 365). One may ask, as I have asked often in these pages: Is Eigen describing a "representation of relation" or, at long last, a *"living,* relating object represented"? If it objectively relates, in what sense does it relate? That is, does it "relate" as a psychological representation providing a sense of psychic relation, as might other endopsychic products like teddy bears, dragons, superheroes, and pink elephants? *Or does it relate because it is the image of a being who relates even while seeking and achieving psychological representability,* who provides in one form or another sufficient hints to real existence—caring, concern, distance, responsiveness, patience, anger, love, and so on—that may be experienced and represented?

Eigen's own point of view can be surmised, I think, from the phrase I emphasized in the above quotation. Namely, Eigen speaks of God as a living object. He is willing to describe God as a being having an "independent nature," to refer to God not merely as one who could be totally comprehended in human terms, not merely as yet another endopsychic projection. For if God is to have an independent "nature," then surely a mature, existential relationship with God would need to begin with an index of reality beyond the limits of human projective mechanisms.

But one ought not romanticize. The psychotic's experience is chaotic, typically confusing, catastrophically mordant or freakishly manic, or inertly concrete and undifferentiated. Unlike the artist, or the true prophet, a psychotic's entrenched pathology limits his or her ability to utilize such perceptions creatively. Nonetheless, the psychotic's unconventionality often seems to yield special access to an enviably real, sensual, luminous, and palpable godlike dimension beyond human consciousness.[4] I emphasize the term "beyond" because it is of utmost interest that, despite all the autistic closeness, self-other undifferentiatedness, concrete personification, and apparently unbridled subjectivity of psychotics' experience of hallucinated objects, it has often been observed that their god images succeed in remaining at some remove from the world (cf. Atwood 1978; Stolorow and Atwood 1973).

David Bradford, a clinical neuropsychologist, writes of this, drawing from his observations of schizophrenics' religious experiences:

> God is not experienced pantheistically. He is transcendent, much more so than immanent. Generally, God is experienced as a person in the theological sense of the term. He is a divine subject, in other words, and is able to enter into relationship with humans in a way not totally unlike that in which humans enter into relationships with one another . . . Finally, God is experienced as autonomous; there is not a simple correlation between the credulity of the patient, on the one hand, and either His presence or its form on the other. (1984, p. 221)

Bradford is willing to take these observations to an uncommon and I think astounding conclusion, (p. 222, emphasis added):

All of this recalls certain basic notions about God held by the Judeo-Christian tradition, and it is tantamount to saying that the phenomenological integrity of the experience of God extends beyond the simple matter of prevalence *and includes His nature as experienced during madness and sanity alike* . . . [p. 223] The phenomenological psychopathology of the experience of God may now be raised to the level of a cultural critique which focuses attention to the poverty of an era which restricts the psychological scope of religious experience to an incomplete shadow of its former outline.

Thus, analogizing for the individual as well as for our culture, Bradford views the torturous religious experience of the schizophrenic as a kind of painful revival of the "atrophied organ of religious experience." This idea has echoes throughout the major religious and mystical literature, to be sure, yet, who could deny the more profound insights gleaned through the specific metaphor of psychotic disturbance and its remission, particularly the notion of God's nearness and influence even when humans have sought to expel God from their minds in the most contorted and violent of ways. In this, too, God looms immortal.

Critique of the Object Relations Approach

Even in the object relations approach, as I pointed out in the case of each writer, one can sense remnants of psychological positivism. Overall, there remains the assumption that the aboriginal image of God is in actuality a product of perceptual and emotional revelations that transpire during self-other differentiation. But if the first "Other" is in actuality the earthly mother, or some aspect of early experience with her, when and how does it become divine? More important, if there really is an objective divine other awaiting relationship, when and how does the human differentiate it from the human or interpersonal other? At what point, in other words, does the purely human contribution to images and representations of God cede to some special other contribution that is utterly nonhuman? Can we reasonably detect areas of overlap or parallel?

My critique threads into one of McDargh's summary comments. He notes that he can be challenged: "Are you saying that God is nothing but a cosmic teddy bear?" McDargh claims he is not, adding, "But I *am* saying that we cannot fully understand what compels human beings to seek after that which they name 'God' until and unless we understand something about our relationship with our teddy bears" (1983, p. xiii). Fair enough. Yet following such understanding as he provides through his object relations approach, McDargh states that

> [representations of God] are not produced by actual encounters with a perceptual object of the concreteness of a parent or sibling [but rather are] imaginative creations or active constructions . . . drawn from the same place and in the same way as the material for superheroes, and devils, monsters, and imaginary companions. (pp. 122–23)

McDargh does not say that God is *not* a material object and, hence, he does not conclude that God is a different *but nonetheless real* object "out there." Instead, he seems to place God right on the shelf with assorted other endopsychic creations whose essence one can adequately comprehend through interpersonally derived models.

This bias will fail to clarify at just what point God ultimately might be distinguishable from the cherished teddy bear or other transitional experiences. A childhood concept of God, to be sure, is a *childhood* concept. But it is also *of God*, just as a childhood concept of a father is nonetheless of *a* father. Indeed, some writers have gleaned from the approaches of Winnicott, Rizzuto, McDargh, and Meissner that god concepts, upon maturing beyond their transitional phase, ought to achieve a point of maximum abstraction and internalization where the personified, imagelike, "magical" God ought to fade altogether. On such assumption, as I noted in the introduction, many have come to view God-less religiosity as still less advanced than humanistic spiritual belief systems.

This misunderstanding, in fact, is sufficiently important to merit a rejoinder while the issue is before us. In response, one must recall that the total abstraction-into-nothingness of a fully internalized object may be a correct description of what happens to this or that specific transitional object, such as the child's comforter, but it is not the fate of objects whose role is more than transitional, such as the child's parents. Transitional objects are, indeed, fully internalized so that their *function* rather than their concrete qualities recede into the overall personality. On the other hand, primary love objects, such as parents, are internalized in a manner that more evenly straddles reality and fantasy, allowing for the retention of form and other qualitative features beyond functionality (Hong 1978; Tolpin 1971). Maximum internalization of *parents* does not entail the absence of their image or object representation, but rather a deconcretization and depersonification of the image. The same may be hypothesized of the image of God, unless one assumes *ab initio* that God is more akin to the child's blanket than to his parents.

Alternative Formulations by Religious Psychotherapists

One might then suppose that religiously oriented psychotherapists fare better in mapping the relation between human personality and its religious object representations. In fact, many fare no better at all despite making use of a welter of new terms designed to "speak to" religious issues. A small group, however, has taken important strides forward in grappling with the psychologistic hypothesis, although even among this group the status of the divine object representation remains incompletely identified.

The counterideology to the Freudian approach to religion is generally considered to have begun with Gordon Allport's *The Individual and His Religion* (1950) and continued with the Christian existential psychotherapists of the 1960s up to the present. In the then climate of general critique of psychoanalysis, on the one hand, and the rise of contemporary ego psychology and Rogerian counseling, on the other hand, these writers strove to emphasize the non-neurotic, adaptive, and creative qualities of religion. As we have already seen, however, the mere emphasis on the so-called conflict-free elements of religious experience—or the willingness to ground the genesis of religious objects in a knd of tautological "need to believe"—does not necessarily or sufficiently yield a method for conceptualizing the reality of divine objects (namely, Ostow and Scharfstein 1954, p. 148).

Interestingly, it was a non-Freudian but nevertheless triumphantly psychoanalytic and religious observer who must be considered an earlier herald of unambivalent efforts to welcome God as objective object back into the therapy room. I refer to the consistent and eloquent writings of Carl Gustav Jung. If, for the sake of contrast, one were to posit that Freud viewed the persistence of religion as evidence for a universal neurotic process, it was the *absence* of religion, in Jung's purview, that counted among the chief causes of neurosis (1932a, pp. 334–38). Jung was deeply interested in introducing religion into the lives of his patients, and he, also a student of psychotic imagery, believed that the powers humans usually projected onto gods are still active in the unconscious psyche (1931, p. 375). But from such theory—and even from his well-known axiom that "the symbol means the God *within*" (1932a, p. 72)—there did not necessarily emerge a view unilaterally distinct from Freud's.

Fortunately, Jung was willing to reveal his deepest commitments more succinctly. For Jung, the true state of health, to which the psychotherapist endeavors to bring a patient, was what he called the "individuated state," and its definition is unambiguously antithetical to Freud's secularist *summa bonum*, love and work: "*Individuation is the life in God.* . . . The symbols of the self coincide with those of the Deity. The self is not the ego; it symbolizes the totality of man and he is obviously not whole without God" (1976, p. 719; see also 1931). Jung boldly expounds the thesis that ideas of God are a basic component of the human psyche and unabashedly advocates religiously oriented psychotherapies. This attitude emerges poignantly in Jung's reflections on the course and outcome of a particular clinical case. In the case at hand (Jung 1928), Jung wondered why the transference was so powerful and so resistant to the usual analytic interpretations. In fact, the energy of the transference was so strong that it gave the impression of being an instinct. Jung then pondered:

> Or, I said to myself, was it rather the case that the unconscious was trying to "create" a god out of the person of the doctor, *as it were to free a vision of God from the veils of the personal,* so that the Transference to the person of the doctor was no more than a misunderstanding on the part of the conscious mind? . . . Was the urge of the unconscious perhaps only apparently reaching out toward the person (the doctor), but in a deeper sense toward a god? Could the longing for a god be a "passion" welling up from our darkest, instinctual nature, a passion unswayed by any outside influences, deeper and perhaps stronger than the love for a human passion. Or was it perhaps the highest and truest meaning of that inappropriate love we call transference, a little bit of real "Gottesminne" that has been lost to consciousness since the 15th century? (1928, p. 130)

Jung adduces proof that this "passion" was not due to the patient's own Christian views of God, for she was agnostic, and that, in fact, the god she created was an archetypic one—the wind, gigantic, primordial, Wotanic; a god more akin to a primitive nature-demon. Thus, Jung himself dared to evaluate the gods and, most probably, would not have granted the coveted status of objective reality—other than our hobgoblin "psychological reality"—equally to every kind of god! Even more interestingly, Jung records that he shared his speculations with the patient and although she did not accept his thesis out of hand, her subsequent dreams revealed that the God-father transference was being undermined. At about the same time, the patient withdrew from analysis. Unfortunately, Jung does not provide a more thoroughgoing methodology for discriminating between human transference paradigms and the "deeper" transferences based on the putative longing for an objective deity.

After Jung, two directions among religiously oriented therapists appear. Some attempted to continue speaking in theistic terms, whereas others became more comfortable with generalities about human "spirituality" and "faith." McDargh (1991) offers a recent conceptualization of these schools. Contemporary existential schools are often considered allied with the nonreductionist approach to religious belief, even though most existential psychotherapists tend to speak only generally of the cure of neurosis via the substitution of "meaning," spirituality, and Logos (Frankl 1955 and 1975; Fromm 1947, 1950, 1963; May 1953). However, the image of or the belief in an objective God *per se*, and certainly a concrete or personified God, is not viewed by these writers as more veridical than any other belief (or its object) that may be accorded existential status by virtue of the fact that it lends meaning to being. Moreover, despite a generally persuasive style and some definitely meaningful turns of phrase, a substantial proportion of these attempts to supplant standard psychotherapeutic doctrine with metaphor-drenched ideologies come across as predatory to modern psychology.

On other occasions, such cosmetic terminological transformations seem blissfully unaware of the complex kinds of marbling that take place between pathological processes and religious beliefs, and, hence, of the complex kinds of work that are requisite in order to effect therapeutic disentanglement. It has been observed more than once that the case studies presented by these alternative schools (for example, Klein 1979a; Popst 1987; E. Stern 1985) tend to depict not very seriously disturbed patients, whose cures consist in exchanging states of relatively mild tension for a more creative form of tension (DiCaprio 1974). Not a bad thing in itself, but one is left with the impression that the depth of the religious dimension cannot properly be assessed in the case of more seriously disturbed individuals until more extensive, "standard" kind of work is completed deep in the chambers of the mind as Freud or others have described it. Existential-didactic therapies for essentially healthy if distressed minds run the risk of evolving psychotherapeutic or developmental theories dislocated from the torturous realities of contemporary psychopathologies. In the end, these will be clinically inefficacious, and "psychotherapy" will become a bloated concept that includes all forms of verbal suggestion and religious education.

Absent good clinical theory which could bring the divine object as a multidimensional reality into psychotherapy, some religious therapists perforce rejected formal psychological theory. Henceforth, it was thought, only religious terminology would be deemed legitimate for understanding the plight of the distressed soul. Unfortunately, there is no evidence that this approach achieved greater success, religiously or clinically, than its predecessor. The extreme position, on the one hand, was consequently reached wherein the therapist and his or her clinical technique—the key operational variables in psychotherapy—came themselves to be looked upon as undesirable interferences between humans and God. Such an approach must be deemed essentially antitherapeutic, as Oden (1967) pointed out.

Most recent Christian authors, on the other hand, have sought to bring the image or at least the influence of God directly into the consulting room, but with insufficient subtlety or respect for the ephemeral psychic pathways the divine image may travel. Stapleton (1977) and Adams (1970) argued that the Holy Spirit "enters" therapy and works through the medium of imagery. Tyrrel (1975) insisted directly that what he termed Christo-therapy includes "the entire saving work of Christ in all of its aspects." Wapnick (1985) viewed the Holy Spirit as communicating through psychoanalyticlike processes. In the work of evangelical psychiatrist Heinrichs (1982), Jesus Christ directly and objectively enters human development and, thus, is equally subject to Sullivanian "parataxic distortions" which must be corrected by the accepting therapist. Yet Heinrichs often writes as if what God *really* is, when humans are not busily distorting his image, should be readily apparent to all. In my estimation, the resulting "psychotheologies" (Stern and Marino 1970; E. Stern 1985) do not yet adequately formulate just where the deocentric relation transpires ("internally" for nontheists? "externally" for theists?) or what conceivable kinds of intersection between the normal and pathological trajectories of anthropocentric and deocentric relations exist.

My final criticism of the present psychotheological approaches highlights an irony. Reading this material, the impression forms that God is being too literally *proclaimed* during the therapeutic session. Psychotherapy is, in effect, pushed aside in favor of kerygmatic counseling. That is, having wished so fervently for a professional approach that would acknowledge the relevance of God for human personality and psychotherapy, the above approaches seem almost to *inject* God into the therapy. The god that eventually emerges from the modicum of therapeutic transcription such authors provide is, in a sense, *too* real, fitting in too pat a way into ready-at-hand theological frameworks. It seems forgotten that the god who *initially* emerges during psychotherapy, to a large degree and in significant ways, is, after all, still an "idealized object," a representation in flux, a psychic residue of myriad forces, motives, internalizations, and perceptions. For a variety of conflict-free as well as conflict-bound reasons, most persons' "God" is only an approximation of the God who truly deserves to be proclaimed. Rather, the nature of God's influence and identity must carefully be distilled from the patient's overdetermined motives and wishes; God's internalized communications must be culled and filtered from prefabricated teachings; and the multidimensional traces of the presence of God teased conscientiously from the patient's apparently interpersonal metaphors and representations.

A psychotherapist, therefore, can ill-afford to trade boldly in the patient's religious terminology understood at face value, whether or not the God to whom such terminology refers is psychologically real or really real!

Summation: Beyond Reductionism

I wish to summarize what we've learned about the psychologistic bias by way of one final, particularly complex attempt to contend with it. Anthony DeLuca, though himself a religionist, initially applauded Freud's reductionism insofar as it clears away much of the primitive encrustation around religious belief. He states:

> Man, in trying to come to the "Wholly Other," makes use of "religion," which treats the sacred as being in the sphere of objects. [But] the objectification of the sacred makes it an object along with the objects of culture. We are left with sacred *objects* and not *signs* of the sacred. Thus, religion reifies and alienates faith. Freud, through his reductionism, brings about the death of the religious *object*. On the other hand, faith is the realm of the symbolic which points beyond, but which always runs the risk of being objectified. (1977, p. 13)

By "sacred objects" DeLuca apparently means concrete things-in-the-world, or in-the-mind, which humans transform into sacred things-of-worship, thereby displacing the true or pristine experience of the divine. In so saying, he has anticipated something akin to Ernest Becker's notion of the "fetishistic object" (1973) which ossifies rather than conceptualizes in a heroic way humanity's deepest feelings, needs, and aspirations. Becker and DeLuca would concur that, "Where objectification takes place, an idol is born" (DeLuca 1977, p. 13; cf. Arieti 1981, p. 53).

Now, evidently, DeLuca *means* to leave us with God in the end— the One who transmits "signs"—but in that case, one must admonish, he has created too extreme a dichotomy between "object" and "sign." For, if God exists, then from both the psychological as well as religious point of view, God *is* an object! Something about this being and its relationship with humankind must be representable, even if ephemerally and precariously. Knowledge of such a God may achieve the highest level of abstraction, but some initial meeting point between the human mind and a perceptually veridical object must remain implicit throughout. It does not even matter if the individual can ever consciously recollect perceiving this primordial object as an objectively external one.

Roy Schafer, for example, leaves ample room for this hypothesis when he conjectures:

> It is conceivable that some objects have existed as internal objects from their beginnings. The differentiation between self and other is not identical with that of "inside" and "outside" the self-as-place. Some objects may be discriminated before the outer boundaries of the self-as-place are defined. These may be included *within* the boundaries once they are defined. (1968, p. 118n)

Schafer is actually addressing here a complicated aspect of a larger issue, but his contribution to the present problem is explicit. Schafer offers a perfectly cogent theoretical space for God as an object and, at the same time, as something more than merely an endopsychic product. His contribution will be more obvious if we remember that terms such as incorporation, internalization, externalization, and projection are all relative to a boundary, to the existence of at least two enclosures or circumscribed areas in space, and to a subject and object engaged in some form of exchange. Schafer is saying, then, that even prior to the establishment of firm self-other boundaries which would allow us to discriminate such terms as "internal object" versus "external object," certain objects—Schafer does not inform us which kind—may find their way inward and there await identification, representation, and further conceptualization. For example, one could imagine specific kinds of intrauterine influences upon the fetus which would have to be spoken of as affecting a not yet differentiated mind, but whose impact nevertheless registers, can be inferred, and in certain instances even empirically demonstrated (see Rosenfeld 1987, pp. 185–88, n. 3; Tustin 1981). At some point posterior to self-other differentiation and the demarcation of internal-external boundaries, these "resident" objects may be (mis)perceived as if new, or, under other circumstances, they may be in some way recognized, giving rise to the sense of timelessness. In short, we are referring to the place or the register of *a priori* objects, and certain *a priori* sensations they inspire, and to the possibility that prementational impressions of God are among these. We shall reconsider this topic in chapter 5. In any event, it seems to me that if DeLuca can acknowledge this minimum possibility, if we can imagine that "God" is a sign *in the sense that* the term and much of what is represented points to an objective referent whose existence is independent of human representational capacities, then and only then have we moved beyond Sigmund Freud's psychological positivism.

DeLuca's dilemma, I think, falls fully within the purview of both the religionist as well as the psychologist. As van der Leeuw taught (1963, p. 174), "God cannot be represented in his external nature, but in his revelation to man he has a 'face' and *it* can be described. Otherwise, the divine revelation could not have taken place." And yet, it is precisely the vividness of God's image, and the degree and quality with which it is internalized, which challenges religionist and psychologist alike. For, continued van der Leeuw, "We know that natural human life is nothing but the creation of images. Yet we know the danger that threatens us: the taking of the image we have formed as the image of God which was given us. It is the primal, and actually the only, sin: idolatry" (1963, p. 323). In other words, the very conceptual categories of both psychology and religion—such as the "object representations" of psychology or the "thirteen divine attributes" and the "Face of God" of Jewish mysticism—threaten constantly to turn the conceptualized object away from its very nature. This sort of idolatry, or commoditization, is not measured simply in terms of the primitiveness of the conjured object one supplicates through religious ritual or of the anthropomorphic qualities of the language with which one addresses this object. In fact, the same idolatry, the same tendency to mistake and misconstrue our projected and transfered representations of the object for the veridical object—supplicating, taunting, and seducing the self-imposed object in terms of our own needs, and in essentially ritualistic patterns—exists throughout the gamut of human relationships and is indigenous to the limitations of language.

For the psychologist, the question is not only: To what degree has the divine object matured from "thing" to "concept?" It is more so: What has happened to those earlier preconceptual psychic registrations from which the higher concept of God has evolved? What functions might thse pre-mature representations of God continue to serve? Under which circumstances might the earlier, "infantile" God concept or the later, "mature" God concept be the more significant, psychologically meaningful concept? How can one arrive at some kind of phenomenologically pure (or "experience near") description of the divine object representation without reducing it to a psychological commodity?

The questions for the religionist are essentially similar insofar as he or she, too, must reckon with the internalized qualities of the imaginable image of God! As the talmudic rabbis recognized, idolatry consists fundamentally not only in the institutionalization of the totemistic object, but also in the imposition of pathological self-structures that nullify the relationship with God:

> Said Rav Abin: What does the passage mean, "There shall be in you no strange god; you shall worship no foreign god" [Ps. 81 : 10]? Who is the 'strange god' within the self other than the evil inclination [yezer ha-ra]! (Talmud, Shab. 105b)

In contemporary terms, idolatry is inherent in all narcissistic structures and their various projected and introjected extensions inasmuch as these cancel out true interpersonal encounter, true recognition of the self and the other, be that other God or fellow person.

In order to take the next fledgling steps toward outlining the overlap between the anthropocentric and deocentric dimensions of experience from the point of view of Jewish belief, a specific substructure must be described. This substructure is the halakhic metapsychology. Inasmuch as this substructure is internalized and represented in the personalities of those who adhere to Jewish faith and practice, it can be considered the psychic plane within which transpires the overlap of interpersonal and human-God relations and of psychotherapeutic and theological constructs.

4 | The Halakhic Metapsychology

There is not a single theoretical or techno-logical discovery, from new psychological insights to man's attempts to reach out to the planets, with which the Halakhah is not concerned. New halakhic problems arise with every scientific discovery. As a matter of fact, at present, in order to render precise halakhic decisions in many fields of human endeavor, one must possess, besides excellent halakhic training, a good working knowl-edge in those secular fields in which the problem occurs.

—JOSEPH DOV HALEVI SOLOVEITCHIK
(1965, P. 52N)

Perhaps the most important yield of the early research in psychology and Judaism was the germinal form of what was to be called the halakhic metapsychology (Spero 1977 and 1980). As denoted by the term, this metapsychology is intended to postulate certain working principles which logically precede the study of psychology or psychotherapy as pertains to religious belief and its objects. This metapsychology is not a testing device per se, although it is capable of submitting itself to testing: it is first and foremost a "framework of meaning" (Rychlak 1977), defining what can occur rather than predicting eventualities in every instance.

The central working principle of this metapsychology is the hypothesis of analogy between the conceptual terms of psychology and Halakhah. Second, by logical extension of the hypothesis of analogy between psychological and religious language, the metapsychology concerns itself with the intimate similarity between the psychotherapeutic relationship and the relationship between God and humans. These hypotheses enable us to speak further of a sense in which psychotherapeutic processes have an inherent redemptive actuality, being complementary and in some ways parallel to the relationship between humans and God. By franchising the therapist to search among halakhic structures for frameworks analogous to psychotherapeutic processes and phenomena, the therapist can hope to find inherently religious solutions for practical dilemmas. By this expedient, the therapist is enabled to concentrate on the *technical* aspects of a shared language for working with the religious patient and his or her unique modes of expression with the knowledge that the therapist's *clinical* language is viewed simultaneously as a religiously sound endeavor.

Problematization of the Relation between Psychotherapy and Religion

Ultimately, the halakhic metapsychology is intended as an iron tool for breaking the deadlock created by the prevailing psychologistic models reviewed in the previous chapter. To this end, the proposed metapsychology adopts as its initial task to problematize the relationship between psychotherapy and halakhic Judaism. That is to say, it underscores four unacceptable aspects of earlier approaches to the relationship between psychology, psychotherapy, and religion—specifically, halakhic Judaism—qua belief structures (Spero 1983).

The metapsychology seeks to disallow, first, the tendency of religiously oriented counselors and therapists to rather arbitrarily harvest "safe" (that is, philosophically or theologically nonobjectionable) practice techniques without regard for the overall fit or integration between Jewish law and these pirated techniques or schools. Second, it criticizes earlier models for not evolving a *modus operandi* for resolving practical, halakhic problems encountered during psychotherapy. Third, it considers as misdirected the energies expended on evolving so-called "Torah psychologies." These haphazardly organized collections of rabbinic statements about human behavior, though useful as such, tend to evince little regard on the organizers' part for the complexities of motivation theory, cognition and perception, interpersonal dynamics, or psychopathology. Little effort has been made to unpackage the embedded rabbinic wisdom or to reframe rabbinic opinions in contemporary terms (which was partly due to the fact that the contemporary framework had been rejected *a priori* by many such writers).

Finally, the metapsychology cites the previous three problems as the major contributors to the intractable perception of psychology as foreign and somehow threatening to the religious community. By dissolving these dilemmas—by bringing to light the inherently psychotherapeutic mechanisms and values of religious belief and the inherently religious nature of the psychotherapeutic process—it is believed that the inhospitable perceptions might thaw.

In particular, for the case of halakhically oriented Judaism, I argued for an outlining of the intrinsic halakhic status of psychological phenomena and psychotherapeutic methodology, thereby enabling "linkage" or analogy between the *languages* of psychotherapy and religious law. This approach, in other words, proposes an inherent identity between the basic mechanisms, processes, or objects both systems believe themselves to be conceptualizing. This, in turn, legitimizes the idea that their languages, terms, and motifs address a single reality, or a single set of objects, in ways that are essentially analogous. The practical challenge remains the enumeration of a large enough group of halakhic models, paradigms, or homologues for therapeutic mechanisms and processes. Each of these needs to be sufficiently rich in detail so as to enable examination and confirmation. Further, each has to be not only heuristic but also at least potentially practical.

Different than the traditional approach, the halakhic metapsychology demands thorough delineation of the intricacies of both the religious as well as the psychotherapeutic concepts so that there might emerge more fully the religiously relevant essence of a given psychological datum or concept as well as the psychologically relevant essence of religious doctrine. This goal is not fulfilled by positing, for example, simply that the Judaic-rabbinic concept of *yeẓer ha-ra* (the "evil" inclination) is *identical* to, say, the psychoanalytic concept of the id or the instinctual drives (see Spero 1980, chap. 5). For, notwithstanding all apparent and intriguing similarities, a too quick or premature *identification* of these terms risks vitiating the actual uniqueness of the two systems and their worldviews.[1] Moreover, it fosters the radical substitution of essentially educational or theological terms and practices for psychotherapeutic ones. As we saw above, this encourages the proliferation of "psychotheologies" of dubious merit. *Instead, the halakhic metapsychology instructs that analogies between psychotherapy and religion cannot reach full utility unless the latent psychological understructure of religious terminology and the latent theological understructure of psychotherapeutic terminology are brought to light.*

Returning to the example of the psychoanalytic notion of the id and the Judaic concept of the *yeẓer ha-ra*, and, for another example, psychotherapy and the Judaic concept of repentance (*teshuvah*), one would state better that both terms represent analogous efforts to grapple with a single motivational-behavioral reality subtended by qualities, characteristics, and processes that are morally as well as psychically interrelated. The fuller personological or existential import of the id—say, on the level of the discovery of the "Other" at the end of the spectrum of "instinctual cathexes"—might emerge by analogy to the theological or halakhic qualities that subtend the term *yeẓer ha-ra*, since theology tends more fully to conceptualize "human drive" and "will" as purposive responses to the call of God. At the same time, a more insightful comprehension of the dynamic subtleties represented by the *yeẓer ha-ra*, and all this might mean for the dynamic relationship between humans and God, could emerge by analogy to the parallel processes that have been more completely fleshed by id (or ego) psychology research.

The halakhic metapsychology, in other words, opposes the old model, which sought a merely extrinsic and at times artificial "alliance" between the fields. The older model, such as adopted by Outler (1954) and, subsequently, by a few Jewish writers (Hankoff 1979;

Klein 1979a, 1979b; Levi 1970 and 1979), led, at best, to occasional nonbelligerence pacts between what were still viewed as essentially irreconcilable mates. The proposed approach suggests that each field stands to be elucidated by its partner. In the case of Judaism, by working with the system of Halakhah, the fundamental ethic and praxis of Jewish religion, such mutual enlightenment can be extended beyond the realm of shared metaphors to the domain of actual practice and technique.

Thomas Oden's Approach to the Psychotherapy-Religion Dialogue

There exists only one similar effort at synthesizing psychotherapeutic and religious language. Its merits and basic flaws must be noted since they will provide a contrast for the potential advances of the halakhic metapsychology (and whatever similar model might be constructed for other religions). This is the approach of Christian pastoral therapist Thomas Oden (1967).

Oden's approach was groundbreaking and far-reaching and greatly relevant to religious Judaism. Oden's observations led him to reject the traditional "secular *versus* sacred" bifurcation of reality in favor of the principle *omni in ipso constant* ("All things in Him consist," Col. 1: 17), which he defended on Christian theological grounds. This puts at center stage what is essentially the Old Testament doctrine that God is the locus of the physical world and its structural properties (Gen. R. 68: 10 to Gen. 28: 11, "He is the place of the world . . ."; cf. Ps. 90: 1). Even more specifically, from the point of view of Judaism, this intimate nexus between the transcendent God and the physical world is schematized within the formal structures of Halakhah. As the rabbis portray, "What has The Holy One in this world but the four cubits of Halakhah!" (Talmud, *Ber.* 8a).[2] Hence, a biblical-halakhic framework for what the modern mind knows as "psychotherapy" would link the therapeutic process directly to an underlying religious structure with built-in potential for relationship with God.

Oden then asserted that psychotherapy must maintain its identity as a science of human understanding and cure, even as, from the religious point of view, this very pursuit must be conceptualized as a divinely intended instrumentality of change. In the given moments when psychotherapy is implemented, in effect, developments unfold that not only touch upon psychopathology or other elements of intra-

and interpersonal behavior as construed "secularly" (neurologically, psychiatrically, etc.), but also reach into the depths of the human spirit, resonating on the level of real relationship between a human and God. The interpersonal (anthropocentric) relational matrix, in contemporary terms, is always parallel to a deocentric relational matrix.

Psychotherapy, it follows, has an intrinsic capacity to reveal and clarify the possibility of relationship to God through a relational process similar to religious *gnosis*. Oden acknowledges exactly this and argues:

> Like gnosticism, psychotherapy views the human predicament under the analogy of a radical imprisonment to unseen (unconscious) and demonic (self-destructive) powers that have taken hold of man's volition and delivered his body over to death. Just as in gnosticism, man's problem is that he has irretrievably forgotten who he is and his salvation is a process of breaking down resistances and breaking through to a new memory, so in psychotherapy the man in trouble has so completely forgotten or misplaced his identity that he needs help to "find himself" again through a process of anamnesis, and must renegotiate the wrong turns in his past traumas. (1967, p. 110)[3]

I believe that Oden was not merely implying that a patient might perchance undergo religiouslike experiences or seek theologically relevant insights through the helping relationship. Oden went further to suggest that the patient-therapist relationship, in its fully psychiatric or psychoanalytic psychotherapeuticness, partakes of ways of relationship that are analogous to the relation between humans and God.

We are to imagine a reciprocal process, in other words, whereby in the process of helping one's neighbor, the therapist is participating as well in the restoration of the divine image in humanity. This process, however, has two facets. The first, to be sure, focuses on the provision of effective helping per se (that is, the mechanics and dynamic contingencies of the helping process), which becomes known from developments within psychology and psychiatry. Yet, Oden sought a process that was intrinsically religious. Thus, in addition to the empirical aspects of cure, the uniquely religious element had to be discovered. For Oden, this meant that the possibility of participating in the helping process *had to be in some way mandated by a prior act of grace*. Oden offered Christian sources for this. For example, he posited that in ministering effectively to the pain of the human, the therapist exercises a divine prerogative, echoing Jesus's last parable, "As you did it to one of the least of these my brethren, you did it to me!" (Math. 25: 31, 32). In the provision of caring, patient helping or *therapeia* to the troubled, declares the Messianic Judge, the righteous have fulfilled a divine expectation and have actually ministered to God.[4] In earlier rabbinic sources, as well, God is depicted as benefiting from human consolation (Talmud, *Ber.* 3a; cf. Talmud, *Kid.* 30b to Ex. 20:12)[5] and assistance (Talmud, *Shab.* 89b).[6] Thus, the willingness of God to share and be assisted in the helping process, as it were, is personified in the particular form of reciprocal "relation" potential in every therapeutic act.

The contemporary psychotherapist, of course, has long since accepted that the therapeutic *relationship* itself is an important curative factor in addition to learning, "anamnesis," catharsis, and gradual accretions of insight (Strupp 1968, 1983). But this kind of relationship does not mean merely the giving of oneself as such, as "friend" to the patient. The factor of the therapist's personality in psychotherapy is subjected to a great many processes taking place within the patient, including a multitude of cataclysmic as well as subtle introjections, idealizations, rejections, and identifications along the arduous and winding path toward a more realistic perception of the therapist and a mature defining of the self (Fairbairn 1958; Greenberg 1986; Goz 1975; Guntrip 1961; Spero 1990; Wallerstein 1989). However, this needs constant reiteration since, as we saw earlier, through the overenthusiastic analogy to gnosis and the apostolic function of therapist, one incurs the risk of an imbalanced emphasis on "learning" or "knowing" that would be decidedly nonpsychotherapeutic.

Even so, if the encounter itself between therapist and patient is to be analogized to religion, and specifically to the religious encounter with the divine object, one would seem to be inviting dismal frustration. If one wished to insist on the analogy, one would need to find some acknowledgment on the part of religion for the idea that relationship between humans and God is also predicated upon moments of neutrality, not only upon presence but also upon absence, and that it, too, involves discriminating the illusory, projected, or transferred perceptions of the divine object from objective ones.

Psychotherapy teaches, for instance, that the therapist's incognito role and the careful safeguarding of personal self-disclosure are prerequisites for the deep kind of self-discovery the patient needs to be enabled to undergo. Oden's approach would beg us to emphasize two facets of this basic aspect of psychotherapy. The first would focus upon the effective implementation of "standard" techniques and taking professional postures as defined by empirical considerations. For what is relevant to the individual providing psychotherapy, as opposed to pastoral counseling or education, is only such kinds and qualities of "disclosure," "attention," "empathy," or "unconditional positive regard" as have been objectively discovered to actually modify psychopathology (cf. Bollinger 1985). The second facet, operating at parallel, would seek the intrinsic link to God within the *religious* dimension of the self-same incognito role. That is, on the parallel level one may experience through psychotherapy something of the relationship between the human and God. This dimension becomes even more comprehensible, other than through a suitably informed psychotherapy, by seeking additional analogies between therapeutic mechanisms and postures and similar aspects of the divine relation with a fellow human.

Oden strikes his analogy in Jesus's cry in the ninth hour on the cross—"My God, My God, why hast Thou forsaken me?" (Mark 15 : 34)—and recasts the *religious* value of the therapist's neutrality thus:

> Likewise in therapy, it is the one who is for us, the empathic therapist, who in a sense "forsakes" us, leaves us to ourselves, lets us radically choose ourselves without overweaning guidance, permits us to be ourselves even amid anger, anxiety, and emptiness, and who thereby allows us to discover our own humanity . . . therapeutic help similarly emerges only after a certain sort of crucifixation; namely, the death of the therapist's own imperialistic desire to control the decisions of the other, the burial of the inclination to shape the destiny of others. (1967, p. 37)

This is a great profundity in this apparent homiletic. In fact, Oden's description anticipates A. Fayek's (1981) recent Lacanian interpretation of the therapeutic process, with its equally robust clinical and existential implications. Relating so-called narcissistic object relations to Freud's concept of the death instinct, Fayek showed that the narcissistic patient must eventually acknowledge that all of his relationships with others take place, in fact, not truly with objective others but rather with "counterparts," extensions of projected aspects of the needy self. The sense of being desired by such objects is obviously imaginary, a tragic and hollow mirroring, a reversal of the narcissist's enraged and unmet demands on his or her own inner objects (or a projection of the miserable inability to requit the introjected demands of others). Such demand is essentially a closed loop within the self. In therapy, this entire narcissistic dynamic is eventually projected upon the therapist. Thus, in order for therapy to effect lasting change in the patient, these projected "counterpart" images and idealizations of the therapist must virtually *die!* In a sense, the therapist-as-construed-by-the-narcissistic-self must truly cease to exist before the patient can ever discover himself in the presence of an object objectively encountered!

Oden's conceptualization, in this light, is simultaneously technical and religious. Continuing with the example of the therapist's self-disclosure, the moment of *non*intervention in therapy is an acknowledgment at once of a bridge between the therapist and God and spans a simultaneously deocentric and anthropocentric element of their relationship. Existentially, it is a realization of the discovery of self via the "death" of the psychotherapist no less than through God's "destruction" of his otherwise predetermining will and foreknowledge. From the theological viewpoint, it is the *a priori* divine self-limitation that mandates the possibility of human self-limitation, *a particular form of which is manifest in psychotherapy.* And it is the therapist's *a priori* self-limitation, developed through an assiduous personal analysis, which enables the patient's self-discovery, *a particular form of which is manifest in the quality of the patient's religious experience.* As M. Masud R. Khan (1969) put it, the therapist's interpretations must occasionally include not-interpreting! As such, the patient's self-discovery in therapy is simultaneously one which enables the gradual rediscovery of the therapist, to some degree to perceive more accurately the objective reality of the person of the therapist beyond the pale of the patient's projections and transferences. Finally, this mode may also enable the patient to rediscover some of the objective aspects of God.

Critique of Oden's Metapsychology

There are two main limitations with Oden's approach, which I forward only so that his contribution may be made sharper still.

First, due to his prior rejection of the so-called "natural theology," which had looked to science to provide facts for theology, Oden came to a rather extreme conclusion: "In our view it is not the therapeutic process which clarifies the love of God, but the love of God which finally clarifies the internal reality of the therapeutic process" (p. 135). In fact, Oden here may have underestimated the full therapeutic power he himself had just restored to the God whose presence is known, among other ways, through human perception. It is precisely because one believes that God reveals religious truths through the empirical world that one may expect to find in the belated discoveries of psychotherapy some of the fullest insights to date into the depth of interpersonal and deocentric love and hate. God's love, empathy, and so forth may be *implicit* in numerous other commandments and injunctions in a general way, and whether or not the human being is conscious of it. Certain additional, very specific forms of love may emerge only in *specific* divine commands, such as the command to *heal* (Ex. 21:19) and to *restore* (Talmud, *Sanh.* 73a to Deut. 22:2), or in other, seemingly unlikely commands. However, for such love to take perceptual form, the inner, technical religious structure which programatizes specific acts of healing and restoration would need to be unpackaged as best as possible and subsequently compared to the techniques of psychotherapy. This leads to the second criticism.

Oden realized that he needed a more complex approach to the actual "linkage" between interpersonal and human-God relationships. He had, in effect, sensed the ideological parallel between the work of the therapist and the work of God and highlighted those biblical passages which he felt expressed this parallel. Even these intuitions directed him to only a few of the most general elements in psychotherapy: unconditional positive regard, empathy, self-restraint. To truly link secular and religious dynamics—to guide the practitioner through the hundreds of problematic moments and technical quandaries in clinical life—there is needed a highly complex, formalized structure, representing God's analogous activity or desire at each step of the way. Sufficiently formalized, such a structure would, at once, enable theology or religion to exert a concrete or practical demand upon the empirical world (that is, the technique of therapy) as well as bind psychotherapist and believer to the faith structure in which relationship with God is implicit. This means that beyond procuring the skeletal biblical passage that hints at analogy, there must take place a full exegesis of the freshly posited analogy in accordance with the formal properties of the religious system. For this to occur, one would have to become familiar with the linguistic conventions, deductive and inductive methodologies, hermeneutic principles, and other fine details of exposition that are particular to the given religion. Here, I shall illustrate some of this kind of unpackaging in the case of Halakhah.

There is an additional reason to bring forth the formal structure of the religion-psychotherapy or religion-psychology analogy. The formal structure of a belief system—and the specific formal structures of each religion—is perhaps the most important and multilithic *internalizable* property of the system. It represents an architectonic whose influence, from earliest life, affects everything from language formation, psychological differentiation, cognitive style, imagination to complex concept formation and values development. (I shall not take up here whether these structures *precede* language or are encased in it.) To be sure, myths, lore, and rituals are also internalized in the religious personality (see Arlow 1961; Spero 1982), but they take their most advanced form primarily in relief against the broader integument of a living meaning apparatus (cf. Richards 1989 pp. 119–22). What typically is called "religious identity," it is clear, is only a relatively discrete aspect of this internalized structure (Ostow 1977). As such, the internalized formal structure—and the *quality* of its internalization—gives volume, form, variety, diversity of emotional tone, and richness of representational texture to primary religious objects, to the not-evidently religious objects with which these interact, and, ultimately, to the overall psychic interior they constitute. To fully comprehend an individual's god, pathological or otherwise, is to do so against the background of the formal structures within which fabric god representations reside.[7]

We may now reexamine the aforementioned problem of the therapist's self-disclosure, for which Oden offered an elementary analogy in Mark 15:34. Through it, Oden sought to join the realities of the consulting room and the cross. Certainly, the religious ideal of self-restraint, even as understood in the most rudimentary manner, already instigates heightened sensitivity to the parallel between the anthropocentric and deocentric dimension. As such, however, it cannot satisfy the clinical need for structures and paradigms that apply even more immediately to the realities of the consulting room. These are, in fact, the links Oden suspected he lacked. To provide such links—from the standpoint of Halakhah, for example—one initially might begin with comparatively elementary analogies, such as the biblical concept of *hastarat panim* (Deut. 31:17; cf. also Ps. 22:1), that is, the constraint and veiling, as it were, of God's direct Providence. Numerous other rabbinic statements portray the tension between a finite, self-limiting versus omniscient, omnipotent God (see Rosenthal 1990). However, the practical links—the more procedurally specific analogies between the religious and therapeutic processes—are delineated by exploring further the intricate halakhic parameters and rules bearing upon love, disclosure, ethical remonstration, confidentiality, and guidance, some of which, in fact, *restrain* under specifiable conditions the active role of the "guiding other" (see Spero 1986).

Presumptions and Tenets of the Halakhic Metapsychology

The halakhic metapsychology provides a glimpse at the internalizable formal structure of Judiasm. In order that it be possible to study the broader applicability of the kind of metapsychology I am proposing, I shall first devote some attention to its basic assumptions.

The most basic assumption of the proposed approach, obviously, is that the Judeo-halakhic worldview can and ought to accommodate the concepts and data acknowledged by the "secular" psychological worldview. Of course, even this assumption is objectionable to some schools of thought within Judaism, which, if they appear disinterested in synthesizing Judaism and modern science in general, are especially vociferous in their abnegation of psychology and psychotherapy. Nonetheless, the present work subscribes to the possibility of such synthesis (see Klahr 1976; Schimmel and Carmell 1989; Soloveitchik 1965). There is even greater novelty in the fact that the metapsychology assumes there cannot be an unbridgeable epistemological gap between the elements of psychology and Halakhah *since at root both systems are different but related schematic frameworks for a single, divinely conceived reality.* And if, from the point of view of Judaism, all aspects of reality are underwritten by a specific halakhic structure, *then psychological dimensions of reality must have their appropriate halakhic structures as well.* Mermelstein (1976) was the sole other writer on psychology and Judaism to suggest a similar type of synthesis (others may have simply presumed one, but the literature, as noted, does not reflect this), although he published no further work on this topic.

Let us put this formally. The halakhic metapsychology is predicated upon three prior axia:

1. Axiomatic to the basic worldview of halakhically oriented Juda-

ism is that the Torah and its postulatory ethicomoral legal system, the Halakhah, precede in an *a priori* way reality as we know it. This is taken to mean, simply, that fundamental halakhic principles are *a priori* like mathematical truths. Proponents of this approach are sometimes satisfied to assert the logical or moral supremacy of Halakhah in its parallel relationship with other, independent aspects of reality (see S. Spero 1983). According to another prominent interpretation, however, Halakhah is actually temporally anterior to reality as we know it (that is, prior in time to Creation). I documented in chapter 1 some relevant sources for the second interpretation.

2. All entities of reality, including abstract values, have their basic halakhic identity, although this fundamental halakhic identity or structure does not exhaust the possible extended forms or applications of a given entity. Hendel (1976), for example, utilizes a mathematical model to illustrate the relationship between pure halakhic structures and their applications in the real world (see also Lichtenstein 1969 and 1975; Tendler 1969). According to all approaches, in any case, a *non*halakhic world—that is, a world in which there is no *a priori* halakhic form for a given subject matter or vice versa—is inconceivable.[8] Nonetheless, a *pre*halakhic state of affairs—one in which halakhic forms have simply not yet been comprehended or applied by the human mind—is certainly conceivable, but this would be viewed as a temporary or indefinite, unredeemed state of reality. Even states or phenomena that Halakhah considers "impure," "abominable," "alien," or simply "wrong"—including behavior often incorrectly referred to as *non*halakhic, when what is intended is "halakhic, but forbidden by Halakhah"—are by this status alone held to be placed within and subject to the halakhic reality. It follows that basic psychological structures must, as well, have a halakhic understructure, whether or not such understructure has yet been brought to light.

3. Finally, Halakhah assumes that all religious obligations or *miẓvot* are designed ultimately to influence the human being in a salutary manner, intrapersonally as well as interpersonally (see *Sefer ha-Ḥinukh*, introd.). Maimonides establishes the point categorically (*M.T., Hil. Temurah* 4:13):

> The Torah plumbed the depths of human thought and restricted
> man's evil inclination [*ve-kiẓet et yiẓro ha-ra*] . . . All these laws are [in
> order to] compel his nature and to correct his personality. And so it is

that most of the Torah's laws are essentially recommendations from
afar, from the Great Advisor, to correct personality and to straighten
one's deeds.

This implies that there *must* be psychological mechanisms of *some*
kind deep within the structures of the law that facilitate or express
such change at every level. However, aside from the operational details and parameters of these laws, it would seem as if the codes generally do not (and never in great depth) outline the actual nature of
such psychological interflow or its permutations and limits. Here is
precisely where emerges the expository power of halakhic analogies
to allegedly extrahalakhic structures.

The Nature of the Identity between Psychological and Halakhic Constructs

One cannot amble into the immense domain of psychotherapy and
Halakhah armed solely with a hypothetical template such as the proposed halakhic metapsychology and push immodestly for a total equation of identity between halakhic and psychological constructs. Owing
to the Law of Transferable Epithets (If, $x = y$; Then, for F, $Fx = Fy$—
an extension of Leibnitz's Law), it would only be warranted to identify a given psychological element x and a given halakhic (or religious) element y if it could be said that every aspect of x is also true of
y. We would have to be able to prove (although it certainly makes
sense to state), for example, that for every id impulse x there is a
corresponding halakhic state y; for each incidence a of projection
or incidence b of therapist self-restraint, there is a corresponding
halakhico-spiritual state a—I shall identify which in the discussion of
arevut that follows—or a moment of divine elusiveness b! We plainly
are not yet able to do so.

At the current stage, one must be satisfied with *correlation* between
halakhic and psychological analogies, or with state-to-state identities.
To illustrate, the halakhic metapsychology would acknowledge that
ensoulment may indeed have its complementary biological and neu-
rochemical characteristics, and it may further accept that spiritual,
psychological, and biochemical states co-exist to a certain degree,
even though this cannot yet be proven because we cannot empirically
demonstrate the actual linkage. As Ernest Hartmann once demonstrated quite effectively (1966), it is possible to use metapsychological
categories as "indicators" of the potential objective links between

psychological and physiological systems even though the precise relationship between these two systems directly is not otherwise known. And this relation holds without implying any causal relation between the metapsychological system itself and either the psychological system or the physiological system. One searches for *cohesion* between the systems rather than solid identity. Hartmann was working with psychoanalytic metapsychological terms: we will coin halakhic metapsychological terms. Rabbinic tradition declares, for example, that the soul nightly leaves the body and returns to its Source; a belief which is incorporated into the mandatory daily practice of ritual washing of the hands upon arising after sleep (Talmud, *Ber.* 57b, 60b; *Mid. Rabba* to Lam. 3:23; *Sh. A., O. Ḥ.*, 4). The ritual act is an empirically observable aspect of everyday life, and perhaps so also are some of its sociological (or microbiological?) causes and effects. Even so, whether or not souls leave bodies, or how states of spiritual "morbidity" and vitality are exchanged, or how God and the human relate to each other via this exchange is not observable. And the psychodynamics of this affair, at best inferable, occupy a middle ground. Yet once these multiple interpretations of "reality" are interwoven in the formal, empirical meaning structures of Halakhah, their *internalized* dimension becomes real and it becomes possible to speak of a true psychological identity among these dimensions.

For another example, the Midrash (Gen. R. 20:15) enumerates four "yearnings" (*teshukot*) or tropisms: between male and female, the evil impulse (*yeẓer*) and the ideological descendants of Cain, rain and the earth, and God and Israel. This rabbinic teaching *may* be interpreted as portraying the *yeẓer* as an elemental biological or organic pulsion, in addition to its spiritual qualities. Indeed, in the commentary of Rabbi Judah Löwe of Prague (d. 1609), the *yeẓer* is typically spoken of as a partly intellectual, partly physical drive (for example, *Netivot Olam: Netiv Ko'aḥ ha-Yeẓer*). Based on such analogies, correlation may appear likely between the evident biological-id-impulse-aspect of *yeẓer* and many of the psychoanalytic principles relating to the id. This would invite (by virtue of $Fx = Fy$) psychoanalytically oriented interpretations of the vicissitudes of the *yeẓer*, on one hand, and ethicomoral or *yeẓer*-oriented interpretations of psychodynamics on the other hand. But there are evident problems with the $Fx = Fy$ junction here. For example, one does not customarily think of id impulses as "evil" in the sense that the *yeẓer* is sometimes spoken of as "evil." Furthermore, in what sense would man's biological pulsions mark him, as the Bible put it, "but evil continually from his youth" (Gen. 6:5, 8:21)? Perhaps, one might argue, custom and usage are the only real impediments to the tightness of our analogies, and language substitution ought to be viewed as the panaceum. Thus, by such substitution, one might suggest that the term "evil" in the biblical and rabbinic lexicon be reinterpreted to mean "untamed," "unsublimated," "split-off and narcissistically rageful," or "psychopathically chaotic." But if we grant this, then the identity of these terms depends upon other factors (such as linguistic conventions) not intrinsic to the terms themselves. Once again, while the postulated analogies or even occasional state-to-state identities do provide useful links between psychotherapy and religion, and between the deocentric and anthropocentric dimensions, the links must be regarded probationally.

Because this new approach is so dense, I will offer one more illustration, this time hinting to the manner in which the $Fx = Fy$ problem can be resolved, and which I will expound in the next section. In this illustration, the reader will note, we will seek to make use of factors that are intrinsic to the terms under comparison.

How might one discover a halakhic analogy for the psychological phenomenon of empathy? One method would be to find a biblical or midrashic episode whose theme or major teaching either directly refers to the value of empathy (first-order evidence) or which can only make sense if we deduce that the episode presumes the existence or operation of empathy and that no other interpretation explains the episode as well or completely (second-order evidence). This is precisely what Oden sought to do in grounding the psychotherapeutic role in the biblical *therapeia*—that is, the teachings of the Messianic Judge in Matthew 25 can only be comprehended by *empathic beings*, from which one deduces that human empathy is implicitly assumed and addressed by the biblical word. We have now examined some of the superficial problems with this approach. Essentially, we have admitted that a tighter fit is needed between the theological and psychological terms.

In the case of Halakhah—and remembering that we are assuming *arguendo* its view that the basic understructure of halakhic principles are *a priori* and, even when they are *a posteriori*, point to truths of objective reality—one might offer the following. The halakhist, too, would begin, perhaps on intuitive grounds, with the best *prima facie* link to contemporary terms that can be located in biblical literature. However, at this point the intuitive phase of the search ends and the fairly empirical-inductive phase begins, as the incumbent biblical analog must now be examined thoroughly from within the fullest possible complexity of its structural characteristics. This means that the biblical (or rabbinic) term, passage, or episode must be analyzed contextually, semantically, and by all legitimate hermeneutic rules that might bring forth the implicit or latent truths and applicabilities of the materiale.

Consider, accordingly, two samples of this:

> 1. From the passage "'Unclean, unclean!' he shall call out" (Lev. 13 : 45), which is ostensively limited to the grim context of the laws of the leper, the Talmud (*M.K.* 5a, cf. *B.K.* 92a) draws forth the following Masoretic ethic: "This [passage] teaches that he must publicize his agony [so that] the community can beg for mercy on his behalf."
> 2. The Talmud (*Sanh.* 104b) inquires into the wording of the passage "You shall surely cry in the night" (Lam. 1 : 2): "Why [specify] 'in the night'? To teach that one who cries in the night, his voice is heard! Another teaching: When one cries in the night, others will hear his voice and they will cry with him."

In possession of these two derivations, one stands upon firmer ground for positing that the two biblical passages cited *in fact* refer to or presume an empathic potential. At the very least—that is, assuming only that the rabbinic interpretations are to be viewed as an entirely *a posteriori* contribution—we may claim to have located a consensual approach to the biblical word that tightens the $Fx = Fy$ criterion and commensurately legitimizes the relevance of the modern notion of empathy to the theological framework. In addition, if one adopts (or wishes to accommodate) the point of view that even *a posteriori* rabbinic exegeses reflect links to *a priori* halakhic truths, then derivations such as the current two samples help forge an intrinsic synthesis between psychological-technical and religious language *and between their objective referents* (which, in this argument, are ultimately variants of a single halakhic reality). Both conclusions, moreover, permit the adduction or prediction of additional instantiations of the given $Fx = Fy$ analog.

In retrospect, we will see that the halakhic metapsychology has large aspirations, but must content itself with humble accomplishments. It may be asked: What *is* gained by positing an identity between the concepts of these two great systems, aside from perhaps eliminating a bit of unnecessary duplication? Does not the proposed metapsychology merely enable psychologists and psychotherapists to "pass off" their professional constructs in religious cloaking?

In response, I believe preparatory groundwork has been initiated, which will make it increasingly possible to *imagine* the kind of homologous relationships that might be discovered someday, in terms compatible with the ways of thought of both great systems. For the fact is that many persons *do* already imagine a God or a soul and tend to speak of these concepts as having actual, objective existence within and influence upon human personality. It is therefore entirely acceptable to try to imagine the kinds of perceptual, neurotransformational, psychodynamic, or object-representational "reception" such religious constructs (and the objective objects they represent) might receive within the psychic system. Of course, the various subspecialities will need each to present its slice of the pie and to interrogate the analogies they propose to the fullest. I shall limit our analysis to the object-representational dimensions of religious objects. Given that it is precisely the patient's beliefs, feelings, and imagination with which the psychotherapist works—these being the formal structures and representations of psychic interiority—then the very fact itself that persons have a certain unique subset of *religious* beliefs necessitates an attempt to correlate such structure with "standard" psychological structure.

An In-depth Illustration of Halakhic Analogy: Psychotherapy as *Arevut*

The halakhic metapsychology brings together states, structures, and values which would otherwise elude comparison. Such comparison philosophically expands the meaning and relevance of the structures of both systems and also contributes practically to the accessibility and assimilability of the structures of one system into the other. I will illustrate this with the psychoanalytic concept of transference, the key therapeutic fulcrum, and the halakhic concept of "*arevut*," or the legal transfer of executive power or financial responsibility.

As noted above, the researcher begins his or her efforts to incorporate the transference phenomenon, as understood by psychotherapists, into the halakhic metapsychology by linking it with its most likely halakhic analog, which I will suggest is the concept of *arevut*, the provision of surety, and the relationship that inheres in serving as an *arev*, a guarantor, custodian, or agent *cum locum tenens*. The concept is derived from at least two biblical passages (see Talmud, *B.B.* 173b): From Genesis 43 : 9, in which Judah guarantees to Jacob the safekeeping of the youngest son, Benjamin,

> I shall be surety for him, of my hand shall you require him; If I bring him not to you, and set him before you, Then let me bear the blame forever.

and Proverbs 6 : 1 – 2,

> My son, if you have become surety for your neighbor, If you have struck your hands for another person; You are snared by the words of your mouth, You are caught by the words of your mouth.

However, in order to avoid Oden's dilemma, the researcher must include the biblical and also the rabbinic foundations and permutations of *arevut*. The value of the rudimentary biblical analogy (that is, at the level of Oden's analogies) would be only to direct attention to the probable existence of further *a priori* halakhic bases for the psychological concept of transference, which, if validated, would then reveal an intrinsic deocentric dimension to the phenomena described by the term psychological transference. The additional formal details of *arevut* would illuminate the more complex common (identical?) legal and psychological mechanisms of transference and *arevut* (such as, displacement of object, exchange of energic, executive, or even emotional communication).

Halakhah hints, for example, that the small parcel of jointly owned foodstuff, known as the *eruv ḥazerot*, used as symbol to create the objective halakhic domain of a communal courtyard (to permit carrying on the Sabbath) simultaneously maintains *interpersonal* intermixing (*arevut*) and domestic harmony (see Jer. Talmud, *Erub.* 7 : 9; also *Erub.* 81a, the view of R. Yehoshua; *SMaG, Hil. Erub.* re: *Shab.* 14b). Yet, in still other discussions, Halakhah restrains the influence of *arevut*, setting the tone for a parallel kind of inhibition of this otherwise natural tendency during psychotherapy (Talmud, *B. B.* 173b). That is, Halakhah painstakingly clarifies the conditions under which the *arev*-bond undertakes almost completely the role and obligations of the other, and when such bond is limited by consensual norm to specific degrees of liability. But above all else, the halakhic structuralization of the concept of the *arev*, or the *eruv* itself, rendered it not simply an external act whose quality is deemed complete upon proper execution, but rather is viewed by Halakhah itself as intimately dependent upon a corresponding mental structure: "One who does not acknowledge [the concept] of *eruv*, his *eruv* is not a [valid] *eruv*" (Talmud, *Erub.* 31b). The point is—and this is crucial—Halakhah considered its forms to be subject to internalization and to play a role in the formation of psychic structure. Such a notion removes the study of halakhic analogies or metastructures from the purely heuristic realm and into the realm of eminent practicality.

Sight is not lost of the fact that, in terms of common usage, *arevut*, strictly speaking, refers to specific kinds of legal instrumentalization and that transference, strictly speaking, is not identical with other kinds of psychological "transfer" mechanisms (for example, Laplanche and Pontalis 1973, p. 455). Leibnitz's Law looms forbodingly before us. Nevertheless, by *analogy* to the state of psychoanalytic transference, one begins to comprehend the empathic, interpersonal foundation of a law such as *arevut* and the potential it has for enhancing the ability to "hear" religious structures in transference phenomena.

In fact, two important classes of identity are licensed by the analogy (that is, even if we cannot claim complete Leibnitzian exchangeability between *arevut* and transference): First, one would state that every act of *arevut*—such as the recitation of ritual blessings on behalf of one's neighbor or taking ownership by proxy of material goods for one's neighbor—evokes, at least marginally, a commonality of feelings between two persons. This commonality of feeling may be denied ("It's just an artifact, a ritual act!") or extended no further than a barely conscious experience of fellowship, or trigger a deeply empathic bond (in the sense of "All of Israel are bondsmen [*areivin*] for each other," [Talmud, *Sheb.* 39a, *Sot.* 37b, *Sanh.* 27b to Lev. 26:37; *R. H.* 29a, Rashi, s.v. "*af al pi*"]). This is psychology's contribution to the exposition of Halakhah, *or the psychological identity of Halakhah.*[9]

Second, one would state that every instance of transference, say, during psychotherapy, evokes dynamic mechanisms or object-relational potentials that extend into the deocentric dimension, into the reality where the relationship between the human and God is mediated by *arevut* structures. By virtue of the analogy, bringing the kaleidoscope of object-relational elements in personality into range—the complexities of proxy relations and sharing in the mother-child interaction (Wangh 1962), the mechanisms of displacement and stimulus generalization, the role and function of mutuality and empathy, and so forth—multiplies one hundredfold the meaning of *arevut* and, hence, expands the potential of this formal aspect of internalized religious structure to elicit meaningful representations of God and the God-human relationship. Quite simply, those key psychological properties that are, in fact, more useful in order to comprehend deeply the sphere of *arevut* in its *broadest* sense are better described by the psychoanalytic concept of transference (or numerous other concepts drawn from the variety of psychological systems) which, in turn, illuminates the halakhic construct. Both concepts can now be viewed as basic psychic structures or drives; not entities to be "resolved" in the simple sense, even though they may under certain circumstances take on pathological characteristics (Bird 1972). And when in the course of everyday religious life something goes awry in those interpersonal domains that a given religious patient conceives through and encompasses by the structures of *arevut*, the halakhic analogy of *arevut*-transference helps flag initial points of intervention. This, then, would be Halakhah's contribution to the religious dimension of transference, *or the halakhic identity of transference.*

In addition to demarcating two classes of identity, the analogy allows direct entry into the practical dilemmas of treatment. Let us consider, for example, the paradoxical aspects of the patient's "freedom" within psychotherapy, one of the more well-known and irksome moral dilemmas facing psychotherapist and patient alike. The psychotherapy patient desires freedom, yet cannot exert such freedom, but must freely will to participate in his or her own therapy, only to then partly surrender his or her freedom to the therapist, who in turn works with the patient, eventually helping the patient to regain a greater range of freedom! Typically, students of the topic construe these paradoxical aspects as an overall philosophical dilemma perplexing all therapists generally, to be resolved in a once-and-for-all manner. Such resolution generally necessitates the application of some form of "agency" model, whereby the therapist is viewed as only temporarily assuming some of the patient's freedoms until the patient's self-knowledge has actually expanded his or her own perception of freedom (Brierley 1951; Burnham 1985; Meissner 1984, chap. 10; Olinick 1959; Smith 1978; Waelder 1936).

A similar view has been adopted by the few writers who have considered the halakhic-philosophical implications of the dilemma, approaching it as a "values conflict" that might be inherent in one technical aspect of the treatment process (Ahren 1980; Spero 1986, chap. 6; S. Schimmel 1977). The problem for Halakhah in attempting to respond to dilemmas such as these is that one will not find anywhere in the vast ancient rabbinic tomes direct technical discussion of "the problem of freedom in *psychotherapy.*" The robustness of the halakhic metapsychological analogy gets tested at precisely this point. And one finds that the *arevut*-transference analog contributes in at least two ways: the first, primarily technical; the second, primarily existential.

Technically, the *arevut*-transference analogy licenses conceiving of the therapist as an *arev* or proxy for the patient's will or ego during the course of the therapeutic journey. As such, the laws which hitherto were confined solely to the domain of *arevut* in its ritual-legal applications now may be extended to its homologous situation; namely, the transference context in psychotherapy. In other words, one derives from the analogy a practical halakhic response to the dilemma of free will.

The following is illustrative of the kinds of parameters one may extract from the *arevut* analogy. Halakhah generally nullifies the value of rituals enacted under coercion, although a key set of exceptions exists. Most germane is the power conferred upon rabbinic courts to coerce a recalcitrant husband to grant a writ of divorce, despite the very specific biblical stipulation that a divorce be freely executed and delivered (Lev. 1:3). Halakhah formally resolves the obvious dilemma here by ruling, paradoxically: "We coerce him until he says: 'I consent!'" Maimonides explains (*M. T., Hil. Gerushin* 2:20) that Halakhah views the individual's *earlier* state of *un*willingness to follow the law (that is, to not grant a divorce) as the state of relative coercion, a state of pathological self-involvement to the point of losing sight of the needs and rights of others. An individual's motivational conflicts, Halakhah would have it, compel him to violate the law against his deeper desire to comply with the word of God. The rabbinic court, in effect, is simply restoring freedom of will.

Critical to the applicability of the proposed analogy is that (1) this power of the Jewish court to coerce is philosophically derived from the principle of *arevut* (see *Ḥiddushei ha-Ritva* to Talmud, *Git.* 52a), (2) it actually extends to a wider variety of religious obligations than just the laws of divorce (*Netivot ha-Mishpat* 3 : 1); and (3) it generally applies as well to officers of the court (as psychotherapists and physicians are halakhically considered) (Talmud, *Sanh.* 5a; *Tos.*, s.v. "*dan*"; cf. also *M.T., Hil. Sanh.* 2 : 11, 4 : 14).[10] In all, it seems to me that this model fits psychotherapy hand-in-glove (discussed in greater detail elsewhere [1986, chap. 6]), for it teaches anew that human freedom is perpetually, and often willingly, compromised by *arevut*-type phenomena; that freedom is a crossroads entity, a matter of constant oscillation between conscious and unconscious modalities of motivation, sometimes rhythmically and somtimes not, emerging from behind the umbra of dependency, bondage, and isolation in grand cadences themselves ironically determined by a host of causal factors.

Ontological Aspects of the Transference-*Arevut* Analogy

The second level of contribution, as noted, is existential and bears upon the fullest aspects of the individual's sense of being, for it is not only the patient's conscious, intellectual understanding of freedom or specific beliefs about freedom with which the therapist intervenes. At the most fundamental level, the psychotherapist is involved with the autonomous qualities of the patient's self-perceptions and identifications. The patient's sense of freedom cannot be simply a philosophical aspect tangential to psychotherapy. It is, in fact, an intrinsic aspect of the qualities of autonomy, mutuality, reciprocality, and so forth that are constituted by the internalized, structured dimensions of object representations. That is, no matter how one understands the problem of freedom philosophically, it is in the nature of the human being who presents himself during psychotherapy to envelop himself in the workings of freedom in ways that are characteristic not simply of his conscious beliefs but also of his unconscious experiences and dynamic conflicts. We may also say that an individual's sense of freedom will be derived not simply from the manifest teachings and beliefs (the "contents") offered by the surrounding religion or culture, as from the "degrees of freedom" expressed much more subtly within the linguistic structures and conceptual pinions which carry these teachings and beliefs. We must understand freedom, insofar as the patient is concerned, as a quality of particular kinds of internal relations among self- and object-representations, which is then abstracted in the form of ideas and beliefs and externalized in the form of "free" actions and autonomous forms of relationship and speech. Along with this line of thinking, the psychopathic personality, for example, is considered beyond moral reasoning not because he or she is unreasonable, but because there exists within such personality a basic flaw in those dimensions of human life which enable an individual to have values and to identify freedom within interpersonal relations (Duffy 1979). Freedom is thus a quality some may view as granted by God— and it may very well be—but the way in which freedom indeed moves from grant to actuality may be as an outcome of certain kinds of intrapsychic developments.

As researchers, we enjoy the privilege of approaching the problem of freedom externally and objectively as a metapsychological "issue" that is removed from living dialogue and requires some kind of morally appropriate deliberation and resolution. But for the therapist and patient during psychotherapy, the problem of freedom is a felt constituent of the very internal psychic structures the patient has submitted to treatment. It is an ontological problem.

Wilfred R. Bion (1959), for example, considerably deepened the understanding of the problem as well as its potential solution when he reconceptualized the patient's freedoms in the light of his unique post-Kleinian point of view. Bion perceived freedom not merely as one of many abstract values in which persons "believe"—of the kind so many therapists supposed one could either include or exclude from the treatment focus. The patient's freedoms are in essence an object-relational motility or tendency in constant search for certain kinds of objects and a certain kind of object relationship. Bion's terminology here is suggestive of what we have been calling the proxy aspects of *arevut*. During psychotherapy, Bion wrote, the patient's freedoms temporarily "repose" in the therapist, undergoing healthy transformations in the safe confines of the therapist's mental apparatus, much the same as the infant's terrifying fantasies and its will to destroy or love omnivorously undergo "detoxification" and "extenuation" in the mother's containing, benevolent mental structures and through her capacity for reverie. Neither the healthy mother nor the therapist shall take over completely the child's or patient's identity, nor will the healthy child or patient achieve freedom and autonomy simply by incorporating the mother or therapist. Rather, their health-inducing functions must gradually be internalized as an aspect of the self and take the form of the patient's own, new autonomous sense of freedom and the capacity for choice.

In any kind of depth psychotherapy, while dealing with the problems of the patient at hand, the therapist quickly begins to recognize the revenants of the "neuroses" and "psychoses" of the surrounding culture and society. At the very least, this is due to the fact that psychotherapy situates itself squarely within the same existential duality that is, in the best of circumstances, an element of basic human nature. Guntrip expressed this duality most clearly:

> The schizoid person, to whatever degree he is schizoid, hovers between two opposite fears: the fear of isolation in independence with loss of his ego in a vacuum of experience, and the fear of bondage to, of imprisonment or absorption in the personality of whomsoever he rushes to for protection. (1969, p. 291)

Almost identical assessments have been made by writers from the disparate fields of social psychology (Fromm 1955; Maslow 1954), existential psychiatry (May, Angel, and Ellenberger 1958), cultural anthropology (Becker 1973), and religion (Spero 1987a). The struggle with this ontologically ingrained schizoid compromise is, of course, virtually unmanageable in disturbed personalities, even though in other circumstances it adds some of the most exquisitely meaningful nuances to healthy self-other relations (Guntrip 1969, pp. 278–79; Khan 1972). And this struggle can certainly be reconceptualized from the halakhic point of view as the basic shifting in the depth, range, and texture of *arevut* between persons. Through mastery of such shifting, pseudo- or false- or simply premature-freedom is modified and true freedom gained. The problem of freedom, then, has become elevated by sensitive psychological explication of the object-relational structure of freedom.

On the strength of the halakhic analogy, *arevut* proper can be viewed as but one expression of a single, divinely ordained empathic phenomenon known in *other* contexts—say, psychotherapeutic ones—as transference. In the light of the halakhic metapsychology, each incidence of transference bears within it the developmental potential for interpersonal and emotional responsibility. Ultimately, the level of responsibility painstakingly tutored by the "working through" of transference, clinically conceived, could take on proportions relevant to the relationship between humans and God, leading to a transmutation of the schizoid breaches between humans and the image of God within.

Of course, this distinctly "moral" dimension may seem irrelevant for psychotherapy during certain early stages. Indeed, at some points it may need to be ignored outright in order for therapy to achieve its clinical goals (say, if there were a far more occlusive resistance to address clinically which took precedence over the moral content itself of the behavior or material as such). At these points, the psychosexual, psychosocial, resistive, or other clinically relevant quality of the transference will be the focus, underscoring only *indirectly* the psychological impediments or proponents of higher moral achievements. At other times, the priorities may be the reverse. In either case, this balancing is observed in every single incident of psychotherapy. For morally appropriate behavior is simply not conceivable without a basis in practical psychological dimensions such as consolidated intrapsychic structuralization (ego-superego), mutuality of autonomy, separation-individuation, self-other boundaries, sublimation and neutralization of instinctual energies, and so forth (Compton 1987; Eagel 1983; Plaut 1986; Post 1972). But at some point, the powerful overlap between the patient's superego maturation, the level of his or her internal object representations, and the quality of object relationship expressed via transference may begin to show advanced characteristics considered necessary for ethical mutuality and moral responsibility. Achievements such as these must take place on the anthropocentric level before they can be used to negotiate a healthy relationship with God. At this juncture, then, theologically or morally relevant aspects of the *arevut* dimension of transference may become an appropriate therapeutic focus.

The problem of emotional and moral proxy-taking—which I hold subtends the transference-*arevut* analogy—is perhaps *the* ontological axis of psychotherapy. Psychotherapy intentionally initiates a process that draws the therapist away from the role of paraclete simply construed. In therapy, the therapist will come to represent for the patient a variety of additional personna that are important in one way or another to the patient and, on some of these occasions, will appear to absorb and "contain" the patient's identifications, thoughts, or personified feelings. Moreover, as therapy evolves, the patient will reinternalize some of his or her transference-oriented perceptions of the therapist, taking in the therapist as a "good" object—or psychological bondsman (*arev*)—that functions in a new and healthy way within the patient's personality. This process, as well, raises the question of whether psychotherapeutic "cure" has been the result of a new development within the patient's identity or of an artificial attachment to the therapist's image within the patient. Are the newly acquired autonomous capabilities merely borrowed from an internal relationship with a new "good" object, or has the patient *internalized* such autonomous qualities more fully and reformed his or her self-structure accordingly (see Bird 1972; Klauber 1972)? Is the patient as "free" in the former case as in the latter? [11]

There is, in fact, another practicable halakhic model that can be derived from the laws of *arevut*, relevant not only to the proxy relationship as such but also to the therapeutic stance regarding the patient's projections during treatment. We begin, again, with the biblical text, this time Deuteronomy 24: 10–11: "When you lend your neighbor any manner of loan; You shall not go into his house to fetch his pledge. You shall stand outside, and the man to whom you did lend shall bring forth the pledge outside to you." In addition to instilling civility and compassion into the harsh realities of lender-borrower relations, these laws argue for maintaining boundaries even though the lender has a legitimate financial claim upon the borrower. Halakhah certainly honors the debtor's obligation to repay, but at the same time disallows intrusion into the debtor's private domain. Even an authorized agent of the court may not enter the house of a borrower uninvited when collecting the debt (Talmud, *B.M.* 115a). Halakhah allows one exception (based on Prov. 6:1, 20:16): it is permissible to enter the domicile of an *arev* to collect a security, since the *arev*, after all, willingly opened his boundaries in order to assist another.

As with the previous analogies, one could extend these laws to psychotherapy and restate them as an instruction to respect the patient's boundaries, to not invasively extract unconscious or hidden ideas and feelings in moments when either resistance or weakness causes the patient to withdraw into the relative safety of his inner spaces temporarily. But, one might fancifully suppose, when the patient has entrusted his material to the psychotherapist-as-*arev*—in the sense that patients transfer certain feeling states and memory patterns into the mind of the therapist via the mechanism of projective identification and other well-known phenomena—the psychotherapist must take care to, on the one hand, protect the patient from premature return of yet undetoxified affective states, but, on the other hand, the therapist must enable the patient free access to his or her own projected material through what the patient will for a while experience as the therapist's "true" feelings or states (for example, the narcissistic patient's sudden conviction that the therapist uses the patient in order to bask in the patient's idealizations).

To all of the above, the professional's immediate associations will be: these are plainly manifestations and vicissitudes of projective identification, or, perhaps, transference. But from the standpoint of the formal structures wherein morality and psychology, and deocentric and anthropocentric relations, are interwoven, this is also *arevut* personified. And not simply because the religionist would like to see this terminology under bright lights, but because *arevut*-transference (in and of itself merely an apt cognomen) refers to objective structures whose internalized forms can be empirically verified. In the case of a personality whose intrapsychic structures have been established in part upon *arevut* and related concepts, we may expect the vicissitudes of the internalization of certain clusters of "good" objects to align themselves to the *a priori* forms of *arevut*. And if, for the religionist, *arevut* further implies an objective deocentric bond or relationship, the psychotherapist who is cognizant of the analogy will be more sensitive to the objective potential of such relationship precisely during his or her work with interpersonal transference.

Critique of the Halakhic Metapsychology: I

An initial criticism of the halakhic metapsychology may come from the general critique of halakhic methodology per se. It has been suggested that conceiving of halakhic living as the scientificlike ordering of behavior, feelings, and the material aspects of the world in accordance with predetermined halakhic structures, is tautological (Shihor 1978) and witheringly antithetical to human subjectivity. Perhaps halakhic investigation does take on this cast when one observes its most abstract, semimathematical operations (see Sosevsky 1976). However, it has been counterargued that the very development of halakhic applications, albeit linked to *a priori* halakhic structures, actually enhances and expands the effective range of human subjectivity (S. Spero 1983; Wurzburger 1962; cf. Lichtenstein 1975).

Pastoral psychologist Levi Meier recently carried this criticism directly into the psychology-Judaism arena (1988). In his exposition of a greater role for the subjective conscience in an alternative halakhic approach to therapy, Meier summarizes my earliest explication of the halakhic metapsychology as he understands it (1980, chap. 1), and then concludes:

> But this *Halakhic a priori* model objectifies man, and does not allow for the subjective human experience. The psycho-*Halakhic* man of conscience [Meier's model], however, incorporates the basic *Halakhic* guidelines of human behavior, and allows man to utilize these norms in a manner that will allow the subjective man to emerge as well. (Meier 1988, p. 31)

Meier may be indulging here in an exaggerated celebration of subjectivity. Meier apparently condenses one of my defensible assertions—that halakhic *a priori* forms substantiate basic psychological states or norms—into the mistaken notion that the *a priori* forms *as such* totally exhaust the range of human emotional experience or psychological reaction in any given situation. To the contrary, the halakhic metapsychology seeks out the complex and subjective elements of human experience which bring to life the specific halakhic *a priori*; while the *a priori* structure, in turn, guides psychic development and interest toward certain objectifiable structures.

Halakhic *a priori* forms may be understood as serving a reality testing function, from the religious point of view, predisposing or demarcating fundamental aspects of human perception and its boundaries. Taking the example of the laws of mourning (*hilkhot aveilut*) to which Meier refers, I agree that it would be ludicrous, and incorrect halakhically, to conceive of the mandatory seven-day immediate mourning period (the *shivah*) as an absolute baseline or ceiling on the expression of grief. But not less absolute than any other time frame against which major developmental milestones are charted and within which temporally bound complexes are believed to unfold (such as when we state that latency "begins" around age seven "plus or minus one year" and "ends" around puberty!). Objective details and formal structures are necessary, even in the domain of belief and feeling, in order to establish a specific kind of internalized representation that may eventually achieve a high degree of objectifiability (see Fromm 1966). As an *a priori* schema, *hilkhot aveilut* must strive for a fairly specific, objective, and normative structure for the psychological processes that underwrite mourning (and as such, serves as what Cattell liked to call a "specification equation"). But even once classified, and even when yoked to concrete ritual acts, these processes retain their variability and subjective meanings.

Moreover, the great contribution of psychology to Halakhah is precisely to expand the uniquely anthropocentric and deocentric relational elements implicit in halakhic reality. If my interpretation of Halakhah is correct, it means that *relationship*—even if only at the representational or conceptual level rather than yet at the fully experiential level—is implicit in every moment of halakhic living. This is ever the realm of idiosyncracy and subjectivity, even if it cannot be felt in the moment of religious action. The view of many scholars on this point (see Bleich 1989; Lichtenstein 1963; Soloveitchik 1971) is well phrased by religious philosopher David Hartman:

> Halakhic man always translates belief into behavior. Just as the Rabbis recognized that an acceptance of the kingdom of Heaven is incomplete if it does not lead to the acceptance of the commandments, they may have also recognized that belief in God is void of significance if it does not lead to the shaping of character. (1976, p. 27)

Halakhist and psychologist alike readily concur that relationship with an object is trivial, or must be considered dominated by narcissistic interest, if it does not yield to change in the subjective self (or in the reciprocating object).[12] Halakhic observance will always be to some essential degree a subjective affair because even during the most objective and exacting study or punctilious execution of one's quotidian religious duties, *the individual's thinking processes and relational tendencies are an insuperable partner to action.* Anything approaching objectivity in religious living remains at all points a constituent of a subjective human mind!

Utterly *a posteriori* levels of self-understanding or relationship or other forms of character change may *or may not* be achieved through execution of halakhic acts, depending upon the extent to which halakhic structures succeed in bringing about subjective change in human nature and perception and depending upon the quality of such structures. Or, such understanding as is achieved may appear fleetingly and temporarily in moments influenced by a combination of "subjective" perceptual experiences passing through "objective" internalized halakhic structures. For still other persons, such understanding may be more likely to accrue during the halakhic aspects of the process of psychotherapy, as a relatively more objective image of God moves into view from behind veils of transference. The overall process of halakhic living and knowledge, it would thus appear, is really a balance between subjectivity and objectivity, a true *enantio-dromia* (in Jung's lexicon), a constant shifting between complementary polarities rather than their dissolution into union.

A final consideration. Rabbi Joseph Dov Soloveitchik, a religious philosopher readily identified with the critique of subjectivism, himself excoriates any inert, behavioristic "orthopraxis" for failing to recognize the very nature of the norms it seeks to uphold (1976). He appreciates that inasmuch as the God-human relationship is to a large degree subjective, it implies various complex, sometimes contradictory emotional states (wrath/love, immanence/remoteness, flight/return). This subjective element typically will be expressed either in the form of logico-cognitive judgments or in ethicomoral religious norms, which by nature lie in the immediate proximity of the psychophysical threshold. I cited in the epigraph to chapter 1 Rabbi Soloveitchik's observation that, "Ostensibly, religion, though flowing in the deepest subliminal ego-strata, is in eternal quest for spatialization and corporeal manifestations" (1944a, p. 69). This acknowledges expressly that the psychological aspects of inner and external experience will seek housing in religious structures, along lines that, of necessity, will be simultaneously subjective and objective. And this must therefore enable us, evidence permitting, to infer psychological processes and structures from religious ones.

In the main, Rabbi Soloveitchik suspects and mistrusts only the explanatory power of theory grounded in subjective data, which attempts to portray the subjective as primary to objective halakhic norms. We shall return to this shortly. His dilemma with the subjective dimension per se seems to come about primarily because he rejects the validity of most observations about subjective aspects of feeling and belief that emerge from the social sciences (and, of course, the methodology through which such observations are drawn). Partly, this objection reflects an outmoded bias (see Soloveitchik 1944a, p. 128, note 87, pg. 131, note 109; cf. note 82), and, most certainly, only what is divinely revealed about human nature can be regarded with complete confidence. Yet, if one adopts the position of the halakhic metapsychology, then it becomes possible to view transference qua Halakhah (that is, the analogue *arevut*-transference) as a reliable informant about a specific domain of human "subjectivity." This much is reaffirmed when Rabbi Soloveitchik adds that it is only "when religious subjectivity is crystallized into forms of ritual, [that the] subjective and objective lie within the framework of religious consciousness" (p. 69). Clearly, then, one can expect precious little from an objective ritual that did not ensconce within it some element of human subjectivity. Religious objectification does not, indeed, *cannot* eradicate the subjective.

Critique of the Halakhic Metapsychology: II

Reversing the direction of the critique, some may object to the desirability of linking psychological states, specifically affective or emotional states, to the law in order thereby to expand the meaning of the ritual act. This school will argue that the necessary and sufficient emotional exchange between two humans or between a human and God during religious practice is brought about simply by the elementary, exacting performance of *mizvah* acts and has nothing to do with conscious appreciation or deep cognitive insight. Regarding the analogy of *arevut*, for example, it would be argued that simply constructing an *eruv* or executing a benefactory act via *arevut* instills automatically an "*arevut*-type halakhic state of mind." This net state needs no further unpackaging. It is not sought but, rather, acquired and has very little to do with any conscious emotional investment other than basic intentionality to act. There is, therefore, simply no need for the entire enterprise of explicating the underlying psychosocial aspects of *mizvah* performance (see Leibowitz 1975).

Although not totally false—because, in fact, Halakhah does not directly enlist emotional or other psychological states as required conditions for the performance of *mizvah* acts as such—this explanation is essentially tautological and bespeaks religious behaviorism. It locates its basic support in the following attitude recorded in the Mishnah (Talmud, *Ber.* 33b; see also Maimonides, *Guide* 3:26 and *Sefer ha-Mizvot: Shoresh* 5): "If a man prays, 'To a bird's nest do thy mercies extend [in reference to Deut. 22: 6–7],' . . silence him! For such a person conceives of Divine attributes [in terms of human] mercy, whereas they are naught but Divine edicts." Nevertheless, even if the ultimate meaning of *mizvot* is beyond human comprehension, the fact that persons, as individuals and in groups, draw psychosocial benefit from *mizvah* performance—and, indeed, take on certain psychological attributes—must be considered relevant to God, who fashioned the *mizvot*. Maimonides, himself, encourages exactly this line of thinking, and, it is important to point out, troubles to formulate his view in the Code (*M. T., Hil. Teshuvah* 10:10–11):

> One only loves God in terms of the knowledge with which one knows Him. According to the knowledge, will be the love. If the former be little or much, so will the latter be little or much. A person ought therefore to devote himself to the understanding and comprehension of those sciences and studies which will inform him concerning his Master, as far as it lies within human faculties to understand and comprehend.

Maimonides, in fact, formally encourages the discovery of "reasons and meanings" for the commandments (*M.T., Hil. Temurah* 4:13, *Hil. Meᶜilah* 8:8; *Guide*, 3:32–33), and we have every reason to seek *psychological* meanings as well.

Accordingly, the halakhic metapsychology must be viewed not as an attempt to introduce new functional requirements into elementary ritual observance, nor to posit that emotional change of a specific kind be considered requisite for complete fulfillment of *miẓvot*. Qua ritual, with delimited demands upon human behavior and intentionality, *miẓvah* acts remains essentially autotelic and mysterious. The metapsychology's sole concern, rather, is the nexus of meanings *within* the body of law, their structural properties, and their object-relational potential. As such, it is not an antipode to the objectifiable aspect of Halakhah; it represents its complement. As the structures become more intimately interconnected and complex, the influence of Halakhah upon personality manifolds.[13]

Critique of the Halakhic Metapsychology: III

Related to the above is a potentially more substantial criticism of the explanative element in the halakhic metapsychology drawn indirectly from Rabbi Joseph Dov Soloveitchik's incisive analysis of the halakhic process.

In his early thesis *The Halakhic Mind* (1944a), Rabbi Soloveitchik examines earlier attempts to offer exogenous rationale for religious obligations, comparing in particular the approaches of Naḥmanides of Gerona (1194–ca. 1270) and Maimonides (1135–1204). Rabbi Soloveitchik considers *causal* explanation of *miẓvot*, with its emphasis on the necessary reduction of religious concepts or truths to the terms of some extrinsic explanatory system, invalid and irrelevant because it, by nature, tends to eliminate its own object. Maimonides's *Guide for the Perplexed* is fairly replete with such explanations (see *Guide* 3:26, 51). It is this kind of obviation of the explicand that is believed to occur, for example, when psychologistic explanations reduce God necessarily to an endopsychic artifact.

Rabbi Soloveitchik favors instead *reconstructive* explanation, which offers *symbolic* links between Halakhah and subjective experience, and which postulates suggestive rather than necessary truths. This form of explanation he associates more with Naḥmanides's approach to *miẓvot* (see Commentary to Lev. 19:19, Deut. 22:6), and, interestingly, with Maimonides's approach in his formal Code, *Mishneh Torah*. To wit, Maimonides emphasizes throughout his Code that the *miẓvot* are essentially divine or scriptural decrees (*gezeirot ha-katub*) and beyond human ken, yet proceeds to offer rationale based on "hints" and "suggestions" derived exegetically or intuitively (for example, *M.T., Hil. Teshuvah* 3:4, *Hil. Mikvᶜot* 11:12). Soloveitchik argues that Maimonides in his Code adopts what are, at best, subjective correlatives for *miẓvot* as opposed to any form of explanation that posits a necessary cause or basis in phenomena or systematic properties to be considered primary over Halakhah. Only the latter approach, Soloveitchik opines, vouches safe the primary status of the religious object and religious truths over all alternative systems.

Thus, in his review of the controversy over the purpose of animal sacrifices (1944a, p. 131, note 108), Rabbi Soloveitchik leans toward Naḥmanides's didactic categorization over the sociological and anthropological rationale found in Maimonides's *Guide*. As a causalist, Maimonides appears to render the sacrificial order secondary to other, more primary causes, such that sociological or anthropological motives appear to *precede* the halakhic command to sacrifice. Naḥmanides, on the other hand, rejects the possibility of causal explanation and, instead, interprets sacrifices as "nothing but a mental sacrifice, symbolizing the internal act of self-negation." Naḥmanides's approach is a retrospective "elaboration," whereas Maimonides's is an instrumentalistic attempt to establish a truth parallel to Halakhah.

It is obvious that the present attempt to link halakhic paradigms with *a priori* psychological forms could, by extension, be viewed as a similar kind of instrumentalism or as an effort to posit psychological givens as a set of truths parallel to halakhic truths. For have I not tried to show that Halakhah responds intimately to the multiple and complex psychological needs and tendencies of the human mind? Have I not postulated the immediate, *a priori* nature of transference, empathy, separation-individuation, psychic structuralization, and other psychological phenomena?

My response begins with the reminder that I have argued that Halakhah *corresponds*, and not merely responds, to psychological needs. There is in this alone no imputation of primary status to psychological phenomena or secondary status to halakhic phenomena. More to the point, the halakhic metapsychology is designed above all else to realign our perspective on so-called *non*halakhic entities or processes and to reinstate such entities as primary precisely because they, too, have intrinsic halakhic identities. If, as the Talmud relates (*Kid.* 30b), God fashioned man's "*yezer*" at the same time as the Torah was created as its antidote, this must mean that the very *a priori* psychological, sociological, and anthropological structures that are to be addressed by the Torah have their own special claim on an *a priori* halakhah status. Indeed, these "scientific" structures are implicit in formal halakhic structures at every level and, thus, are part of a single language. Causal interpretations such as Maimonides sought, accordingly, cannot be accused of alloying *extrinsic* material to halakhic material, nor of improperly elevating *non*halakhic causative factors to a role primary to Halakhah. To the contrary, such explanations help correlate the variegated dimensions of Halakhah.

The *arevut*-transference analog, for example, informs us that transference does more than just elaborate or reconstruct the meaning of *arevut*. Rather, transference and related processes become reclaimed as bona fide constituents of a complex halakhico-psychic structure which, for convention's sake, I have given the cognomen *arevut*-transference. From God's point of view, as it were, there exists some single, quasi-conceptual "whole entity" that is no more and no less "*arevut*" than it is "transference." In the extended world, however, the mind encounters phenomena that, in some circumstances, are recognized more clearly through the halakhic principles of *arevut* and, in other circumstances, through the psychoanalytic principles of transference. In the light of the halakhic metapsychology, a third set of circumstances can be distinguished wherein both dimensions are brought into focus—such as during psychotherapy—permitting attention to the deocentric and anthropocentric aspects of psychological structure and relationship.

Summation

On the practical level, the halakhic metapsychology seeks to make it logically untenable to state any longer that psychology, psychotherapy, and religion (Halakhah) are *in principle* antithetical or incompatible. Halakhic analogies are now available which serve as springboards for recasting therapeutic theory and procedure in halakhic terms and also for conceptualizing the structure of the formal, internalized aspects of the deocentric and anthropocentric dimensions of psychic experience. Traditional attempts at synthesis tended to snare in the face of this, that, or the other specific psychological practice or ideology which turned out to be halakhically unacceptable, either as a piece of theory or as it took form in the field. Against the new framework, however, such problematic components can be viewed individually as inadequate or ill-formed extensions of a more basic and steadfast halakhico-psychological parameter or paradigm, without doing major damage to the overall synthesis between psychology and Jewish ethics.

On the larger conceptual level, by bringing to light the combined psychological and ethicomoral dimensions of human motivation, the preemptory and controllable qualities of human drive, and the redemptive as well as curative aspects of intense interpersonal relation, the metapsychology brings into bolder relief the qualitative differences between the kinds of objects presumed by psychology and religion.

Via both revolutionary achievements, the metapsychology offers the potential for resolving the traditional dichotomy between religion and psychology that, paradoxically, drove Freud and others to summarily conflate the two. This conflation deprived religious objects of their independent status and value beyond psychological experience per se. In the past it had seemed as if psychological concepts, as originally, positivistically explicated, brought the person into closer contact merely with his or her instinctual nature and its wish-related, endopsychic objects. Theological or religious concepts, as originally explicated in their context, brought the person into closer communion only with his or her external ethicomoral norms and declared but unfathomable objects of belief. Now, the two levels of perception can be viewed as parallel processes, reflecting variant yet contiguous dimensions of a single experience, leaving room to discriminate, if only conceptually, between an earthly and a divine object.

Still lacking, however, is a pictorial model to aid in conceiving more precisely these parallel levels of experience and their objects. I shall supply such a model in the following chapter.

5 | A Model for Anthropocentric and Deocentric Dimensions of Psychological Experience

We have become so bashful in matters of religion that we correctly say "unconscious," because God has in fact become unconscious to us. This is what always happens when things are interpreted, explained, and dogmatized until they become so encrusted with man-made images and words that they can no longer be seen.

—CARL GUSTAV JUNG (1933, P. 264)

By this point there lie before us a number of potentially objectifiable aspects of the representation of God that might lead one closer to understanding the parameters of the god object in psychotherapy and everyday life. I have been interested particularly in professional thinking that explicitly makes room for a real God. The search continues for a model that acknowledges a relationship between humans and God and that such a relationship undergoes developmental changes. Such a model must show that the human personality influences this relationship, but also that the real God object influences it and that this kind of relationship, on some level, has an independent status that cannot be completely understood from the perspective of anthropocentrically derived models of behavior alone. In short, I am interested in a model which does not reduce all aspects of deocentric conflict or relationship to the terms of interpersonally based conflict or relationship.

It bears reiterating that, after securing from the professional community a modicum of interest even to consider the aforementioned possibilities, the chief problem has been to conceptualize these possibilities. Even the so-called practical dilemmas in working with religious patients and material, for all the exigency with which these beg for handy technical remedies during therapy itself, are in large measure conceptual dilemmas, as we saw in the introduction and in the first chapter. In an early paper (1960, p. 115), neuropsychologist Paul Pruyser acknowledged straightaway that the psychology-religion problem was conceptual: "James realized that religion has a human and divine side and that psychology can only study the former . . . Religious life involves images, intuitions, concepts, and the human history of all these about God. *But, above all, it involves an object relationship with God.*" Unhappily, Pruyser never returned to work on the necessary machinery for conceptualizing an object relationship with a real god object, save for some clinically spun musings toward the end of his life (1985). Overall, Pruyser joined the ranks of those who ended the search with the discovery of God, transitional object *par excellance.*

It is possible to further refine our understanding of the conceptual deadlock and the steps necessary to move forward. I shall pick this up again in the final chapter by way of a reconsideration of Jung's and Freud's comments on religious experience. At this point, I wish to consider some models.

The models to be presented demonstrate several aspects of anthropocentric and deocentric representations and relationships, and the areas of overlap between them, in a manner compatible with the religious view that an objective entity known as God exists external to the psyche. These models do not solve the problem of how, ultimately, one gains full knowledge of God, and they do not portray certain other simultaneous aspects of the developmental process (such as cognitive or neurophysiological factors), owing to the unnecessary complexity this would add to what is still basically an introduction. The models also have not been tested for applicability to other religious worldviews. The value of these models is in portraying the mechanisms of perception and psychological maturation that have as one of their characteristics the ability to elicit changes in sensitivity (regressive or adaptive) to the spiritual and religious dimensions of experience. Second, these models highlight new dimensions of meaning and pathways of analysis for the transference relationship in psychotherapy. They supply a plausible and *clinically useful* rendition of parallel anthropocentric and deocentric dimensions of the transference relationship in psychotherapy, thus enabling therapists to better track the multiple levels of meaning inherent in religious material.

A word about the mechanisms of perception and maturation mentioned above. This set of mechanisms includes such factors as cultural networks of meaning, social schemata, linguistic styles, psychodynamic patterns, and so forth. As should be clear from the preceding chapter, the Jewish believer must include halakhic structures and metaphors among such mechanisms inasmuch as from the earliest moments these are interwoven into the development of affective styles, object-relational tendencies, cognitive schemata, judgment, perceptions of time, and so forth. Halakhic categories compose a great deal of the *a priori* meaning network through which parent and child encounter each other even for the first time and cast a significant imprint on the intersubjective linguistic and conceptual as well as larger cultural patterns into which the child's own inner perspectives are drawn (see Daniel Stern 1985). Ultimately, such meanings become part and parcel of the object representations and other internalized structures through which an individual comprehends and relates to the world.

Halakhic categories, precisely by virtue of their categorical bridging of the spatiotemporal properties of the world and the *a priori*, divine structures, may serve as priming mechanisms for bringing basic psychological faculties into the orbit of the divine object. Or, to relate this to Laor's contribution (1989), they may repose as deep meaning structures (after Ogden 1984) at the periphery of the "religious register." This bridging function is brought to light by the halakhic metapsychology. In considering the broader influence of Halakhah upon this process, it is clear that loristic-aggadic traditions are of equal importance to the narrowly formalistic halakhic traditions, since both are needed in order to illuminate value concepts and to provide a fulcrum for conceptualizing and ultimately internalizing the objects that lie beyond halakhic observance.

Models of Anthropocentric and Deocentric Overlap in Psychological Experience

Figures 2, 4, and 6 are pictorial renditions of the relationships between objects outside the self and their internalized, representational forms in the self. Figures 3 and 5 portray graphically the kinds of empirical and hypothetical structural-conceptual factors which may modify the initial perceptions of the object as it develops toward its final representational form. Throughout, the following definitions will be adhered to: Object *image* refers to an unorganized, unstructured, whole or part perception, whereas object *representation* refers to a more organized, structured, and internalized image, which at the highest levels of internalization exists independently of need states. Object *concept* refers to a larger consolidation of many related object representations (Moore and Fine 1968; Sandler and Rosenblatt 1962).

Figure 2 depicts the basic situation of human object representation: the relationship between an objective human object (namely, a real person existing veridically in the external world) and its intrapsychic complement, the object representation (O. R.). Of course, we are rarely, if ever, dealing with a photographic kind of representation inasmuch as the objective self and the objective other are each encountered in a predominantly *subjective* context, that is, the phenomenological sense of object and self as it is perceived by the other. However, the subjective aspects of experience, initially registered as isolated, unorganized images which precede full recognition of a differentiated object world, eventually take the form of "representations" distilled from real experience, fantasy (drive-determined) elaborations upon such experience, and later transitional experiences (and objects).

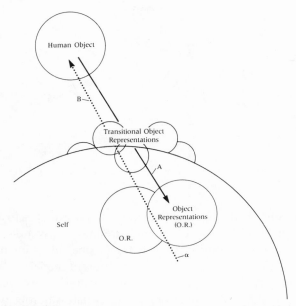

Figure 2   Psychic Representation of Objective Interpersonal (Human) Objects

Line A in figure 2 depicts the psychic translation of the perceived objective human object into the form of an object representation. Dotted line B depicts the fact that the human object is primarily perceived or experienced through subjective object representations that are formed over a lifetime and in ways that are commensurate with the overall quality of internalization, psychic differentiation, dynamic balance, and so forth. Line B is portrayed as beginning from outside of the object representation itself (the area marked *alpha*) to indicate that interpersonal perception may begin prior to, independently of, or beyond formalized object representations, such as in other structured (language) and nonstructured (drive) sources.

Following Winnicott's elegantly simple diagram (1953), I have depicted transitional objects in figure 2 as if they occupy the psychic space "between" the external and internal world, thus coloring in some important way the perceptual relationship between the objective object and the self. Transitional objects have been included since so much of the inner world of object representation is derived from perceptual experiences that have already been filtered through pre-existing transitional representations, providing continuity with very

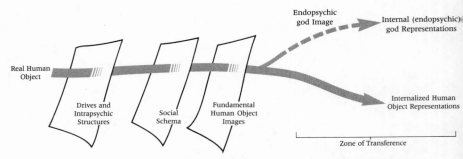

Figure 3   Standard Psychological Model of the Development of God Concepts
(the Anthropocentric Dimension)

early experience and lending unique transitional qualities to adult experience. Since at least one of the main traditional psychologistic approaches views the god object as a transitional phenomenon, it is
useful to clarify this identity through the present models.

Figure 3 is a companion to figure 2 and illustrates the developmental trajectory of a real human object on its pathway toward ideally
complete internalization. The objective object passes through at least
three major types of templates or perceptual mechanisms: (1) the biological drive and psychological-motivational intrapsychic structures
(ego, superego), (2) the gamut of social schemata and related meaning
networks, and (3) the repository of previous object-representational
modes and tendencies. This listing is by no means exhaustive but
rather illustrative. Figure 3 introduces the standard psychologistic
model of the god image and the eventual god representation conceived as endopsychic products whose primary germinus is human
interpersonal relations. Thus, I have depicted the "endopsychic god
image" as a splintering-off from the main pathway of human object
internalization. Thus, if such god images eventually amalgamate into
a representation, they are properly referred to as an internal rather
than internal*ized* representation, since the latter indicates the taking
inward of an object that was once external, and which, according to
the psychologistic approach, God is not. I have also marked this
forked area as a "zone of transference" since it is precisely at this
point that anthropocentric and deocentric representations and dynamics either collide, merge, conflict, or continue toward parallel
destinies. However, no matter how multifarious their pathways, the

standard model will, in principle, seek to reduce the latter to the terms of the former.

Also operating within the confines of the standard psychologistic model, figure 4 illustrates the object-representational aspect of the development of religious imagery and representations of God. For example, psychoanalytic developmental psychology and most object relations approaches teach, in general, that subjective aspects of representational experience can be combined to form new endopsychic objects. Such objects are not truly to be found in the external world, but they are experienced as such after being projected outward and subsequently introjected. This mechanism is in operation, for example, when children "invent" imaginary companions and in the process of artistic creation. Figure 4 depicts a particular projected endopsychic object known as "God." Following traditional theory, "God" is conceived of as the result of the conglomeration of split-off aspects of subjective experience and the coalescence of many already-

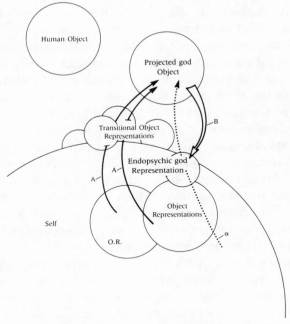

Figure 4   Psychic Representation of Endopsychic "God" Objects

existing representations that serve dynamic needs and conform to varying sociocultural definitions. The precursor religious "objects" or schema (they may be purely cognitive), founded on early qualities of parent-child or family-child experience, serve as the crucible or register from which "God" experiences emerge.

Both of the lines marked A in figure 4 depict the internal generation or amalgamation of suitable material, some of which is supplied by family and societal input (see fig. 3), which is then projected and given quasi-objective form. The god object of figure 4 is thus only experienced "as if" outside the self, and it is only this "as if" experience itself, as opposed to the object as such, that can be empirically discovered. Sufficient experience with one's own projected religious images eventually crystallize (line B) in more complete form as endopsychic god representations. Obviously, analysis or interpretation of this type of god representation ultimately leads back to human interpersonal experience (*alpha* is as in fig. 2).

Figure 5 takes us a major step forward. It is a modified model in that it assumes two distinct lines of development (and parallel, initially, only for ease of illustration). The first line indicates the trajectory of an objective human object moving toward internalization, including the splintering-off of endopsychic religious objects as per the traditional model. The second line indicates the trajectory of an *objective* God object moving on *its* representational pathway toward internalization. As before, the human object traverses a series of modificatory mechanisms (as in fig. 3). In addition, figure 5 depicts a novel set of mechanisms that are of special relevance from the standpoint of religion and of special value as regards the perception of God. I have listed: (1) certain innate, unconscious (archetypal?) endowments that orient the human toward God (such as the "image of God" given in humans, or the "special love" which reveals God's relationship to humans); (2) immediate conceptual structures, such as halakhic *a priori* forms; and (3) the repository of previous deocentric object-representational modes and tendencies.

Thus, while the line of development for the objective *human* object may, indeed, yield anthropocentrically based, internal or endopsychic gods, only the line of development from the objective object known as God can legitimately be said to yield an internal*ized* God representation. For only in the latter case has something *really* external and objectively of God been taken inward.

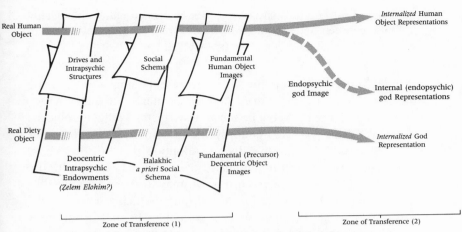

Figure 5   Modified Model of the Development of God Representations (the Anthropocentric and Deocentric Dimension)

I have accordingly demarcated two zones of transference in figure 5. The first zone of transference actually amplifies the second zone of transference, which has been indicated in figure 3. The first zone of transference illustrates that the sets of mechanisms which individually influence the developmental trajectories of their respective objects often overlap, which explains the inclusion of anthropocentric features in the objective God representation and deocentric features in the endopsychic god representation. The second zone of transference illustrates overlap between the more completely formed human, endopsychic, and objective God representations. Even the objective God image, for example, may take on knowable traits through common descriptors such as the "hand" of God, which, in turn, draws its meaning from the context of human hands and the linguistic concept of "handiwork." It is also possible to draw from other, direct, somehow perceivable objective divine handiwork (for example, "The heavens declare thy handiwork, O Lord . . ."), which may be further conceptualized through *a priori* halakhic structures. And from the overlap of deocentric over anthropocentric templates, one derives expressions such as, "he has hands of angels," or "the Lord's apprentice, that one is!" Pruyser anticipated these possibilities when he wrote,

> To me, the statement that God is a father figure may also imply its complement—that biological fathers have numinous qualities. In

other words, psychoanalysis has established a new affinity (not identity) between God and man which cuts across the technical
distinction between God's transcendence and his imminence. (1960,
p. 117)

Finally, figure 6 depicts the object-representational aspect of the
emergence of a truly internalized God representation. It depicts a moment of experience between the self and two distinct religious objects,
one identified as projected-endopsychic (as in fig. 4) and the other
newly identified as objective-divine. Adopting the religious viewpoint, it has been conjectured that any divine object holding forth the
possibility of being discovered or known may further be assumed to
have created mechanisms or faculties through which discovery is indeed possible (fig. 5). Figure 6 further enables us to illustrate four
imaginable pathways to God representation. On one hand, all of
these pathways are *psychological* in that they are experiences which
transpire in the mind and submit at least partly to lawful explanations
having to do with cognitive and emotional properties. On the other
hand, three of these pathways are distinctly *nonpsychologistic;* that is,
they do not necessitate the belief that mental structures and experience tell us only about the mind and nothing about a distinct objective reality that might, in fact, share some parallel relationship with
mental structures and experience.

The first pathway depicted in figure 6 (line A) adheres to the psychologistic assumption, portraying a psychically created endopsychic
god representation as discussed in figure 4. The modified model, in
other words, accommodates the phenomena of transference gods and,
borrowing from Kohut's classification, narcissistic self-object gods.

New vistas are illustrated by lines B–D. They illustrate levels of experience parallel to mundane interpersonal relationship (fig. 2), and
even to the type of religious experience depicted by line A in figure 6.
Following a sufficient number of experiences with special perception
(via halakhic structures) of the objective divine object, one could
imagine the direct internalization of an ideal "divine" representation,
as depicted by line B. While a divine object could conceivably present
itself to the human mind in some immediately knowable and comprehensible form (such as prophecy or revelation), it is equally conceivable that the divine object becomes known in a developmental
manner, mediated *through* parallel interpersonal mechanisms, expe-

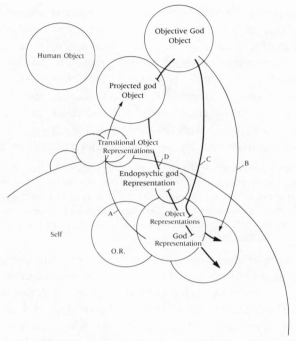

Figure 6   Psychic Representation of Endopsychic "God"
Objects and Objective Divine Object

riences, and object representations that are in some way preparatory
to an encounter with God (line C).

It is likely that these preparatory interpersonal experiences are not
random and that they tend to be grouped or in some way identified by social convention as particularly relevant to religious experience (such as the belief that loving one's parents leads to love of God).
Because these particular interpersonal experiences are associated early
on with religious connotations, endopsychic god representations tend
to form early (for example, Freud's oedipal god), preempting the perception of the objective divine object. Yet whereas according to the
model in figure 4, this level of endopsychic representation was the
conceptual terminus of human religious experience, figure 5 allows
(line D) that the divine object may be initially, if dimly, recognized
through previously existing, interpersonally based endopsychic representations that are particularly suitable for the discovery of God.

Such representations may be precursors to objective religious perception by virtue of being "primed" with important family, tribal, or universal mythic material pertaining to God and religious belief.

In the last analysis, however, even the representation of an objective God, qua representation, is not God. *This remains the sense in which religious object representations (not the objects themselves)* are *illusions.* This provokes the question: Then to whom do we relate, to God or to the representation of God? And the most suitable, defensible response must be drawn from Sandler (see also Sandler and Rosenblatt 1962):

> The internal image of the mother is thus not a substitute for an object relationship, but is itself an indispensable part of the relationship. Without it, no object relationship exists. It is not in itself a source of real satisfaction to the child. The real source of gratification is the mother or any other object who can conform to the child's "mother schema." (Sandler 1960, p. 156)

The god representation, in other words, is an essential component of the relationship with God and is one possible way of understanding the "special endowment" that talmudic sage Rabbi Akiva referred to as given to humans by God with "special love" (Talmud, *Avot* 3 : 17). It is an instrumentality that enables the individual psyche to relate *to* God *through* representations of God, aided perhaps by additional deep preconceptions on the order of an "archaic heritage" that disposes the psyche toward God's presence.[1] A representation can, in fact, supply certain gratifications and most probably guarantees mental stability in a variety of critical situations. But a relationship solely with one's mental representations as such, and to the exclusion of the object itself, is endemic of either pathological autism, schizoid isolation, or bereavement.

Contributions of the Modified Model

The modified model makes five contributions to the intersection of psychology, psychotherapy, and religion. Foremost, although most generally, it enables the conceptualization of coexistence between psychological and religious approaches to object representation and relationship, particularly *religious* objects and experiences. A main demonstration of this new form of conceptualization lies in the ability to create a shared language between psychology and religion. This shared language will be more easily described after consideration of the other three contributions.

Second, the model does not require wholesale abandonment of current psychosocial, psychosexual, object-relational, and cognitive conceptualizations of the qualitative aspects of divine object representations. On the contrary, these remain necessary for assessing and interpreting the qualitative and functional aspects of religious objects and the parallel relationship between anthropocentrically modeled and deocentrically modeled objects of religious experience.

Third, it accommodates the traditional psychologistic notion of endopsychic god concepts and representations, emphasizing that these may serve special priming and transitional functions in turning the personality toward noetic or spiritual phenomena during early developmental stages when the distinction between earthly and transcendent objects is yet incomplete. Such precursor religious object representations serve crucial bridging functions until more mature god representations are available.

Parallel Aspects of Transference

The fourth contribution of the present model is to enhance perception of various kinds of overlap between human object representations and endopsychic and objective God representations, enabling one to speak of a new kind of transference that moves in the completely reverse direction than that originally postulated by Freud. With figure 6 in view, one can now imagine *human* object representations that have been displaced from their rightful context in objective *deocentric* experience onto interpersonal ones (such as being displacedly angry at another human being when one is actually angry at God). These qualities of experience in the interpersonal or anthropocentric plane provide, in a sense, a pseudo-focus because they are experienced in the context of the wrong object, and will be unalterable if an intervention fails to deal with the true objects and the true contexts of these emotions or conflicts after all other aspects of analysis have been properly undertaken.

The practical relevance of the preceding approaches to transference can be illustrated simply. Many persons are angry at God for one or another reason (Stamey 1971), and the relevant therapeutic intervention can take three turns. According to the first technique, the patient's god concept is arbitrarily partialed out of the therapy—since it is "really" just another displacement concept—and the basis for all aspects of the problematic emotions would be sought within the human interpersonal context. Yet, if God in fact exists, such psychologistic clarification may leave such patients angry, or they may be led to forfeit their God for the wrong reasons.

The second technique also follows the traditional psychologistic model, but would endeavor to accept at least the psychological reality of the patient's God and to include this God-artifact in the therapy. Through it, the therapist may enable the patient to perceive his or her human-God conflict in terms of transference *from* the objective realities of the interpersonal realm *onto* a split-off, endopsychic creation known as God—a displacement of anger which would be interpreted as belonging rightfully to some significant human object relationship. Provided with this new perspective, the patient may thereafter resolve anger through the analysis of transference, eventually discovering that he or she has no real problem with God. However, as I have noted frequently, if the therapist truly believes that god concepts nevertheless *really* are endopsychic creations, a certain solipsism, perhaps even a dishonesty, must pervade the therapy.

In fact, there is a third possibility, which follows precisely from the willingness to grant objective reality to the divine object behind the formal god representation. Take, for example, a chronically angry and depressed survivor of the Holocaust in treatment, and imagine the patient resolving his or her transference-based conflicts, slowly healing the impact of objective trauma, and then choosing to maintain enmity with God! This struggle might continue to cause pain, and in dealing with it the patient might even cease to practice his or her faith. Does one assess the anger in this scenario as infantile spitefulness, neurosis, a pocket of unresolved transference anger, or an aspect of a special kind of relation that must seek its resolution on a plane beyond psychotherapy?

To enliven the illustration of the "reversal" of transference, suppose this embittered, depressed patient has retroflexed his or her *objective* anger at an *objective* God over the destruction of his or her family during the Holocaust and relates to all significant persons as per the introjected image of the wrathful, paranoid god representation of his or her reality. From the moment such material surfaces in therapy, the clinician would need to respond clinically to the same question that troubles the philosopher: "Why is this person depressed and angry at God, whereas many identically traumatized persons are not?" The clinical challenge, all agree, will be to discover the degree to which

Holocaust trauma retroactively evoked childhood traumas having to do with faith and interpersonal dynamics. These dynamics may over-shadow the patient's perception of the objective God's otherwise kindly, forebearing, suffering characteristics or may re-evoke an early, endopsychic god object linked with small-scale intrapsychic holo-causts throughout the patient's earlier years. In these instances, the patient may be said to have a valid emotional reaction *given the kind of god he or she is relating to.*

Continuing the illustration, assume that a stage has been reached where thorough analysis of oedipal and purely post-traumatic as-pects of the patient's depression has significantly lightened but some-how not eliminated the angriness and related symptoms. At this juncture, existentially oriented practitioners might rightly speculate about the existence of an *ontological,* nonpsychiatric guilt or anger, "having to do with something basic about existence as such" (May, Angel, and Ellenberger, 1958). I wish to adapt this modification to the self's relation to objective *religious* objects. What if the patient, in other words, believes he or she suffers simply from the sheer experi-ence of the force of God's objective wrath? Depending upon the reli-gion in question, the patient might need to learn to accommodate, or attempt to change, an *objectively* wrathful, or perhaps even paranoid God, and to comprehend his or her depression from within the con-text of relationship with that objective divine wrath.

Now, some religions feature gods who spew forth pure brimstone and hellfire, before whom persons are believed fated to ineluctable doom. The god of Abraham, Isaac, and Jacob is described as capable of wrath as well as forgiveness. The Christian god is generally por-trayed as unconditionally loving, virtually incapable of such wrath. If *objective* qualities of God are under consideration, could a psychother-apist ever be justified in relaying to a patient the implicit message that his or her perceptions are based wholly upon intrapsychic or inter-personal dynamics? More unconscionable: Dare a therapist holding religious belief X offer his impressions or skepticism based upon his experiences with *his* God and *his* beliefs to a patient of religious belief Y? If, however, the patient's God is objectively not responsible for the Holocaust—presuming such a theological view—then perhaps a pa-tient's persistent blaming of his or her God could legitimately be viewed as a neurotic mechanism which allows displacement of a feel-ing of powerlessness onto God and a repetition, in a pathologically compulsive way, of a losing battle with an unseen enemy. Clinically, a therapist would acknowledge that the patient's feelings indeed have to do with God, but also with the patient's individual perception of God and the unique dynamics of that interaction.

What transpires as anthropocentrically based displacements and transferences are divested? Is it possible for the psychotherapist and patient to fold back the anthropocentric aspects of a god representation or concept sufficiently so as to allow a glimpse of the objective God? Perhaps one must be content to glimpse the image of a closer-to-objective god representation and expect nothing more. However, speaking for the case of Judaism and, given the assumptions of the halakhic metapsychology, I believe that the closer one moves toward working with unfettered halakhic structures—which, ideally, presumes a nonpathological state of mind—the closer one is to the person's representation of the objectifiable aspects of God. It will come as no surprise to the reader to learn that this folding-back of displaced and distorted images, revealing the record of a more objective perception that has taken place simultaneously, is the lynchpin of the therapeutic process.

Psychotherapists are familiar with this idea: they participate in a similar phenomenon whenever they experience that a patient has removed or lifted from the therapist the heavy weight of projection or transference in order to reclaim the formerly projected feelings, attitudes, or images. For both the psychotherapist as well as for the patient, there follows a moment, sometimes longer, of relatively objective perception of the other. Sometimes the recognition emanates not so much from acknowledging *content* that is newly comprehended or known as from the new experience of *being* comprehended or known by the therapeutic object, or of *becoming* comprehensible, in a way that would not have been possible if the therapist was in actuality identical with the projected and displaced images the patient originally apperceived in the therapist.

This in its own right can often be an existentially tragic experience, including its own special form of depression, inasmuch as a patient discovers that, projections and transferences aside, he or she really knows very little about the person of the therapist. What has been gained, and, one hopes, becomes internalized, are the "goodly" functions of and experiences that have been gleaned from working with the therapist. The patient, in other words, retains healthful and useful structures that have been built up in the course of the experience with the "goodness" and "badness" of the psychotherapist, even though the therapist as a person in his totality remains a largely unknown and unexperienced domain to the patient.

This process is the subject of innumerable contemporary clinical papers, and I shall return to it in discussing the case presentations in chapter 6. I will now illustrate the salient points here with some material drawn from literature and conclude with some perspicacious theoretical reflections drawn from the clinical setting.

Perhaps the most masterful articulation of the folding-back process is found in Melanie Klein's (1955) classic description and analysis of the literary character Fabian, of Julian Green's *If I Were You* (1950), who repeatedly adopts and sheds the introjected identities of other persons. This he does compulsively until he contemplates taking over the personality of his unrequitted lover, Elise. He imagines he could make her happy by loving her, then wonders that if this were so he could become even more happy by *turning himself into* Elise. He dismisses these thoughts with the realization that he cannot be sure whether Elise's current lover, if Fabian were to become Elise, would continue to love her (now *him*). After a moment of hesitation, Fabian discovers that what he loves in her is essentially a reflection of himself, that Elise's sad eyes are a reflection of Fabian's eyes and his own inner emptiness. This sudden insight effectively terminates his need to merge with other objects and initiates the process of reclaiming his own soul. In real life, of course, psychotherapy is hardly immediate or simplistic in this way. Yet the process of self-discovery often takes essentially this route through the various byways of provisional images of the psychotherapist and experimental levels of residence within, respectively, the therapeutic space, the therapist's mind, the transference relationship per se, and, ultimately, the therapist's therapeutic functions.

One example of the reversal specifically of anthropocentrically based god representations is found in Gosse's autobiography (1909, pp. 33–34). What transpires was not the result of intensive psychotherapy, yet in the description that follows one witnesses a "grand disillusionment" on par with what Freud described as occurring at the end of the oedipal stage.

> My mother always deferred to my father and in his absence spoke of him as if he were all-wise. I confused him in some sense with God; at all events, I believed that my father knew everything and saw everything. One morning in my sixth year, my mother and I were alone in

the morning room, when my father came in and announced some fact to us. I was standing on the rug, gazing at him, and when he made this statement, I remember turning quickly in embarassment and looking into the fire. The shock to me was as that of a thunderbolt, *for what my father said was simply not true!* Here was the appalling discovery, never before suspected, that my father was not as God and did not know everything. The shock was not caused by a suspicion that he was not telling the truth, as it appeared to him, but by the awful proof that he was not, as I had supposed, omniscient.

For Gosse, this terribly painful realization marked the beginning of what he termed the "humanization" of his image of his father, and, at the same time, an eclipsing of his idealized image of God. Yet, he remained all his life with a devout belief in God. It would seem at the very least incomplete to state that Gosse discovered that the entirety of his god concept was merely a projection of an omniscient, idealized endopsychic father imago. If that is all God is, then, indeed—why believe?

One can argue that Gosse is clinically naive, and that in reality he experienced only an initial level of clarification, having not undergone something like psychoanalysis, which might actually have further purged his god representation of all endopsychic contaminants. Freud, for instance, certainly would have hypothesized that Gosse retained a god representation in order that he might thereby preserve some encapsulated remnant of the childhood sense of paternal omniscience. Perhaps. But clinical experience, in fact, leaves room for alternate expectations, such as the possibility that, post-analysis, Gosse would be left with a vital interest in a more objectively perceived God, bereft of all endopsychic dross. As I have tried to emphasize, however, even in the latter case, it is possible that a sense of oedipal-type awe, omniscience, and so forth might remain, since these feelings may develop from experiences with the structural aspects of an objective God in a manner identical to their development in the interpersonal context.

Consider also the following vignette tucked away in Father Joseph Nuttin's *Psychoanalysis and Personality* (1962, p. 195). Nuttin describes a young man about twenty years old who gave the following associations to the word "God": "A powerful force which shatters me; I cannot escape from it. I have the impression that a man is pushing me forward; he is pushing me in the back with a stick; I must walk. I can see my father; he is pushing me; I cannot escape from his anger, he is spoiling my life." The patient then adds: "I no longer have this idea about God. I know quite well that God is utterly different, but when I was young I was afraid of God and of my father . . . without them I could have done as I liked." Nuttin does not address the obvious psychosexual symbolisms in the patient's associations. He is more concerned with the significant qualitative differences between the God of this man's childhood and that of his adulthood. Yet Nuttin's comments are problematic:

> On the intellectual level this young man had 'liberated' himself from his father and from his infantile idea of God, but the emotional state experienced so intensely in childhood went on echoing in his psychic life. *Nevertheless, his actual idea of God was neither the continuation nor the development of his infantile experience.* "If there was only that," he had once said, "I should no longer believe in God." There were, in other words, emotional echoes which went on resounding in him, *but besides there was a mental content within him corresponding to another idea of God. The latter had a different origin, although it was not completely differentiated from the first;* it was in fact an intellectual understanding of the necessity of a first cause or a final explanation of the world. (p. 196, emphasis added)

Like Gosse, this 20-year-old recognizes that the God of his childhood could not possibly sustain nor merit his continued devotion. But has the patient exchanged this god for a representation more true to God's objective qualities, or has he instead accommodated a childhood concept within the wider blanket of advancing intellectual developments? Nuttin apparently is satisfied with the idea that the patient's intellectually satisfying God indicates a development far and away beyond the "God" of childhood. He accepts it as evidence for the persistence of some "mental content within corresponding to another idea of God . . . of a different origin." Once again, however, it is not unambiguously clear whether this "different origin" is, indeed, "different" in kind, process, quality, or object. We have conceded that both endopsychic god representations as well as an ideal representation of an objective God will be *psychological* inasmuch as they are experienced in the mind. Even so, the fact that god representations of later life tend to be more complex, abstract, and intellectualized is not alone what makes them more "real," since such transformation is to be expected during the development of many kinds of internal objects.

Perhaps the childhood god who is a "punctillious cattle prod," as one patient of mine put it, is intended to vacate a place for a god "with gentle hands," if this *is* closer to what God objectively is like.

Or, maybe the god who is eclipsed by the frightening paternal phallus is intended to become transformed into a god with a more objectively perceived divine "phallus"—a guiding pillar of light, a towering fortress in the storm, the might of right, an awesome "Thou shalt *not!,*" a probing *herm*-eneutic. That is, the mature change in religious representation is neither necessarily nor logically toward rendering God more abstruse and unfathomable, but rather toward being more accurately known to the degree that God is knowable! The missing criterion, as with the earlier analyses, seems to be a clear statement regarding the assumed truth value of the religious structures themselves, against which the individual patient's god representation can be compared from a variety of qualitative and object-relational perspectives.

A more complex example of the rediscovery process can be discerned in an interesting illustration offered by Harry Guntrip. It is unique, I believe, because it provides a more complex picture of the object-relational torsion inherent in the individual's representations of God and humans.

Guntrip was discussing his view, popular among early object relations theorists, that the psychotherapist must be available as person for the patient, enabling the patient to experience some sense of personal reality in the therapist, so that the patient will eventually be able to surrender his or her spurious reality filled with "bad" objects. He then records a patient's dream:

> I'm looking for Christ on the seashore. He rose up as if out of the sea and I admired His tall, magnificent figure. Then I went with Him to a cave and became conscious of ghosts there and fled in stark terror. Be He stayed and I mustered up the courage and went back in with Him. Then the cave was a house. And as He and I went upstairs, He said, "You proved to have greater courage than I had," and I felt I detected some weakness in Him. (1969, p. 351)

The patient's subsequent associations included a comparison between his admiration for both Christ's and his own father's athletic figures, and then with the therapist's. The patient continued:

> I also associate Him with you. I've got the idea that somehow you may inveigle me into [having the] courage to face ghosts and then let me down. Mother was a menacing figure. Father was weak, mute before her onslaughts. He once said it wasn't a good thing to have one parent constantly dominating the other in a front of a child, but he never showed anger at all.

In his analysis of this dream, Guntrip suggests that the patient os-
cillated between an old fear that the father disappointed the patient
whenever he tried to stand up to his violent mother and a new waver-
ing hope that the therapist would not let him down as he prepared to
confront the "ghost" of his angry mother. In technical terms, the
psychotherapist was being gradually internalized (more correctly, *introjected*) as a reliable parent-substitute and was lent divine, saviourlike characteristics. Clinically, I believe it would be wrong simply to
assume that the therapist in the dream is Christ or that Christ is the
therapist. Each, in the given dream moment, represents a pole of a
moving force, of an intrapsychic or interpersonal transmutation,
which may in fact reflect a larger number of sponsoring objects and
representations. Perhaps the emotional give-and-take of "fear" and
"courage" is even more significant for this patient than the objects
who give and take.

Practically speaking, a transference interpretation of this material,
were one to be appropriate, would need to take account of several
vectors: patient-therapist, therapist-Christ, parent-therapist, parent-
Christ, etc. The saviourlike characteristics of the therapist might have
been drawn from an endopsychic god representation or from an objective God representation. At the same time, the patient's image of
Christ may have been swayed by the prevalent power of current interpersonal experiences. That is, his image of Christ was colored by a
similar sense of disappointment or anger from previous letdowns (an
anthropocentrically derived displacement onto Christ drawn from
the patient's parents) and perhaps also by the hope of future courage
(an anthropocentrically derived displacement onto Christ drawn from
the patient's experience with the therapist).

What is most important is to observe the overlap between two dimensions of the transference, the oscillating movement between an
objective therapist, an objective God, and the patient's internal and
internalized object representations of them. For Guntrip, the patient
is conferring divine qualities upon the image of the psychotherapist.
One does not learn how much farther Guntrip carried this implication, yet his style of analysis happily does not foreclose the interpretive options.

If the therapist works from within the framework of the modified
model presented here, it becomes easier to entertain a new adven-
ture: that the divine qualities the therapist apprehends have been
placed upon him or her may allow both participants to infer and, per-

haps, experience the presence and influence of a Third. Moreover, it is equally likely, from the religious point of view, that Guntrip's patient's god representation is becoming more psychotherapeutic, as McDargh concludes (1983, 1991). By this McDargh means that the god representation itself can become a more able "good" object, infused with new strength derived from psychotherapy, to counter pathological objects. Even this, however, is a restrained exegesis. According to the metapsychological view propounded here, it is God's actual presence in the therapy room—per se, if one's theology demands, or consubstantiated in the *corpus mysticum* of the therapist (cf. Leavy 1988), or more implicitly in the fabric of deocentric structures—which is transmitted via the therapeutic process. As such, the additional psychological nutriment gained for the patient's representation of God derives directly from God as well as from the "goodness" of the psychotherapist.

The Modified Model and a Shared Language for Psychology and Religion

I now return to note a fifth contribution yielded by the modified model. There have been many attempts to articulate a "shared language" for psychology and religion that would enable psychology to speak in a less reductionistic way about religious experience (Assagioli 1956; Bradford 1984; Havens 1968; May and Van Kamm 1963; Van Kamm 1985). In search of the same, many religious therapists have ignored the root issues and, instead, have supplanted standard therapeutic technique with idiosyncratic religious terms and ideologies, yielding either mere cosmetic alteration or a welter of polysyllabic appellations of minimal therapeutic efficacy and dubious explanatory value. I reviewed some examples in chapter 2. It was, in fact, the existential psychoanalysts, the first group to introduce the search for meaning *beyond* psychodynamics, who explicitly warned against bifurcating "mundane" psychological and higher spiritual or noetic levels of meaning and most assiduously did not envision their perspectives replacing basic psychotherapy (for example, Frankl 1955, pp. xi, xii, 17). Unhappily, in other therapeutic circles this deference was not sustained as new "psychotheologies" began to proliferate.[2]

The proposed model maintains that the constructs of contemporary psychology, with minor modification, must be retained for use in referring to religious objects and experiences since it is through constructs such as these that even the objective God may be discoverable. There would be little value in dismantling the material (psychological) structures of the mind in favor of so-called psychospiritual or psychotheological categories. Terms such as "noetic conflict," "peak experience," and "formative authenticity"—when they replace rather than supplement standard working terminology—actually tell little about the experience of the objective divine object. At worst, such languages lead to superficial interpretations, which, in turn, generate disturbed empathy and no greater sharpening of the basic psychological mechanisms that provide access to the experience of the objective divine object. Terms such as "transitional object," "drive derivative," and "ego introject," however, when they are not simply tacked onto human experience but are allowed to become personally relevant descriptors or human experience, enable one to begin to imagine subtleties of interpersonal experience that bear directly upon religious experience.

Summation

We have seen that the modified model of the relationship between human and God representations, endopsychic and objective, is eminently practical as well as heuristic. It is heir both to the traditional psychologistic approach to the reality of God, whose valuable insights it retains, and also to the halakhic metapsychology, whose hypothetical structures are incorporated to help elucidate additional factors which likely impact upon and influence the development of god representations. Of particular significance is the manner in which the modified model parlays the clinical relevance of the transference paradigm in therapy.

Since the religious focus here has been on Jewish rabbinic thought on psychological matters, one may inquire whether there is an awareness in rabbinic literature of the kind of parallel and overlapping endopsychic, interpersonally based representations and objective divine object representations that have occupied my attention in this chapter. In response, while there is no direct reference to the contemporary mechanism of transference, the following rabbinic exposition simply cannot be passed by.

In the collection of talmudic exegeses known as the *Midrash Tanhumah*, the rabbis expounded upon the biblical episode of God's premier appearance to Moses at the burning bush. Moses suddenly apprehends a voice calling, "Moses! Moses!" (Ex. 3:4; cf. I Sam. 3:4–10). Noting the apparent pleonasm, the *Midrash* (*Tanḥ.* Ex. 19; Ex. R. 3) elaborates:

> "And God saw that [Moses] turned from looking, and the Lord called to him from within the bush, and He said: 'Moses! Moses!,' and he answered, 'I am here!'" Rabbi [Joshua ha-Kohen bar Neḥemia] taught: It is written [in passage 3:6 following] "I am the God of your father and the God of Abraham . . ." [Rabbi Joshua wished to draw attention to the twin references to Moses and to God's own double self-identification]. [This teaches that] God initially revealed himself to him in the voice of Amram, Moses's father. At once, Moses was elated and exclaimed, "My father Amram lives!" God then declared, "I am the God of your father—I lured you toward me so that you not be frightened."

Moses's experience, in other words, is initially processed as an interpersonal one, through anthropocentric templates, at the level of familiar object representations, and only subsequently, as the screen of interpersonally based expectations is moved aside, does Moses discover the presence of the objective God object. Of course, God directly orchestrates the perceptual process here, and one might demur that we really have no idea how Moses might have perceived God had God simply revealed Himself as such without allowing Moses the benefit of an intermediate phase. But that point is probably moot. The rabbis appear to have sensed, in the terms of their own expository framework, that God can be discovered through interpersonal transference and that perhaps this is a necessarily prior stage developmentally. They also sensed that this interpersonally based transference experience and the intrapsychic objects it generates must ultimately be relinquished and the objective divine object differentiated from the endopsychically conceived one. The image of an objective God can sometimes be found in the penumbra of the human object representation, the endopsychic god representation, or, as with Harry Guntrip's patient, in the shadow of the therapist's representation. "Patient! Patient!," the patient imagines the therapist as calling forth, beckoning toward him in the polyphonic voices of father, mother, therapist, and God.

6 | Clinical Illustrations

*[T*he] *believer's standpoint is marked by a twofold excess: an excess of the unconscious significations that, in spite of man's intentions, assert themselves on him, and the excess of hidden significations [which] he apprehends in manifestations of the divine. A truly authentic faith will assume these tensions, but no matter how legitimate the explicit intentions of belief may be, these conflicts, which touch the very roots of man's being, are fraught with snares and delusions, and the religious path remains a confused and risky one.*

—Antoine Vergote (1988, p. viii–ix)

This chapter presents an in-depth examination of the transformations in two patients' god representations in tandem with other important changes that took place during their intensive psychoanalytic psychotherapy. In both illustrations, certain distortions have been introduced to protect the anonymity of the individuals.

The first illustration includes an analysis of these changes in the light of a third factor which is present, I believe, in every psychoanalytic psychotherapy. I refer to the patient's early forms of idealization of and identification with the therapist and the subsequent abandonment of these identifications in favor of more mature, independent, well-internalized developments within the self. This is of particular technical interest since in the course of treatment the therapist's religious beliefs may be swept up by the patient along with these early or later identifications. In fact, however, the early forms of identification tend to reflect pathological or immature components of the object relations process as it unfolds between psychotherapist and patient. Such apparently "objective" identifications are, in fact, lower-level *introjections* and reflect the patient's need for the therapist as an immediate, magical replacement (or, in more disturbed patients, as filler material for the gaps in their psychic structuralizations). Such "identifications" tend to be based on the patient's repressed images and wishes, as projected onto the therapist, rather than on the therapist's true or known characteristics. This is not yet equivalent to the desired, higher-level identification with the therapist's empathic responsivity, analyzing functions, adaptive ego apparatuses, and so forth (Dewald 1976, 1983). It is precisely the different levels of internalization a patient may achieve which distinguish therapies that cure by facilitating direct identification with the therapist's values, by heightening self-esteem by introjecting the therapist's benevolent superego, by providing corrective emotional experiences, and by transference cure (Horwitz 1974, p. 261; see also note 2, chap. 5).

Not surprisingly, therapies which achieve cure by fostering primarily only the early, "objective" kinds of introjection of the therapist are disposed to find themselves often troubled by patients' wishes to "become like" the therapist. Therefore, any indication of the more primitive or immature form of identification during therapy requires examination and analysis, leading toward what may be called "analytically forged" identification. Only the latter, carefully worked-through internalization process is empirically linked to far-reaching, structural change (Wallerstein 1989).

Case A

The movement from objective identification toward what I term analytically forged identification can be traced in the five-year psychoanalytic treatment of a 26-year-old, unmarried medical student suffering from obsessive-compulsive neurosis (featuring obsessive fantasies with mixed hetero- and homosexual themes) with hypochondriachal and somatization traits. He was also a long-time sufferer from some form of irritable bowel syndrome, apparently of psychosomatic origin. There was no history of serious psychiatric illness in the patient's family, although two deceased relatives had had depressive neuroses.

The treatment was particularly amenable to assessment over time since the patient had been seen professionally by myself at various stages in his life, when both he and I lived in the United States and later in Israel. During his late adolescence in the states, I provided almost two years of psychological counseling primarily to resolve school-related crises and test anxiety, and then initiated psychotherapy upon his graduation from high school. While these early interventions were satisfactorily supportive during crises, their analytic potential was snagged by acting-out and impulsivity on the patient's and his family's part and by countertransferential reactions on the therapist's part. True psychoanalytic therapy began once the patient sought out the therapist after both parties had settled in Israel, at which point the patient lived relatively independently from his family.

The patient's family immigrated to Israel during the patient's adolescence, entering into a most difficult transition period. The father, a commodities analyst by profession, found it difficult to secure work and eventually took a professional position which was beneath his skills but which paid adequately and to which he adapted moderately well. The mother, a good and responsible woman, had to maintain control of her own overanxious and hypochondriachal tendencies, since living conditions necessitated that she leave the hearth and pursue work as a teacher. The patient got along with his brothers and sisters, who were generally supportive to each other despite near constant bickering during the many trying years.

Until middle adolescence the patient practiced his family's orthodox Jewish faith, at which point the combined effect of continual family crises, social isolation at school, increasing obsessiveness, and great anxiety over the prospects (four years ahead, at the time) of compulsory military duty resulted in daily panic attacks, heightened somatization complaints, suicide threats, and protracted battles over many religious customs. Owing to this new destabilization, earlier themes bearing upon deep psychosexual conflicts began to emerge in the breach. He became increasingly a loner, yet maintained close if conflictual relations with his parents.

When not withdrawn and depressed, the patient came across as a prematurely sardonic judge of human inconsistency, hypocrisy, and guile, flailing himself no less harshly, and not without a certain literary flair and depth. He lambasted the secularists, religious Zionists, and the ultraorthodox with equal vigor. It was interesting to observe, particularly during these episodes, that while the patient's everyday parlance was in fluent Hebrew, he pointedly referred to *religious* customs and terms with exaggerated English translations or in exaggeratedly Americanized Hebrew, with hard *r*'s and weak *kh* vocalizations, alien to him. Although I shall say more about this shortly, it seemed that when he would pronounce in English, with mocking emphasis, that he saw some people walking to "the *syn*agogue to *pray*," he sought to feign the speech of nonreligious Jews whom he believed spoke this way and whose freedom he secretly envied, and with whom he attempted to identify as a youngster in an effort to escape the constant surveillance by the God of his orthodox teachers. Also, and with particular forcefulness, he ceased formal prayer and obedience to rabbinic authority, yet at the same time avoided violating major Sabbath restrictions and for a long while still wore a small skullcap. I will interrupt the flow of the narrative at this point in order to consider this last seemingly paradoxical development.

Latent Theology and Paradox in Religious Functioning

Apparent paradoxes in the level of religious practice within a single personality are not uncommon. Dissociation from some aspects of religion while remaining faithful to others readily submits to psychodynamic or object-relational explanation, exemplifying the powerful role of what has been termed "latent theology" (Ahlskog 1985) or "precursor religious experiences" (Spero 1989; 1990a).

Latent theology includes the reappearance (such as during treatment) of childhood religious ideas, ideals, and memories discarded in adult life and the continuous search for a religious or theological experience to satisfy tendencies that have been set in motion by a particular set of early psychosexual and psychosocial factors. The first aspect underscores that *all* of the key object-relational and cognitive factors discussed in this text play roles in sculpting propensities toward certain kinds and qualities of religious experience and God representations (see also Almansi 1983; Rizzuto 1979), although an individual may never succeed in actually finding formal religious objects to satisfy these propensities. Thus, one may elect *or reject* religiosity based upon the overall quality of latent theology. I am referring, quite obviously, to the influence of preformal religious structures. The additional term "religious precursor" highlights psychological material which plays a formative role in influencing not only the development of God concepts and specific religious ideologies, *but more importantly the development of certain self- and object-representations that forever retain a certain affinity for or antagonism against dormant religious meanings.*

It also ought to be obvious that the repeated surfacing during therapy of a specific quantum of psychological material (a dream, an association, an anecdote), accompanied by some actual or potential religious meaning, highlights the role of religious themes and memories as linking or "bridging" phenomena in Mahler's sense. Technically, as illustrated above in figure 1, when specific psychological dynamics are in focus during psychotherapy, the associative processes they evoke will likely reconnect with "abandoned" religious artifacts that once bore a relationship to these dynamics. Similar to what are called "organizing" dreams or memories, which are cornerstones of psychotherapy in general, latent theologies and precursor religious phenomena provide a framework around which religious, psychodynamic, and object-relational meanings intertwine, sweeping, as it were, through overall psychic material and accumulating ever new material, permitting deeper understanding as psychotherapy proceeds.

Thus, during therapy, "good" feelings toward a particular religious precept or belief, *which itself may ensconce "good" feelings toward some more significant* interpersonal object, become transferred to the therapist in the form of early identification with or idealization of him. The need to protect the "good" object or belief from other influences or objects that are perceived as "bad," destructive, or otherwise depriving—among whom the therapist may occasionally be numbered due to transference—will often result in particularly sharp and sometimes extreme forms of attitudinal isolation. In more disturbed patients, where splitting within the structure of personality has been a predominant mechanism from early on, religious objects will often be split along the lines of the prevailing defensive modes or faulty psychic structure. The transference, too, will often reveal splits between object-relational tendencies bearing one religious significance and other object-relational paradigms bearing contradictory religious significance. And the initial hint to such splitting will often be the kind of paradoxical religious attitudes observed in Case A.

In the present case, the still sacred Sabbath was a significant part-object representation for split-off "good" maternal qualities and, thus, could be retained, isolated from fearsome paternal qualities and split-off "bad" maternal qualities. The bad, intrusive qualities were projected onto rabbinic authority and their myriad, inescapable by-laws and customs. A similar dynamic underlay the patient's mocking of English-Hebrew transliterations, or his avoidance of Hebrew terms that had a primarily religious connotation even among English speakers. Mere use of familiar Hebrew terminology brought to life painful experiences of phobic apprehensiveness, guilt, and anger, but not in the simpleminded sense that such terms "reminded" the patient of such pain. Rather, Hebrew terms and their complex connotations were linguistic girders around which formed his sense of past and sense of self. Hebrew terms were thus manifestations of particularly painful identifications between himself and specific aspects of the outside world and its cultural meaning systems, such that their use needed also to be subjected to splitting.

For example, the patient recollected teachers joking about modern rabbis who, in their unsophisticated religious discourse (as his teachers saw it), used the term "dairy" or even the Hebrew "Zionistic" term "*halavee*" instead of the more customary Yiddish term "*milikhig.*" He felt these jibes also devalued his parents and their rabbi, who were not averse to using all three terms. If as a youth he heard individuals use English translations of Hebrew terms or poor Hebrew, he identified with them and immediately felt shamed for them. The teachers' critique itself, he recalled, provided an early clue that religious Zionism might represent a less impossible identity for him. While he in no way yet appreciated the ideology of religious Zionism, his early memories revealed that he had come to view Zionism as a link with ritually uncomplicated agrarian festivals, a nationally condoned Sabbath day of inactivity, and the culture of hundreds of Israeli religious scholars who used no English or Yiddish in their discourses.

The Role of Early Identifications

To be sure, these idealizations very quickly wore thin in real life and led to disappointment and increased depression. He assumed, for example, that I was a fellow "modern" and that I shared his disdain of "primitive, uneducated" ultraorthodox Jews. Yet when once discussing his attitude toward some important Yiddish and Hebrew terms, my accurate Yiddish pronunciation plunged him despairingly into the new conviction that I was at heart just like all his early teachers. His naive view of Israel as an uncomplicated agrarian society rapidly bowed under the myriad rituals and entrenched cronyism of its intensely bureaucratic social systems, especially the army. The erstwhile country of philosopher kings gradually revealed its rag journals, underworld gangsters, and unwashed masses who abused the holy language. The issue of simple nuances of speech bore directly on quality of early identifications. Autonomous use of basic Hebrew terms was impossible for the patient without some form of projection (such as wondering aloud whether the therapist himself used these outmoded terms) or splitting. From this perspective, a major development in therapy was signaled when the patient eventually felt more free to use Hebrew terms.

Returning now to the narrative of the case, at age fifteen the patient returned to the states, and he resided with his grandmother, who played the role of a formidable, unswerving, incorruptible, all-knowing, magically powerful, quite godlike character. She was sharply contrasted in the patient's mind with her daughter and son-in-law, although they were no less honest and consistent, because she alone could quell the patient's anxieties. She, along with an ambivalently cathected image of the family pediatrician, represented awesome, yet longed-for idealized parental figures. Their dreaded qualities seemed mostly to coalesce in the patient's image of God, whom he worshipped with obvious counterphobic intensity during late childhood and early adolescence. And yet, he eventually sought to escape this god representation as it became an unbearable guilt- and shame-inducing introject.

The patient, still and all, did not abandon religion altogether. He gradually developed an idiosyncratic religion that espoused the values of justice, freedom, and honesty rather than rituals, obedience, and punishment. Of note, his new religious perception tended to blur any direct representation of or relationship with God. Yet internally he continued to be troubled by certain sexual fantasies that persisted in mixing in a primitive way the metaphors of his childhood religion and his basic psychosexual fixations. In these moments, the harsh, superego-bound "old" god representation burst through the banalities of his recently adopted humanistic faith. For example, while praying on Yom Kippur, he had an intrusive fantasy of the ornamental lions on the Holy Ark copulating and then imagined the face of God, contorted in rage, demanding unspeakable punishment, hellfire, and excommunication. Perhaps one of his most ironic obsessions was that he was not truly free to violate certain cardinal religious proscriptions, such as masturbation, lest he forfeit his portion in the very same hereafter he officially had ceased to believe in! Most of this imagery had an introject-level quality of internalization, reflecting highly ambivalent and disruptive identifications.

Despite this emotional turbulence, the patient matriculated high school and enjoyed fairly steady employment. He became a member of a rather unconventional religious synagogue, which enabled him to resume religious devotion, but he soon became disenchanted and disappointed. At about this time, he began to date girls. It became characteristic for him to select girlfriends with obvious psychological frailties, to whom he felt immediately devoted, identifying with their primitive qualities in a manner suggestive of tenuous self boundaries, championing them against battering fathers, psychopathic former boyfriends, and their own poor judgment. The manifestly shame-provoking quality of these relationships was repressed or occasionally disguised by the sudden appearance of religious guilt; for example, he worried whether it was religiously permissible to use a condom if one was already intent upon having premarital sexual relations (see Lewis 1971; Spero 1984). By identifying with these women and then saving them, he experienced himself momentarily as saved, whole, unshamed. Prior to therapy, however, the patient more generally experienced inevitable confrontations with the repressed "badness" he sought to externalize.

At age eighteen, panicked by unfounded fears of retaliation by an incompetent business partner, the patient returned to Israel precipi-

tously, knowing that army service awaited him. By now quite antago-
nistic toward all forms of religious Judaism, he seemed most desirous
to fulfill military duties in Israel over and against his manifest anxieties and dread about the army. A more militant Zionism seemed to
have become his new faith, and his military commander his god. His
idealization initially was so extreme that he found himself volunteer-
ing for the tank corp, yet it was not long before he was overwhelmed
by anxieties and somatic preoccupations. His less than one year of service was racked with obsessive scruples over exaggerated moral quandaries, what-if situations, and anxiety attacks, although, as before, he
functioned responsibly overall. The martinet and fate-controlling
qualities, objective and projected, of many of his officers fit exactly
into the space vacated by the exiled earlier God image. In particular,
the patient could not tolerate the threat of stockade, the constant
shouting and bawdy humor, the occasional homosexual tension, the
"bad" food, the filth in the washroom, and the seemingly bottomless
waste pits in the field. These concerns followed him even when he
was reassigned to a modern hospital base near home. Clinically, his
lifelong ability to maintain inner balance by dragooning rapid identifications and idealizations was rapidly weakening, and psychosexually
significant themes permeated his thoughts. He was soon discharged.

Disconnected from mainstream religious-ideological lifestyle and
deeply humiliated by his military failure, he sought long-term psychotherapy. In analysis, the patient initially relayed an intense fear of
divine punishment for his lack of religiosity. He ruminated constantly
over whether to reenter the army, to become nominally religious
again, to leave Israel in the middle of medical studies, whether it was
sinful to engage in premarital sex and would he burn in hell for it
even though he had denounced the metaphysics behind all such concepts. He sought often to cast me in the role of benign religious advisor, overlapping with the "good" maternal representations the
patient had projected upon me. He idealized me as a "breed apart"
and wanted desperately to know my opinion on all manner of
religious issues, simultaneously deprecating himself for his dependency. This self-deprecation, however, also hinted to how he would
subsequently treat a helpful object once "secured" via identification.

Ought a therapist to serve this role by answering the patient's questions and solicitations of advice—viewing them as asides whose superficial and direct dismissal or discussion might help cement the

working relationship? We have already clarified that dismissal is simply bad technique. But direct advising is also problematic. My experience teaches that ultimately this stance only evokes "religious" devaluation by the patient who would begin to identify the therapist, in his new role as religious advisor, as another potentially inept, "bad" religious object. Rather, by my retaining the traditional incognito role, the patient was enabled to move from manifest-level religious questions, fears, and obsessions to somatic preoccupations which gave more direct expression to root psychosexual fixations. Instead of playing "rabbi," which itself might have reactivated the archaic image of "forbidder of immodest thoughts," I encouraged projection of early disappointing objects that had been incapable of calming his primitive anxieties. Sequentially, in the past, the patient's parental objects failed in this regard, then the endopsychic god concept created in their image, then the abstract concept of justice, and finally the apparently nonreligious military "objects."

For the better part of the first two years of analysis, the patient ruminated about his military and sexual experiences, to the exclusion of developing other themes (at the same time, his academic progress was fairly steady). These topics ought to have been incredibly shame-provoking, yet the patient masked shame behind depression. The constant recounting of military anecdotes represented the struggle to cope with trauma, to be sure, but more specifically to externalize contaminating "bad" part-objects. However, the patient continued to experience a great deal of pain resulting from the "attack" of "bad" objects which now made their home in projected perceptions of the therapist, the patient's parents, and some of his fellow students enrolled in full military service (Fairbairn 1943). Worse, along with the externalization of the negative aspects of "bad" object representations came an additional sense of loss in the wake of externalization of complementary aspects of self. Even as his depression began to lift, the sense of loss was expressed more directly through panic and anxiety attacks. It soon became evident that he had attempted during his military tour to deal with similar feelings by identifying with "good" officers, yet inevitably fell back to identifying pathologically with the symptoms of malingerers and recalcitrant recruits (often from ultraorthodox religious circles, which complicated his affiliational conflicts to no end).

Toward the late middle of the second year of treatment the patient changed from his very immature identification with me in a generally ideological way (fellow outcasts, fellow nationalist-Zionists, fellow cynic-poets) to a relatively less immature identification with me as a devoutly religious person whose "beliefs" (based upon exaggerated inferences he drew from some of my interpretations) he could use magically to counteract medical and psychological crises. Although he made as yet no obvious change in external religious behavior, he began to explore some popular superstitious religious beliefs (for example, did I believe that Messiah was more likely to come since the Yom Kippur war?) with an eye toward discriminating between his anxiety-ridden motives for belief and his less neurotic feelings toward God. In the course of this new exploration, the patient resumed use of long-forgotten religious terminology and paid attention to religiously germane current events, a practice which was, for him, a constructive religious experience.

Rather than encourage him simply to independently research his religious concerns outside therapy, we explored the multiple dynamic meanings of the religious concepts that preoccupied him, eventually linking these preoccupations to salient themes of shame, exposure, fear of his projections, and his attempted introjection of my views. I observed that tutoring the patient to unfold religious material into psychosocial, psychosexual, and object-relational meanings had two important effects. First, there was a significant reduction of recently renewed resistance through the abuse of religious themes and questions within the monologue, yielding less "convoluted communication" (Langs 1976, 1981). Second, we enjoyed a greater production of new religious metaphors of very *specific* nature and very closely related to the patient's core drive conflicts.

Comprising the work of the following year of analysis, the patient slowly relinquished powerful narcissistic defenses against the transference, now experiencing feelings of shame and guilt toward his father, then guilt and underlying rage against both parents for their not protecting him against their own depression and fearfulness. During this period two new identification themes emerged. First, the patient carefully resumed specific religious practices as a result of the slow detoxification of his primary religious representations. At the same time, he began dating a girl whose own religious attitudes were sharply contradictory to his own. This, I believe, allowed him for the while to continue his splitting, but at some remove from the self. Indeed, he expressly sought to help her renew her interest in religiosity, a motive which we explored in terms of the mechanism of "reversal of passive into active," transference, and other determinants.

In a second effort at identification, the patient considered becoming a psychiatrist, which, at this point in his life, was not only quite unrealistic, but also linked primarily with my curative role. It was also important to note that in tandem with the search for professional identity was a quickening of interest in Jewish rituals and values, albeit rationalized by the patient as "merely" a necessary aspect of what he envisioned he would need to know for his future therapeutic work with religious Jewish patients. Deeper still was a homosexually based motive to provide motherly healing to powerful but wounded male figures. In all, such identification would have been a substitution rather than a meaningful transformation in his own self-structure (see Chused 1987).

This kind of identification, of course, is not entirely unwelcome in psychoanalytic therapy inasmuch as it indicates continuing development in treatment. In the present case, the patient's identification led to more direct work with latent homosexuality within the already existing primitive, dependent maternal transference. The paternal, relatively more mature oedipal transference could then follow. By the end of this segment of analysis he became markedly less anxious and phobic, much less preoccupied with his former sadistic god representation, and better focused on the many mundane, compulsive rituals he had adopted or invented as substitutes for old religious rituals. In some instances, these idiosyncratic rituals expressed conflictual feelings and hostile object representations, yet in other instances they served as a kind of cache where "good" religious feelings, memories, and accompanying object representations could safely hibernate.

The Sense of Mystery and Object Identity

To a significant degree, the most fateful turn in the therapy, deeply rooted to the issue of identification with the therapist, came with the following developments.

The patient began one particular session by wondering out loud about the phenomenon of ESP, relating all sorts of anecdotes from the popular press, his military and other experiences, many of which had a distinctly religious coloring. A select group of stories focused on idealized religious mentors who indulged in all sorts of numerologically based predictions. I highlighted the sense of mystery that appeared to attract his attention the most and wondered about the link between the uncanny tales of ESP and the distinctly religious element in many of these. The patient immediately began to relate supportive associations regarding the mysterious element of religion and spontaneously connected to the "mysterious" aspect of his phobias, the unknown element in his hypochondriachal fears, to the sense of unknown anxiety that so often overwhelmed him, and to the possibility—which therapy had helped him acknowledge—that something very much *known* hid behind the ubiquitous sense of unknown. He ended the session by noting that a sense of mystery also surrounded his relationship with the therapist.

He continued with this theme in the subsequent session, drawing a parallel between the mystery in his phobias and his growing sense that much of his difficulty with religion had less to do with this or that doctrine as with the various "senses" he experienced with religion: improbability, uncanniness, awesomeness, determination, foreboding. He then returned to his similar experiences of the therapist's identity and his attempts to ascertain the truth about the therapist's identity. The patient surmised that his own vigilance for truth and his self-appointed role as uncoverer of hypocrisy were displacements from the need to uncover key sexual secrets, to have certainty about the reality around him. To know the therapist, furthermore, was somehow to ascertain a trustworthy, internalizable object, to no longer be overwhelmed by it, to no longer be ashamed in its presence.

In fact, this transference-based identification represented an attempt to render less uncanny and dangerous—to experience as "known"—the very objects the patient projected upon the therapist. Ultimately, this identification indeed meant coming to know himself, since much of what he "knew" of the therapist was projected from his own inner world. He also realized that there was much less intensity lately in the desire to be like the therapist. There was, however, a proportionately greater interest in a number of personal interests and relationships whose mysterious qualities in the past had complicated his appreciation of them (such as his interest in medicine, on one hand, and his "strange" and paradoxical fear of blood and violence, on the other hand). With this work, the patient felt he was able to discard a major qualitative distortion in his sense of reality that had until now impeded autonomous religious experience.

During this period the patient developed a more clear sense that his knowledge about my own religiosity was essentially scanty, that the few valid inferences he had purloined here and there certainly did not yield an imitable religion. He revealed renewed interest in specific old religious rituals and pursuits, but with a sense of how this religiosity might be a component of an entirely new experience of himself as a physician, as a person in relationship to God, who he no longer perceived as pilloring or ridiculing him. He related that in some ways he felt he had returned to the God of his grandfathers, recalling numerous happy and also bittersweet memories and was prepared to examine the overlap between these beloved human objects and the divine image that was apparently rising in close proximity. He was certainly talking much less about his earlier perceptions and impressions of *my* God, or even the specific images that had coalesced into the god concept he had struggled with throughout childhood.

The more "full" and complete he felt about himself, the less relevant seemed the isolated aspects of the therapist's self or presumed beliefs the patient had earlier sought to internalize. He was aware of a continued interest in me, but my actual religious identity as such seemed far less relevant now than the more obvious oedipal aspects of our transference relationship. Any religious feelings that began to surface in the patient sought dynamically to be integrated into some whole. In other words, the patient understood that the aspects of my personality or beliefs he had earlier idealized had no substance or vitality out of context. The proper "context" had to be a more integrated personality, interrelated with the constructive aspects of the patient's own latent theology. The patient was well enough to accept the fact that he could not have mine. In the end, the patient began to identify not as much with the therapist's actual religion, but with his own more maturely experienced and internalized version of a world of representational objects, drive channelizations, and the religious symbols expressing these components.

Case B

A second illustration is the intensive, four-year treatment of a highly intelligent, combative, and jealousy-prone Roman Catholic nun with a narcissistic character disorder. We shall enter the therapy at a relatively advanced point during the late half of the third year of treatment.

At this specific stage of psychoanalysis, the patient began to focus on her repressed envy of the older men in her present and past life. She particularly admired the gait of tall, muscular men and began to ridicule the "neutered" way of walking she had had to force herself to adopt during religious training. In a remarkable association, she added that she found the therapist's body type and gait effeminate, yet at the same time provocative, mysterious, and dangerous, qualities she readily associated with the lure of the therapist's orthodox Jewish faith. She had always viewed Judaism, and Jewish men, as "dark," shadowy, and had come to realize through therapy that this connoted the projection of a specific qualitative aspect of her repressed sexuality. The patient, at first, preferred to intellectualize that the "shadow" had to do with the Bible and Mosaic law and the Christian doctrine of their foreshadowing the Gospel ("*Umbra in Lege, imago in evangelico, veritas in coelestibus*"). However, she moved stepwise toward acknowledging that the "law" she feared was "Jewish" psychoanalysis's uncanny ability to read her thoughts—which challenged her Catholic supremacy and her omnipotence, and frightened her. Soon, she began to consider the possibility that the "shadow" concept alluded to a screening function over an early childhood trauma.

Until this point in therapy, she considered all such thoughts sinful, and therefore inadmissible, and had kept such thoughts secret not only in therapy but even in formal Confession, which she also managed to rationalize. The parallel idea of keeping thoughts from the therapist by appeal to religious doctrine (that is, their sinfulness) was, in one sense, a rather simple level of "religious" or "catechistic" resistance (Kehoe and Gutheil 1984), not different in kind or quality from her overall narcissistic suspiciousness, and not particularly significant for its religious trappings. The deeper structure of the resistance had to do with the phallic significance of the "sinful" thoughts about men and the conflictual sexual or gender implications of her fear of her "shadow."

The resistance, in other words, defended against the fuller articulation of latent homosexual wishes and other unresolved oedipal conflicts. She not only idealized the male body from a heterosexual vantage point, but wished to inhabit the male body in the fantasy that it would be a stronghold against the intrusiveness of a sexually cruel mother. Even so, she devoutly believed that her closeness with God depended upon somehow offering herself to him in a way that was vaguely sexually exciting; a way which "required," as she expressed it, that she be satisfied with a feminine identity. (I have often heard religious Jewish women patients express a similar unconscious conflict by becoming preoccupied, in generally rather pseudo-philosophical manner, with the masculine and feminine motifs of the mystical Kabbalah, the sexual union between God and Israel, and the like.) Thus, the complex religious structures that had been built upon her god representation, and which for years had remained relatively autonomous or "adaptive," slowly became irradiated with conflict by association to the core conflicts.

It became increasingly evident that religious themes and resistances were inextricably tied to basic aspects of sexual identity and the emergent transference relationship. God, on one hand, was to be approached as an idealized masculine image by the patient's feminine identity, whereas the therapist was to be approached by masculine aspects of the patient's identity as a split-off and projected representation of her femininity. From the standpoint of technique, much of this material emerged rather nicely by encouraging the patient to talk about "sinfulness" and the types of experience this concept included, which led obliquely to a natural abandonment of the ideological rationalizations behind her resistance.

Further levels of conflictual identification came to light as the patient began to report dreams in which she experienced envy toward the therapist, featuring transference-laden depictions of him as a gaunt yet omniscient Jesus-like teacher. She noted that in her fantasies Jesus's head was always covered, which she recognized from certain works of religious art but more specifically identified with priests' skullcaps and then with the therapist's skullcap. Her earthly father most probably was the first object behind this representation, conspicuous in his suffering passivity, which she refurbished and projected onto the image of the nonprotesting Jesus and the neutral (she termed it "absorbing") therapist. She associated the headcovering with the worn-out, dirty fedora her father wore constantly. She detested her father's ignorance, whereas an omniscient being could be passive yet powerful in his foreknowledge. Partly, she had realized this idealized state in her own life through scholarly achievements, transforming herself into an object of envy. This, in turn, evoked a certain amount of shame and guilt, characteristically expressed initially in religious terms, such as constantly doubting the piety and purity of her motives, and only subsequently in a manner thematically closer to the core experience of dynamic conflict.

In reflecting upon the Jewishness of Jesus, both in historical fact as well as in the transference-laden images in her dreams and fantasies during prayer, the patient began to belabor intellectually the odd relationship between Judaism and Christianity, the Father and the Son, the "older brother" and the "younger brother." This we often viewed in terms of the relationship between therapist and patient. Occasionally, there was a hint of her appreciation that these dichotomies expressed indirectly her objective relationship with God. It eventually surfaced that she had fixated on the possibility of converting to Judaism, or at least embarking on a career in Judaic scholarship, even as her sexual fantasies about the therapist were redolent with latently anti-Semitic conceptions, while other of her idealizations seemed blatantly counterphobic.

At this juncture, I interpreted her sudden interest in Judaism in the light of the available psychodynamic picture, underscoring the concurrent ambivalence toward the Jewish faith and the therapist. Yet, despite the high level of functioning of her judgment and reality testing, the patient began experimenting secretly with a few Jewish rituals, especially those which her scholarship had revealed were forerunners of current Catholic rituals, and attempted to not practice certain Catholic rituals. She felt she had become a "Marrano in reverse," and somehow was sure that the therapist's family name suggested Marrano ancestry. However, the history of the Marranos disturbed her as she was sure she would have chosen death over forced conversion. Yet, during one such discussion she remarked in an absentminded way, and all the more chillingly, that as a good Catholic she doubted whether she would have resisted much the orders of the Inquisition. There was an implication in her subsequent associations that even when she had earlier supposed she would face death rather than convert, she was essentially directing murderous impulses toward herself *as Jewess*. These doubts and wonderings suggested the emergence of unconscious resentment toward the introjected idealized representation of the therapist. Further work made clear that this idealization secondarily masked emergent feelings of rage toward her impassive father and toward a God who so relentlessly tested and tried.

Subsequently, the patient began to explore the sexual element conspicuously absent in all of her idealized male representations. In her mind, the therapist's and her own mutual commitments to what she termed "professional and religious celibacy" rendered both parties social mutants, "neutered," capable of a relationship that was at once platonic in a relieving way and, given that she often experienced herself as masculine, also distortedly homosexual. She wondered intellectually about the special satisfactions of the Jewish woman, whom she viewed as enjoying a fully equal relationship with the Jewish male. Her thoughts expressed apparent ignorance of how idealized this view was. She remained unconscious of the strength of her envy and combativeness and of the equally powerful wish to eliminate any difference—sexual, cultural, religious—that might symbolize her preoedipal and later oedipal crises. For example, she was especially attracted to the Orthodox Jewish menstrual laws and fantasized about the great power in being able effectively to keep the lustful male at bay for close to two weeks. Her interest in these particular laws again suggested the continued need to hide behind asexuality. While this clarified another aspect of her attraction to celibacy, it actually caused her to experience a weakening in identification with the therapist since for a moment it seemed as if "Judaism offered not much more than Catholicism."

The resulting dent in her identification with me led to a depressive period. She harangued church leaders and even Jesus for all manner of antifeminine attitudes and policies, but the bulk of her critique, if in some way valid, was laden with oedipal anger and disenchantment. Indeed, she experienced my interventions against her identification with Judaism as an assault, an authoritarian blow, a deprivation, and a castration. Given the feminine maternal identity she projected upon me during this stage of the analysis, my intervention was also experienced as a continuation of her mother's abuses. If the patient venerated Judaism on the phallic level, motivating an intense though ambivalent identification with the therapist, she venalized it on the level of the oral and anal significances its traditions and customs bore for her. Similarly, associations about these themes in her own Catholic devotions and doctrines brought up great emotional turmoil on the dynamic level and disturbingly primitive introjections on the object-relational level.

The eventually successful analytic journey revealed a religious woman who, for the first time in her life, felt an especially close relationship with God, one no longer mediated by theological understandings which happened to cater to her narcissistic, concretistic view of reality and her constricted sexual identity. She became much more devoted to *thinking about* Jesus, whereas for her whole life she had primarily read or learned about Jesus. If until now she felt she recognized God, it was only because he was essentially an extension of familiar object experiences from home. She now began imagining what started as a kind of healthy, girlish relationship with his image and gradually grew into a trusting investment in his newly identified capacity for caring and activity. To a certain degree, the patient's awareness of these potentialities initially emerged during her discovery of such functions in the therapeutic relationship and, thus, might be seen as an attempt, following parallel developmental phases of sexualization and eventual sublimation, to perpetuate these qualities in the safest place imaginable. And to another degree, the bestowal of these potentialities about her image of God also represented an effort to repair her father by proxy. For the most part, however—certainly by the beginning of the fifth year of treatment—her relationship with God, her fellow sisters, and other significant persons had taken on uniquely complex forms of expression. More important, she evinced much less of the earlier tendency for automatic saturation of all of these domains simultaneously and equipotentially with whatever conflict or sexual/aggressive impulse happened to be agitating in one or the other specific domain.

In terms of her neurosis per se, through the transference phenomena and their resolution, specifically including her early identifications with the therapist, the patient was no longer subject to crippling anxiety, fright, depersonalization, and experienced less envy and doubt. In the domain of religious experience, her more recent representations of Jesus seemed to take on characteristics that, to the best of our knowledge, had no obvious, unilateral root in her pathological traits nor in the introjected idealized characteristics of the therapist. Of course, some of the newer traits appeared to be subtle, creative syntheses drawn from hitherto dormant or "trapped" precursor religious objects—and in this sense, they were old/new. But there were exceptions, whose objective or complete source remains unknown.

In saying that certain of the patient's religious objects were "new" and seemed no longer encumbered by her conflict-ridden human oedipal models, I do not mean that these new objects were totally bereft of all characteristics or descriptors meaningful in earthly terms. As the patient began to develop complex, bountiful, and deeply moving representations of and relationships with God's hands and facial expressions, there was evidently a consensual *anthropomorphic* basis for comprehending generally the terms "hands" and "face" even as she moved toward creating a unique category of significance for what she was considering to be God's hands and face. Upon reconsidering the matter at the time of writing, the nagging question returns: At what point can we assume that the hands and face of God-the-objective-object have found expression through human terms?

The answer, again, must be modest and limited to our prior acceptance of the assumptions of the religious believer. One of the assumptions is that God seeks relationship with humankind and the second is that God reveals through the Word something of himself that is representable, internalizable, and the basis for a relationship. Given these assumptions, it is possible to consider "new" religious objects as those which form spontaneously around the structures and contents of revealed doctrines and practices and with which the individual enters into new relationship, or new levels of relationship. It is critical that the sense of relationship and even mutuality remain even when the affective tone of the relationship is weighted with despondency, passion, rage, anger, awe, or mystery.

The patient in case B had innumerable experiences with human hands and faces, but she also had many other good as well as bad experiences with faces and hands whose structures and meanings had remained latent until her analysis (although they were expressed obliquely through dreams). The loving attention she in one session paid to tracing the creases and wrinkles in Jesus's face as featured in a favorite painting did not seem copied from any actual model of relationship we could discern, although for a while this caressing seemed distinctly compensatory and perhaps reparative. At another stage, it bore the developmentally healthy (and theologically striking) significance of a kind of motherly exploration of the newborn child—at an earlier substage, this expressed a mirroring fantasy in which Jesus represented the patient, and only later did the patient presume the mothering role. During a stage later still, under the sway of one particular transference tendency, this caressing became more blatantly sexualized (and at a later stage aggressivized) as Jesus came to represent a highly idealized introject of the analyst modeled upon a wished-for paternal image. Persistently, she completed each successive stage by contrasting and differentiating her new images of God and her experience of self in relationship to God, from all prior experiences.

The point is that we could document empirically that the novel representations and relationships the patient eventually formed with Jesus's hands and face were clearly different than her old representations and more complex and mutual than the transitory representations modeled upon her analyst's hands and face. Progressively—and in tandem with the many other developments and topics that occupied our attention in treatment—her relationship with Jesus grew away from early models, taking on complex forms unknown to other of *her* internal object representations. In the final analysis, even if one were to find, upon the furthest retrograde exploration, that the "new" God representations involved the resurrection of latent primal representations, what remains authentically new is that these primal representations can now develop unhampered along structural pathways that dispose toward relationship with God.

One could say, following Guntrip and McDargh, that the patient's god representation had become more therapeutic. Or, one could state that increasingly more therapeutic experiences with former god representations enabled the objective God to be perceived in a less endopsychically encumbered way. And there are other questions. One may ask, "Would this woman have elected to become a nun had she been successfully psychoanalyzed earlier in life?" One cannot answer this question retroactively (although we certainly pondered it during analysis), but the fact is that the patient chose happily, one might even say *graciously*, to continue her celibate vows even after undergoing all those kinds of emotional expansion that the hypothetical questioner presumes to be *in*compatible with religious extremism! To be sure, the patient did undergo a religious crisis regarding whether or not to continue all of her religious vows. On the one hand, the idea of human sexual experience had regained its normal appeal and she had much less need to disguise and restrain her impulses and hates through religious prohibitions and sectarianism. On the other hand, therapy had also uncovered *healthy* early identifications with echos in her current religious life. She discovered new, less archaic meanings implicit in her religious prohibitions and sectarianism, and her overall sense of religious commitment still pulled strongly in the direction of the type of sacrifice she made as a nun. She had surrendered earlier attempts to gain vengeance against her father and to find a substitute for him through Jesus, and her masochistic drives seemed to have been authentically sublimated.

In fact, it could be said that she no longer *identified with* Jesus—that is, she no longer related to him in terms of some conceptualization of identity formed by pathological projections. Instead, she for the first time aspired to a *relationship* with God, perhaps still modeled upon an interpersonal concept of dialogue and desire for acceptance, yet open to the unique contribution of her self-experience and to the utter uniqueness of the divine object with whom she sought relationship.

Discussion: Identification and Relationship to God Concepts

The discovery of parallel dimensions of experience in therapy, and perhaps even in other forms of encounter, offers special opportunities for examining the relationship between the human and God. A central assumption in early writing on the subject is that the acceptance humans find in psychotherapy can lead to being sensitive to and then seeking acceptance in God. In this assumption we gained explicit recognition from the religious point of view that psychotherapy may bridge the parallel dimensions of anthropocentric and deocentric experience.

Different than earlier approaches, however, the present model does not seek to encourage interpretations that simply appear mystical or religiously "loaded." Rather, it seeks formulations that are truly *anagogic* (Silberer 1912, 1914; cf. Freud 1900, 1922), moving beyond interpersonal dynamics toward the great ethical dilemmas of the human mind and the way in which these dilemmas express qualitative aspects of relationship with God.

Some writers have demanded restraint. Their rationale is particularly relevant for advocates of the possibility of discovering an objective God in therapy behind the sundry interpersonally based transferences. Oden himself remarked:

> [T]he authenticity that can at least partially be *conceptualized* by existential analysis, and at least partially *actualized* by effective psychotherapy, *can never be fully actualized, and, therefore, never fully conceptualized, except in response to a relationship in which one is loved, known, and understood by one in whom mistrust is impossible.* Such a relationship is only fragmentarily enacted in therapy, where one is always dealing with a finite human brother in whom mistrust is always possible. Such a relationship can be possible only if God's own love is made known in history. (1967, p. 119)

In fact, we need not conclude so pessimistically. While the therapist does not proclaim for the patient a specific religious lifestyle or theology per se, and certainly does not offer himself or herself to the patient as a religious object, there inheres in working through the parallel deocentric-anthropocentric dimensions the possibility of clarifying the particular ways in which human and religious objects have influenced personality. In my view, it is precisely because God is unfathomable in essence yet knowable in the realm of his influence on human personality structure, that the objective role of the psychotherapist is so strikingly relevant to religious experience.

In his usual complex phraseology, Kleinian psychoanalyst Wilfred R. Bion (1967) offered some very relevant "second thoughts" regarding the patient's experience of God, housed in the context of his important instruction to practice psychoanalysis, to as great a degree as possible, absent of all biasing memory and desire on the therapist's part. The bias inherent in "memory" and "desire" derives entirely from certain nonconventional meanings that Bion assigned to these terms. Space permits only a brief reminder that in Bion's lexicon, "memory" (usually printed under an arrow pointing eastward) refers to events that *have not* happened—that is, ones that are perceived *psychologically* as having not happened; the invariants of an event which is unconscious because it is obscured by screen- or pseudo-memories *although* it *has* happened—whereas "desire" (printed under an arrow pointing westward) refers to events that *have* happened—that is, ones that are perceived *psychologically* as having happened; an event which is manifest because it is disclosed by an intense desire or wish, even though no such event has in fact occurred (cf. Freud 1912, pp. 115–16).

Bion begins with an unequivocal assessment of the problematic of the religious patient in therapy:

> It is quite common for psycho-analytic students to observe patients whose references to God betray the operation of "memories" of the father. The term "God" is [then] seen to indicate the scale by which the magnitude, wisdom, and strength of the *father* is to be measured. If the psycho-analyst preserved an open mind to the mental phenomena unfolding in the psycho-analytical experience . . . he would not be restricted to interpretations of God as displaying a distorted view of the father, but would be able to assess evidence, *should it present itself,*

> for supposing that the analysand was incapable of direct experience of God and that experience of God had not occurred, because it was made impossible by the existence of "desires" and "memories."
> (p. 144)

Bion has enunciated in a robust way that direct experience of an objective, nonpaternally tuniced God is somehow possible and, therefore, ought to be anticipated by the psychotherapist.

Bion is further prepared to anticipate, in a way that is harmoniously superintended by the parallel models sketched here, that if such direct experience is *not* evident—given contexts where we may be permitted to presuppose such experience—then the therapist must be willing to analyze the possible interference/resistance of "memories" and "desires" regarding this special object as he would any other. Only in this way can we conceive of a corrective experience that is at once psychoanalytically legitimate and religiously authentic. As Bion continues:

> The psycho-analyst accepts the reality of reverence and awe, the possibility of a disturbance in the individual which makes atonement and, therefore, an expression of reverence and awe impossible. . . . It follows that interpretation involves elucidation of evidence touching atonement, and not evidence only of the continuing operation of the immature relationship with a father. (p. 145)

A maddeningly absent, inadequate breast may give rise in the adult to the compensatory preparedness for interminable awe and allegiance to a god representation who, as we have learned to state, has been essentially and fatefully designed by the believer (or culture) to never requite a single one of the hapless petitioner's wishes. Freud taught: abandon such a god! Bion claims: recognize the "desires" and "memories" from which such a god construct suspends and analyze the "desire" that compels one to create *such* a god—or to follow one if one such as this happens to exist!—and become free to search for an experience of God riven of prior anthropocentric biases.

While in agreement with Bion's overall program, I have attempted to take much larger account of those possible anthropocentric factors and dimensions that actually may be desirable as components of the objective deocentric encounter, such as is transmitted through the deep structures of the halakhic *a priori*. Furthermore, we have been intrepid about the possibility that beneath the several layers of the in-

trapsyche and its object-representational structures as humanly conceived lie the imputed demands or "desires" of an Other, reverberating
silently in memories and desires that, for the most part, are only
hazily perceived during a lifetime and whose objective Object greets
us only so rarely as it peers from behind the incohate shadows of life
and death.

Let us reconsider another route to such discovery through the overlap itself. It was noted above, for example, that the personality of the
therapist, which includes his own intrapsychic structures and identifications, plays some role in the analytic process. The therapist's basic
goodness, however, is only recognized through the penumbra surrounding the transference relationship. What is "good" about the
therapist is the way the therapist practices his or her technique in a
goodly way, doing so in a manner that eventually makes the patient
feel good. And inasmuch as the therapist has acquired basic goodness
from relationships with other humans, there is in this basic element
something which automatically, constantly, yet indirectly exposes the
patient to the basic goodness, love, and acceptance with permeates
the reality of the therapist. Thus, although the specific "good objects"
of the therapist's inner or external world are never offered directly
to the patient, and the therapist can never be completely known by
the patient, the patient partakes indirectly of these objects as well.
Through this experience, the patient has the experience of self-
discovery and some taste of relationships.

Bion's above cited reflections contain an even more far-reaching
teaching regarding the discovery of God. Properly understood, Bion
moves us closer to appreciating the importance of what the psychotherapist or psychoanalyst does *not* do and *refrains* from thinking
during the treatment process. In other words, Bion is emphasizing the
significance of certain modulated forms of *absence* in order to maxi-
mize the potential growing and listening space for the patient. This
notion of the "presence" of objects that become explicit precisely
through their absence, and the existential sting of their absence precisely as symbolized by the presence of language (insofar as language
takes the place of the earliest caretaking functions and, eventually,
mother herself), has been brought to center stage by the piquant
work of Jacques Lacan (1964, 1977). For our purposes, only a small
aspect of his complicated work can be noted here.

André Green, a psychoanalyst at one point heavily influenced by

Lacan's insights, clarifies succinctly how the discovery of self—and we will extend this as well to the rediscovery of God—might be possible not only through the overlapping of two sets of objects, but also through the juxtaposition of "presence" and "absence" in the therapeutic dialogue (1978, p. 181; see also Schafer 1983, p. 39):

> *The analyst is not a real object; the analyst is not an imaginary object.* The analytic discourse is not the patient's discourse, nor is it the analyst's, nor is it the sum of the two. The analytic discourse is the relation between two discourses which belong neither to the realm of the Real nor to that of the Imaginary. This may be described as a potential relationship or, more precisely, *as a discourse of potential relationships, in itself potential.*

Indirectly present in the therapy, in other words, are the analyst's parents, supervisor, and analyst, as well as, from a temporal vantage point, the patient's and the analyst's past and future. Green is rendering clinical the Lacanian emphasis on the importance of "absence as presence," such as the way language represents the attempt to overcome the initial separation from parents and the way transference in therapy re-evokes the same trauma.

This differentiation between the projected and real object-aspects of the therapist is developed further in Lacan's revision of the concept of transference and its analysis during psychotherapy (1964). The therapist, in Lacan's terminology, functions as the "third man," for he is neither the *true object*—that is, the missing or conflict-ridden object of the patient's lifelong desire, nor is he truly the *alter ego*—that is, the ego of the subject itself to the degree that this ego itself is a product of being "captured" as an object by other persons. As Wilden interprets in his close-to-the-text rereading of Lacan:

> Although [the therapist] begins the therapy by acting as a mirror for the subject, it is through his refusal to respond at the level consciously or unconsciously demanded by the subject (ultimately the demand for love), that [the therapist] will eventually (or ideally) pass from the role of "dummy," whose hand the subject seeks to play, to that of the Other with whom the *barred subject* [Lacan's term for the negated or repressed aspects of self that have been put aside in favor of the pseudo-I that is mistaken for the true self] of his patient is unconsciously communicating. The mirror relationship of ego and *alter ego* which was the obstacle to recognition of his unconscious desires, which the subject has set up and maintained, will be neutralized, the subject's mirages will be "consumed," and it will be possible for the barred subject to accede to authenticity. (Wilden 1981, pp. 167–68)

The patient's transference, then, essentially is the drama of the patient's struggle to resist the therapist's special revelatory powers as the third person—expressed nicely by the rabbinic hermeneutic as the *katub ha-she*ʿ*lishi ha-makhri*ʿ*a*—and to repetitiously recast him as either the *true object* or the *alter ego*. It is through the fundamental invalidity of the patient's discourse "to" or "with" the therapist—because the patient is generally not talking *to* or *with* the person-who-is-the-therapist—and via the carefully apprehended and scrutinized tendency in the patient's language and associations to slide away from the therapist and toward the true, hitherto barred subjects of his love and hate, that the absent objects of the patient's inner world materialize.

Perhaps, too, the patient's *religious* metaphors and the nature of new forms of religious experience that emerge during psychotherapy, and the direction toward which these slide, can be seen similarly as expressing the indirect influence of the god representations and other religious structures of the analyst and the patient. There may be present in the above, ultimately, the influence of the analyst's objective divine objects or endopsychic god objects. And in the same way, the apparently real absence of god representations in the patient or analyst may reveal, depending upon one's point of view, the real lack of such objects in the world—because in fact *there are no* such objects; or, the very same absence may imply the *presence* of an only imaginary lack, of the god *manqué*, of the traces of the deleted or nullified divine object and of the schizoid compromises and fetishistic substitutes (à la Becker) used to compensate for this lack. In any case, *because this is psychotherapy, such influences are submitted whenever possible to analytic scrutiny.* One is compelled to conclude that patients, upon completing therapy, take away not the objective aspects of the therapist, but rather healthy, new representations of themselves and their historic past that have slowly developed in the transitional space between their objects and the "silent" but available objects of the therapist.

The patient in the first illustration did not come away from therapy with a great deal of factual knowledge about the therapist. All the same, the patient was able to experience the therapist as somehow knowable, knowable at least in his "therapist-ness," the moment he was able to cease *mis*identifying the therapist with projected object representations. This achievement turned out to be sufficient to launch a similar process of exploring and identifying anew the scope and presence of the divine object. Indeed, we can now respond to Oden's aforementioned reservations: It is precisely the working-through of transference and the relinquishing of the uncanny and ultimately unsatisfying experience of pseudo-acquaintance with the therapist that enables the patient to begin the process of properly identifying and coming to know the objects in his or her own world.

If one holds that the "unconditional positive regard," empathy, patience, and acceptance that a therapist offers the patient is ultimately rooted in the therapist's own experiences with regard, empathy, patience, and acceptance, and point to objective objects in the therapist's reality with whom he or she has shared such experiences—one of whom may be the God who accepts the therapist—*then it is also possible, from a religious point of view, that these same object-relational capabilities may point a patient toward an objective divine object.* This is the legacy of the transitional object, and it is the prerequisite for interpersonal and deocentric growth. As the patient slowly perceives how dim and ephemeral his or her identifications with the therapist are, and as he or she learns, first, to cope with a certain necessary sense of aloneness, the patient becomes heroically able to relinquish scattered part-representations and make way for a true relationship with a mutual partner. As the individual learns to accommodate the approximate, to objectify the unseen, to signify absence, to exist between external and internal reality, to abandon, create, and rediscover objects, he or she may be viewed as apprenticing for a deocentric relationship.

7 | Final Considerations on God as Structure

Various religious sects are in fact defined by a common set of symbols having approximately common significance for all members. Yet, the essential psychological situation remains: of all the modes of human discourse, the religious is inevitably the one that is used with the greatest latitude, and the one to which the demand for specifically agreed upon referents least applies. The reason is that the cosmic conditions pointed to in religious language are not demonstrable, not knowable (in their entirety), and therefore not accurately signifiable.

—GORDON W. ALLPORT (1950, p. 136)

There remains only to entertain some final considerations on the main theme of this work.

First, a thought regarding the central contribution, the elaboration of the halakhic metapsychology. This hypothetical yet systematic schematic enables the clinician to conceptualize the weave of intrapsychic structures, specific to each religion, within which both endopsychic and objective representations of God may germinate, and through which they may ultimately be differentiated. It also informs us about the framework of the religious representations themselves. The metapsychology, thus, has heuristic and practical utility. Specifically, the metapsychology allows for intelligible discourse regarding the parallel and sometimes overlapping and conflicting anthropocentric and deocentric dimensions of human object relations. As such, and contrary to Allport's pessimistic appraisal cited in the epigraph, some objectification of the God behind the god representation can be inferred from the nature and quality of the constituent images and structures that attend the representations. I also discussed and responded to some potential objections to the metapsychology.

Still and all, there are limits to the explanatory power of halakhic metapsychological constructs, commensurate with the limits of our understanding of both Halakhah and psychology. This does not mean, however, that we must resign ourselves to mere description. Explanation, it has been said, ought not to be contrasted to description, but only to *mere* description. For, in fact, there are many excellent verbal explanations that are essentially descriptive. Moreover, as Rubenstein (1967) notes, even if a hypothesis is false (such as the notion of the caloric flow of heat), and hence does not properly *explain*, it can still be used to describe metaphorically an empirical generalization (such as the true molecular "flow" of heat), even though it, in fact, is better *explained* by a totally different theory (for example, the *kinetic* flow of heat). The same can be said for the metaphors generated by the halakhic metapsychology. Since we are not yet acquainted with the real or existential aspects of either Halakhah or psychology—what an "id" or an "object" or an "*eruv*" or a "*yezer*" or a "God" *really* is—we can only hope that as we confirm small aspects of the hypothetical-constructive aspects of our theory, it becomes more likely that the existential aspects to which they refer are, in fact, real properties of the world.

In terms of treatment, some interesting conclusions have been reached. Differentiating the transference distortions that take place among interpersonal object representations, endopsychic God concepts, and objective God representations can be a central aspect of psychotherapy. It must matter whether the objects we deal with therapeutically, and whose constructive and destructive influences we interpret, are intrapsychically real, phenomenologically real, metaphorically real, or *objectively* real! And this is so even if the only directly observable difference such distinctions allow is a more profound empathic bond between patient and therapist.

The practical difficulty is just *how* one talks about God, what this unique object is like ontologically, how it relates to humankind, and other aspects which one senses are not captured by existing anthropomorphic categories. The religionist feels aided by sacred texts (and the belief in their divine authorship), legends, and cultural history which render God slightly more imaginable, experienceable, knowable; yet God is apparently known in different ways by different people during different eras. My goal has been simply to demonstrate that the borders of this domain extend significantly farther than we are accustomed to think. To this end, I proposed a model through which therapists can think in terms of an additional, unique level of dynamic activity and a unique set of object representations wherein humankind's deocentric experiences might be envisioned and from which special meanings can be derived for the religious material emerging during therapy.

Identification and interpretation are key elements in the change process, and their proper modulation and direction undoubtedly are central factors in determining whether psychotherapy is an affair of gross manipulation and the fostering of simple imitation, or an entirely more complex process. The clinical illustrations make clear that psychotherapy welcomes the appearance of identifications insofar as this heralds the regressive process upon which therapy depends. Such identifications are bound to take expression in ways that envelope the patient's religious metaphors simply because *both* are underwritten by the same characteristic dynamic activity. This principle will better enable therapists to evaluate and treat religious material in a uniform and consistent manner.

Conceptualizing the Object, the Experience, or Its Territory?

We are now in a good position to ask whether it is most advantageous to view a god representation in terms of the religious experience it generates, the identity of the object itself, or in terms of the kind of psychic space the object occupies? I think we can develop a response by reconsidering the approaches of Carl G. Jung, Donald W. Winnicott, and Sigmund Freud.

As noted in chapter 3, it often seems as if Jung himself vacillated between full acceptance of God's ontological reality, on the one hand, and a somewhat more restricted emphasis of God's psychological reality, on the other hand. This struggle emerges throughout Jung's provocative *Answer to Job* (1952) and other works. Indeed, some critics were impressed that even as Jung rejected Freud's wish-symbol approach to God, he, in turn, fell back upon a conception of God as merely a cognitive structuralization of psychic states drawn from the collective unconscious, "existing" in only the same psychological sense that he believed flying saucers to exist: as an archetype for certain basic psychic strivings (Jung 1958). This left Jung vulnerable to charges of psychologism (see Glover 1956; Philp 1958).

However, the approach adopted here enables one to comprehend Jung differently; closer, in fact, to his intended point of view. Jung, it is true, vacillated, but not between affirming or disavowing that an objective God exists. Rather, in Jung's own words:

> An archetypal image is like the portrait of an unknown man in a gallery. His name, his biography, his existence in general are unknown, but we assume nevertheless that the picture portrays a once living subject, a man who was real. We find numberless images of God, but we cannot produce the original. *There is no doubt in my mind that there is an original behind our images, but it is inaccessible.* We could not even be aware of the original since its translation into psychic terms is necessary in order to make it perceptible at all. (Philp 1958, p. 12, emphasis added)

What fascinated and confounded Jung—apparently because he could *not* tolerate simpleminded psychologizing of God—was his very belief in an objective God *and* in the root inadequacy of our psychological or neurological receptors to "pick up" God objectively. Jung surmises that God speaks to humans in symbols, but feared also that humans cannot be confident about the symbols used. Now this quandary is entirely valid. For exactly how *does* one link conspicuously common archetypal structures to objective divine structures?

At this juncture, one indeed can progress no further unless certain further theological statements or assumptions are declared. Using the example of Judaism, one would need a declaration of belief in God as an image- or structure-producing God, that such structures can be regarded with confidence to reflect some aspect of the divine, that such structures reside in a knowable system (such as Halakhah), that such structures are internalizable. For it only makes sense to pursue in an optimistic way the level of reliability in an archetype, symbol, or metaphor as a path toward God *if* one believes God has forwarded to his creatures a specific quantum of *basic* structures through which God can be known as well as the ability to perceive such structures.

The doctrine of a structure-creating God, a structure-bound world, and a structure-deducing human being is, in fact, implicit in Halakhah. The most explicit reference is surely the view of Rabbi Akiva (ca. 40–135 C.E.) expressed in the ethico-halakhic tractate *Avot* (3:17):

> Beloved is man, for he was created in the image of God; But it is by a special love that he was informed that he was created in the image of God, as it is written: [Gen. 9:6] "For in the image of God did He make man."

> Beloved are the people Israel, for they were called children of the Omnipresent; But it is by a special love that they were informed that they were called children of the Omnipresent, as it is written: [Deut. 14:1] "You are children to the Lord your God."

> Beloved are the people of Israel, for to them was given a special instrument of delight [the Torah]; But it is by a special love that they were informed that to them was given the precious instrument with which the world was created [Talmud, *Pes.* 54a, cf. *Shab.* 88b], as it is written: [Prov. 4:2] "For I gave you good knowledge; do not forsake my Torah."

These observations have been interpreted in a variety of ways through the centuries. No matter what else, Rabbi Akiva has emphasized the *a priori* nature of key aspects of divine design, relationship, and responsibility. Moreover, he has emphasized that God imparts this design and relationship to humanity in a perceptible and representable manner, so as to enable the development of internalized structures.

In search for a similar set of assumptions, I believe, Thomas Oden and Jung labored hard to read a particular kind of structuralism into the rituals and testaments of the Christian faith. They realized, perhaps in terms different than mine, that conceptualizing God means internalizing certain kinds of characteristic structures in addition to undergoing certain kinds of experiences and psychodynamics. Consider, for instance, Jung's (1942) amazingly Lacanian treatment of the concept of trinity versus quaternity, and note how he moves the analysis from latent numeric configurations to the structural infrastructure of the stages of psychological development. As such, these symbols—whether they are the geometric or numeric structures in primitive myth and religion or the geometric, numeric, and temporal forms of halakhic *a priori* structures and kabbalistic numerology—become intricately correlated with human interpersonal (intrapsychic) structures to such a degree as to make possible the subjective-objective experience of relationship with the structure-imposing Other who is God. (Unfortunately in the case of Jung, he again in the 1942 essay does not make explicit whether he viewed the structures he hypothesized as divinely intended or whether he viewed his own interpretations as retroactive reconstructions.)

Donald W. Winnicott, although he did not discuss religion all that much, budged the conceptual frame just enough to capture a new dimension: the *psychic territory* or space occupied by god representations. Winnicott, in his inimitable style, literally sought room for the kind of objects we are trying to conceptualize, even though he did not state directly what kind of god he was referring to (1963, p. 94; cf. with Fairbairn 1927):

> The saying that man made God in his own image is usually treated as an amusing example of the perverse, but the truth in this saying could be made more evident by a restatement, such as: man continues to create and recreate God as a place to put that which is good in himself, and which he might spoil if he left it in himself along with the hate and destructiveness which is also to be found there.

Excellent! For although in Winnicott's "restatement" one unmistakenly hears the familiar refrain of the role humans play in creating God, I do not believe Winnicott intended to emphasize this in an absolute sense. It is inconsistent with the overall body of Winnicott's theorizing to believe that he wished to leave us with yet another endopsychic object extended from biological or social drives and conflicts. Rather, I believe that Winnicott sought to emphasize the human psyche's special contribution to the representation of God and to accept the fact that these contributions have to be "psychological" simply because this is all that the human mind (as best as we know) is capable of contributing. The human contribution is the making available of psychic apparatus and space as dwelling places for structures related to God, even as on the larger scale, God may house all psychic entirety.

A Psychic Space for the God Object

The trial of the human response to God is, therefore, to render the psychic apparatus as hospitable as possible to the potential kind of object representations and relationships God *as object* might require. And humans can succeed in this task only if they have apprenticed healthfully in the "creation and recreation" of God concepts.[1] For it must be expected that even an objectively real God object will undergo qualitative changes in the way the human mind represents such a being during different stages of development.

Rabbinic tradition acknowledged this fact in characteristic fashion. Elaborating upon why the Decalogue begins with the declaration of God's oneness, the Midrash states (*Pesikta Zuta Beshalah,* 15:3; *Mid. Tanh. Yitro;* see Rashi to Ex. 20:2):

> "I am the Lord, your God" [Ex. 20:2]—Because the Holy One appeared to them at the sea like a hero waging war, at Sinai like a scribe teaching the Torah, in the days of Solomon as a youth, and in the days of Daniel like a merciful old man. Said the Holy One to them: "[Although] you see me in many images [*demuyot*], do not conclude that there are many gods! Rather, I am who is the Lord at the sea, I am who is the Lord at Sinai, I am who is the Lord in every place."

And in terms closer still to contemporary theory, the rabbis understood that at least part of the explanation for varying representations of God—that is, aside from special characteristics of divine revelation itself—resides in intrapsychic developmental factors:

> R. Levi taught: Had it been written "The voice of the Lord in *His* strength"—the world could not sustain. Rather, it is written, "The voice of the Lord in strength" [Ps. 29:4]. [That is,] according to the strength of each of them [i.e., according to individual tolerance and capacity] did the Lord reveal Himself; the youths according to their strength, the elderly according to their strength, the little ones according to their strength, the sucklings according to their strength, and the women according to their strength. (Songs R. 6 to Songs 5:16)

Developmentally induced modifications in the god representation expose the resident God object to all the fluctuations of schizoid-to-depressive phase development, separation-individuation dynamics, and the like—all of which is included in the type of creating and recreating envisioned by Winnicott.

We now learn that in addition to undergoing certain kinds of nutritive experience, and the differentiation of certain kinds of objects, the development of a well-internalized God representation also requires the establishment and maintenance of a special kind of psychic territory or apparatus. The "shaping of character" which theologian David Hartman (1976) spoke of as resulting from religious living, surely means more than the salubrious influence of some hypostasized, adaptive fantasy upon ethical behavior. Rather, it refers to the necessary formation of specific kinds and qualities of psychic structure and object-representational space for the sphere of real interaction with God. The development of such psychic space is among the earliest and the most specifically human of the basic psychological developments in people. Of course, the experiential metaphors of religion comprise the very warp and woof of a religiously inculcated individual's style and quality of thinking and conceptualizing (Patai 1977), not to mention the individual's elementary identity formation (Ostow 1982). But even these metaphors are dependent upon earlier, rudimentary, preconceptual cognitive, linguistic, and affective structures that serve as the vehicles for such metaphors. Winnicott (1963) comprehended this when he sought certain basic capacities, such as the capacity to "believe in" and the maintenance of "potential space," within which psychic area the object representation of God eventually settles. In the same vein, we saw that Erik Erikson also sought to isolate certain primary psychic experiences (such as "numinosity") which serve as aliment to later religious experience.

Indeed, probably a great many important psychological developments relevant to religious belief and experience transpire far before the human mind achieves its abstracting and symbolizing functions. Rabbi Levi's teaching in the previous citation suggests that even infants can develop some kind of god image or representation (see also Mid. Ps. 22 end, "Said R. Elazar . . ."). If so, then even these aboriginal formations may have their own rudimentary religious significance. I termed these early influences "precursor religious objects" (Spero 1987b and 1990). Ahlskog (1985), in related work, discusses the role of "latent theology," namely, childhood religious ideas that serve throughout life as vehicles for all sorts of central psychic con-

flicts. Nathaniel Laor attempted to conceptualize an even earlier rudimentary area by hypothesizing a "religious register" setting up during
earliest life, which Laor depicts as some kind of dawning experience
or set of experiences which enable a subsequent God image, of a kind
that is "both very general and also essentially religious at its core"
(1989, pp. 226–27). The result of these kinds of precursor influences
is an intrinsically religious object representation—whether formally
recognized as religious or not (see also Rizzuto 1979, p. 178).

The above underscores the salience of early childhood research and
psychoanalytic-developmental theorizing for getting nearer to the
genesis of the encounter with the religious object. For it is reasonable
to suppose that many of the preeminent early psychic developments
upon which constructive and maladaptive religious beliefs and representations are based are registered even before the human infant is
fully self-aware or conscious, perhaps even prior to the budding differentiation between self and other, inner and external reality, tem-
porality and atemporality, and so on.

The importance of the hypothesis of creating a special psychic
space for the development of the early god image and representation
needs to be related to Roy Schafer's aforementioned speculation regarding the process of internalization:

> It is conceivable that some objects have existed as internal objects
> from the very beginning. The differentiation between self and object is
> not identical with that of inside and outside the self-as-place. Some
> objects may be discriminated before the outer boundaries of the self-
> as-place are defined. These may be included within the boundaries
> once they are defined. (1968, p. 118n)

Schafer leaves room for the influence of very early perceptual forces
of as yet unknown identity. He has explained how it might be possible to experience certain kinds of objects as already "present," as
belonging to the psychic interior and exterior almost simultaneously,
perhaps cloaked in an aura of timelessness and without our ever
being able to recollect the ultimately first empirical discovery of them
in the real world. This would fit God well. For Freud, classically, this
subjective sense of being somehow familiar with an object even upon
encountering it for the first time would be analyzed in terms of an
attempt to create retroactively a sense of perpetuity in time, due to a
variety of idiosyncratic dynamic motives such as to deny that what *is*

in fact familiar is really the return of a repressed oedipal association (for example, Freud 1911, p. 58n). Schafer, however, is arguing, in the case of the types of objects he is describing, that the sense of familiarity is ontologically valid inasmuch as the "presence" of these objects preceded the arrival of consciousness. Schafer's notion would spirit away an early religious object of this kind far from the constraints of the traditional oedipal-wish model and even from the relatively later transitional-object model.[2] Symbolic dimensions of the object's "presence" and "absence" could now be given full ontological weight.

Freud, too, entertained the possibility of the influence of early object images that *precede* full psychic interiorization and differentiation. In his classic *Three Essays* on sexuality, Freud articulates a universal theorem: "There are thus good reasons why a child sucking at his mother's breast has become the prototype of every relation of love. *The finding of an object is in fact a refinding of it*" (1905, p. 222; 1925, p. 237). This is not only a motivational drama. It is also the nutshell of the essential dynamic of the acquisition of language, symbol, and myth: the translation of the "search and refinding" process into linguistic and intrapsychic structure and the transcription of lost or absent objects into pictorial and verbal representations (what Lacan refers to as the "phonemic organization of reality" in "The Function and Field of Speech and Language" [1956/1977, p. 103] and "The Direction of the Treatment" [1958/1977, p. 255], heralding the entry into the symbolic order). Freud had hereby innovated the idea that the "refinding" takes place not in physical reality simply construed, but primarily within the infrauniverse of language and fantasy.

But this immediately drives home the problem that the overall quality of this rediscovery process is dependent not only upon the availability of objects, or even of their representations, but also upon the dimensional adequacy of linguistic structures and their capacity for containment. Unsatisfied wants, unrequitted loves, and, on the highest level, inexorable theological-philosophical dilemmas owe a large percentage of their unique character to the goings-on at this linguistic-representational level. According to this, one would treat the perennial dilemma of theodicy—"Why is there evil in the world?"—in terms of: "How am I able to think/conceptualize/hold-on-mentally-to-the-thought that there is toxic matter inside me that seems capable only of catastrophic effects and permits of no neutralization?!" (at least, in cases where an individual's point of interaction with this dilemma is not simply philosophical but rather, or apparently neurotic, distractional, compulsive).

However one resolves dilemmas such as these, one must conclude, I think, that already at this level there takes hold the possible influence of an objective God—or, at least, of the *a priori* structures through which a God may enunciate. Whatever be the clinical import of the finding and refinding of an object, Freud's notation bears an existential implication that anticipates the profound cyclicity of the yearning, abandonment, and reencounter that characterize human relationship. But to understand the source of Freud's existential insight, we must return to the old problem of Freud's analysis of religion. In fact, I believe it can be shown that one of the earliest object influences he ever described highlights a direct relationship to the so-called religious object.

Toward the end of his life, in *Civilization and Its Discontents*, Freud writes specifically regarding religion:

> The origin of the religious attitude can be traced back in clear outlines as far as the feeling of infantile helplessness. *There may be something further behind that, but for the present it is wrapped in obscurity.* (1930, p. 71, emphasis added)

At first blush, this seems like vintage Freud, reducing religion to infantile dynamics; confining it to some predawn adaptation to trauma. Upon closer examination, in fact, one notes that Freud leaves room for some thing or some experience even prior to his traditional baseline. However, in *Civilization and Its Discontents* Freud does not pursue this obscurity.

A clue to just what it was that Freud intuited in the "further behind" may be discerned in an unlikely place—among his earliest, pre-psychoanalytic writings, the foundational "Project for a Scientific Psychology" (1895, p. 318). In this dense metapsychology, while writing of neurons and psycho-biological quanta, Freud leaps to an observation which I believe lays the groundwork for a major contribution to the psychology-religion interface:

> At early stages the human organism is incapable of achieving this specific action [i.e., relief from a given excitation]. It must be brought about by extraneous help, when the attention of an experienced person [*ein erfahrenes Individuum*] has been drawn to the child's con-

dition by a discharge taking place along the path of internal change (e.g., by the child's crying). This path of discharge thus acquires an extremely important secondary function, that of *communication* [cf. also pg. 366], and the original helplessness of human beings is thus the *primal source* of all *moral motives.*

Freud's official translator James Strachey rendered the key term *Verstandigung* as "communication," but I prefer Jones's translation which is both more precise and closer to the context: "namely, of bringing about an *understanding* with other people." Both terms bring to the fore the notion that "moral motives" or religious concepts cannot be said to germinate from the state of helplessness *per sui,* nor even from the experience of *being helped* as such. *Rather, they germinate in the experience of a self being met* and understood *by the other, from the sense of relationship with a reliable object.* This relational *Verstandigung* itself, the great endowment of comprehensibility, is part of the great "something other" that Freud suspected lay further behind the traumatogenic infantile motives for belief.

We begin life, Freud was prepared to see, with a potentially religious feeling already as profound as anything postulated of "advanced," "mature," Buberian faith. Freud's early, succinct speculation is entirely object-relational, for this early morally relevant sense of "understanding" could not take place if there was not an other present and willing to respond. More important, Freud has left room for an object who understands human need far before such need can be articulated by the human himself, far before the Other is recognized as *ein erfahrenes Individuum.*

Epilogue

"It can't be *light!*" Anna gave that sentence a finality that was irrefutable.

"So, fine," I said, "If it can't be light, what is it?"

"Mister God can't be light." The words flew like stone chippings as Anna hacked away with her mental chisels.

I could imagine Mister God edging forwards on his golden throne and peering down through the clouds, a little anxious to know what kind of a mould he was being forced into now. I had the itch to look upwards and stay, "Relax, Mister God. Just relax, you're in safe hands." I reckon Mister God must get a bit fed up now and again considering all the various shapes we'd pressed on him over the last umpteen thousand years, and I don't suppose we've come to the end of it yet, not by a long shot.

"He can't be light, can he? Can he, Fynn?"

"Search me, Anna. Search me."

"Well, he can't be, 'cos what about them little waves we can't see and the big waves we can't see? What about them?"

"See what you mean. I reckon things would be a whole lot different if we could see by those waves."

"I think that the light's inside us, that's what I think. I think it's so's we can *see* how to see," she nodded her head, "that's what I think. The Mister God Light outside us is so's we can see the Mister God Light inside us."

Upstairs Mister God—if you'll pardon the image—slapped his leg and turned to his angel hosts and said, "How about that! How about it."

—Anna, in *Mister God, This Is Anna* (Fynn 1974, p. 168)

Abbreviations

Scripture

Gen.	Genesis	Jon.	Jonah
Exod.	Exodus	Mikh.	Mikhah
Lev.	Leviticus	Naḥ.	Naḥum
Num.	Numbers	Ḥab.	Ḥabbakuk
Deut.	Deuteronomy	Ẓeph.	Ẓephaniah
Josh.	Joshua	Zekh.	Zekhariah
Judg.	Judges	Ps.	Psalms
1 Sam.	1 Samuel	Prov.	Proverbs
2 Sam.	2 Samuel	Songs	Song of Songs
I Kings		Eccl.	Ecclesiastes
2 Kings		Lam.	Lamentations
Isa.	Isaiah	Esth.	Esther
Jer.	Jeremiah	Ez.	Ezra
Ezek.	Ezekiel	Neḥ.	Neḥemiah
Hos.	Hosea	1 Chron.	1 Chronicles
Obad.	Obadiah	2 Chron.	2 Chronicles

Midrash

Various forms of rabbinic exegesis of the biblical text compiled from the period of the beʿrita and mishnah, until well into the geonic period, ca. 400–1010 C.E.

Gen. R.	Genesis Rabba
Ex. R.	Exodus Rabba
Lev. R.	Leviticus Rabba
Num. R.	Numbers Rabba
Deut. R.	Deuteronomy Rabba
Esth. R.	Esther Rabba
Songs R.	Song of Songs Rabba

Lam. R.	Lamentations Rabba
Eccl. R.	Ecclesiastes Rabba
Mid. *Tanḥ.*	*Midrash (Rabbi) Tanḥumah*
TDE	*Tanna Dévei Eliahu*
PRE	*Pirkei deʿRabbi Eliezer*
Yalkut Sh.	*Yalkut Shimoni,* compiled by Simon of Frankfurt, 1898.

Talmud

Pagination in the Babylonian Talmud, redacted ca. 500 C.E. is according to folios, side *a* or *b,* unless Jerusalem Talmud (J.T.) is indicated (redacted ca. 400 C.E.), in which case pagination, similar to the Mishnah, is according to chapter and paragraph or halakhah.

Ar.	*Arkhin*	*Kid.*	*Kiddushin*
ARN	*Avot de'Rabbi Natan*	*Maksh.*	*Makhshirin*
Avot	*Pirkei Avot*	*Mak.*	*Makkot*
A.Z.	*Avodah Zarah*	*Meg.*	*Megillah*
Ber.	*Berakhot*	*Men.*	*Menaḥot*
B.K.	*Babba Kamma*	*M.K.*	*Moʿed Katan*
B.M.	*Babba Meẓiah*	*Naz.*	*Nazir*
B.B.	*Babba Batra*	*Ned.*	*Nedarim*
Bekh.	*Bekhurim*	*Nid.*	*Nidah*
Beẓ.	*Beẓʿah*	*Pes.*	*Pesaḥim*
DEZ	*Derekh Erez Zuta*	*R.H.*	*Rosh ha-Shannah*
Eduy.	*Eduyut*	*Sanh.*	*Sanhedrin*
Erub.	*Erubin*	*Shab.*	*Shabbat*
Git.	*Gitten*	*Shek.*	*Shekalim*
Ḥag.	*Ḥagigah*	*Sheb.*	*Shebuʿot*
Hor.	*Horiut*	*Sot.*	*Sotah*
Ḥul.	*Ḥullin*	*Suk.*	*Sukkah*
Kallah R.	*Kallah Rabbati*	*Ta'an.*	*Ta'anit*
Kallah Z.	*Kallah Zutreta*	*Tem.*	*Temurah*
Kel.	*Kelim*	*Yeb.*	*Yebamot*
Ker.	*Keritut*	*Zeb.*	*Zebaḥim*
Ket.	*Ketubot*		

Codes and Commentaries

Rashi	R. Shlomo Yizhaki, d. 1105, foremost French expositor and decisor for the text of the entire Bible, Mishnah, and Talmud.
Tos.	*Tosafot,* Franco-German talmudists of the 12th–13th centuries, interlocutors of Rashi, and early decisors of halakhic opinion (*s.v.* [and some Hebrew term], following the talmudic location of each *Tos.,* refers to the heading that appears *ad loc.*).
Sefer ha-Ḥinukh	Major compilation of the miẓvot and their major laws and meanings, by Aaron Halevi of Barcelona, d. 1350.
Minḥat Ḥinukh	Supercommentary on *Sefer ha-Ḥinukh* by Rabbi Joseph Babad, d. 1874.

M.T. *Mishneh Torah,* halakhic codex of Maimonides (d. 1204), organized around major legal groupings; e.g., *M.T., Hil.* [*Hilkhot*] *Shabbat* 3:5 = *Mishneh Torah, Laws of Shabbat,* Chapter 3, Law 5.

Sh. A. *Shulḥan Arukh* ("The Set Table"), halakhic codex of Joseph Caro (d. 1575), organized into four major sections: *Orekh Ḥayim* [*O.Ḥ.*], *Yoreh Deᶜah* [*Y.D.*], *Ḥoshen Mishpat* [*H.M.*], *Even ha-Ezer* [*E.H.*]; e.g., *Sh. A., O.Ḥ.,* 435:8 = *Orekh Ḥayim,* Chapter 435, law 8.

Tur. Sh. A. (*"Arbah Turim"*) Precursor to above by Rabbi Jacob ben Asher (d. 1343), divided into four subsections as in *Sh. A.*

Resp. Collection of halakhic responsa, querries, or novella, generally arranged according to sections of *Sh. A.*

Notes

Chapter 1

1. Winnicott (1958) tended to distinguish between psychoanalysis proper and cases requiring what he termed "management"—psychoanalytic management, of course—where the therapist's personality comes more to the fore. However, the bulk of psychoanalytic treatments of the so-called borderline, primitive, or preoedipal personality involves just this kind of complex therapist-patient bipersonal interaction, with the attendant need for the therapist to very scrupulously "manage" his management.

Chapter 2

1. I may appear cynical, but, having rejected dynamic theories of psychopathology, as well as the deterministic basis of behavioral psychology, without which scientific behaviorism does not make much sense, one must wonder, indeed, how these writers intend to explain the development of behavioral or mental disorders? Merely as the wages of sin? If so, then *physical* infirmity as well? And if "Yes!" to the latter, then disavow all of contemporary medicine—which Judaism quite plainly does not?

2. A few comments are in order apropos Peter Gay's (1987) thesis that psychoanalysis, in its historical context, is inherently and teleologically linked to Freud's atheistic Jewishness (Gay's otherwise extensive bibliography overlooks Vogel's earlier [1975] consideration of this issue). Gay apparently believes that *orthodox* Jewishness encourages some kind of psychic complacency or quietness of soul that would militate against the kind of deep-seated anxious iconoclasm and investigating which, in turn, nurtured the formulation of psychoanalysis. Without rejecting these ideas out of hand, the follow-

ing observations may temper the enthusiasm with which one greets Gay's conclusions.

i. There are no grounds for assuming generally that the religious personality is inimical to psychodynamic kinds of wondering or psychoanalytic soul-searching. Pierre Janet and William James, both deeply religious, certainly plied the waters of the subconscious, while Gay himself noted the passionate psychoanalytic investments of the Reverend Oskar Pfister. See also Wangh's recent analysis (1988) of the roots of Freud's (1930) interest in and reservations regarding the "oceanic feeling" as the basis of religious experience.

ii. Pursuant to this, Rudnytsky (1989) recently compared the opposing attitudes of Freud and British psychoanalyst Donald W. Winnicott as regards religion and linked their differences to contrasting early paternal and maternal experiences. Winnicott, as is known, revealed new dimensions of psychological experience that may seem especially compatible with the influence in his own early life of a maternal, playful capacity for "religious" illusion. And yet he, too, adopted Freud's instinct theory, Melanie Klein's hypothesis of innate sadism, and adhered overall to psychoanalytic speculation.

iii. The voluminous scholastic-didactic literature of Orthodox Judaism could easily be construed as particularly suited for psychoanalytic-type theorizing. On this point, it is unfortunate indeed that most authors seek to compare psychoanalysis primarily to a kind of decerebrate, populist Judaism, shorn of the very intricacies and empirically oriented conceptualizations that singularize it (Bakan 1958). The writings of the ethical-perfectionism movement known as *Musar* (discussed on p. 39), which was in earnest proliferation among Freud's Lithuanian rabbinic contemporaries, readily confirm that the type of anxious, creative self-consciousness capable of leading to the development of a "dynamically" oriented system of behavior change (although far from psychotherapy proper) is distributed among the devout as well.

iv. In fact, not only do many aspects of psychoanalytic doctrine share much in common with the *content* of Judaic teaching, as others have demonstrated with varying degrees of depth and tightness of fit, but also with Judaism's hermeneutic, exegetic, and semantic methodologies. The point is especially important in the light of Lacan's appeal to return to the Freud of *The Interpretation of Dreams* (1900). Thus, while there is no second-guessing history, it is not unreasonable to think that orthodox Judaism could also have produced a Freud! Perhaps not the Freud who doubted (on specious grounds) the Hebrew lineage of his ancestor Moses, but certainly the Freud who plumbed the depths of human motivation and forged a framework for the unconscious.

3. It is certainly noteworthy that there is not more than a handful of published accounts by Israeli psychotherapists of intensive psychotherapy in which religious issues are a main, specific area of focus or technical challenge (cf. Beit-Hallahmi 1975; Greenberg 1984; Mester and Klein 1981; Witztum, Greenberg and Buchbinder 1990; and perhaps Ilan 1977; cf. also Witztum, Greenberg, and Dasberg 1990). In Gorkin's (1986) provocative analysis of countertransference between Israeli Jewish therapists and Arab patients,

sociopolitical and ethnic issues emerged, but apparently not religious issues! Similarly, Hodis's 1986 paper on Israeli *yordim* (émigrés from Israel) living in America discusses psychodynamic metaphors but makes no mention of religious issues. Now these authors don't necessarily *have* to discuss religious issues, yet the focus of their discussions is already fine enough to render the absence of this topic conspicuous. Are we to believe that religious issues could have been nonexistent in the treatments of such clientele? Or, were such issues perhaps present, but in latent or otherwise not readily recognizable forms? Most important, on the possibility that such issues or themes *were* present, were the therapists able to "hear" the religious issues (see Leavy 1990, p. 50)?

Apropos of Leavy's concern regarding the ability to "hear" religious issues, I might add, at slight risk of tangentiality, that a troubling reminder of this possibility appears in Peter Heller's very recent reminiscence (1990) on his early adolescent analysis with Anna Freud. At one point (p. 317), he reflects upon the emergence of some religious material during one session and recalls that Anna Freud simply paid it no interest. In retrospect, Heller felt the religious concerns were and remained quite sensitive issues in his life. Now we don't know enough about the consistency of this kind of attitude to count it as a firm substantiation of Leavy's concern (see recently Koltko 1990; Gartner et al. 1990), and we need special kinds of analysis to study exactly how such clinical attitudes influence subtly the patient's immediate monologue and long-range production of material in treatment. However, Heller's reflections do suggest that even as a young patient he was able to distinguish such indifference from even-hovering analytic attentive reticence.

4. I leave to professional epistemologists whether the inference of God's existence from demonstrable human expressions such as the emotion of "reverence"—as in the so-called ontological argument—may legitimately be considered a *kind* of empirical evidence (cf. Smart 1962, pp. 440–63; S. Spero 1965). Schleiermacher (1830) certainly wished to earn such status for a special class of emotions. In particular, he sought to ground religious piety in a unique form of dependence he termed "*Abhängigkeitgefuhl,*" a form of ontological dependence he specifically distinguished from natural or "psychological" dependence which arises in the parent-child context. Kauffman (1981) similarly distinguished between the "ontological anxiety" of the mature religious personality and the anxiety of early separation. For Schleiermacher and Kauffman, consciousness of being absolutely dependent or ontologically anxious *is* simply and empirically the being in relation to God.

Otto (1917), of course, criticized Schleiermacher for rendering the difference between dependence upon God and dependence upon parents a matter of degree rather than an intrinsic difference *in toto genere*. Later on, in my critique of the object relations school's contribution, I will raise the same criticism regarding Guntrip's (1969) formulation. However, the true dilemma remains that ultimately all human feelings toward an *imaginable* object—and our feelings can be directed only toward imaginable objects!—are psychological constructs. The objects themselves may be objective or fantasied entities, but our feelings qua feelings are objective only as psychic phenomena. I see no way out of this dilemma save by adopting the view that dependence upon parents, for example, as well as other so-called mundane or basic psychological experiences, are already imbued with the holy and, therefore, bear the implicit presence of the One who imbues holiness. This might be taken as the intent of Psalms 139:13, 15:

> For Thou has formed my reins,
> in my mother's womb . . . ;
>
> For my frame was not hidden from Thee,
> when I was made in secret.

The issue in religious experience, then, is not simply the *kind* or *quality* of ontological emotion or sensation, as compared with so-called mundane emotion, but rather: *What is its object?* Schleiermacher-type emotions, one may restate, differ not as much in developmental trajectory as in the ultimate object which absorbs them. The task of the religionist, or the psychotherapist, then, is to delineate as accurately as possible the true object, human or divine, of a given feeling, and, as I shall state in chapter 5, to assess as best as possible the degree to which the penumbra of one object has been cast upon the other.

Chapter 3

1. Leavy (1986) argues effectively that Bergin's (1980; 1983) search for an underlying, lawful "spiritual substance" and Meissner's approach to religious belief as a transitional phenomenon both remain entangled in psychological positivism. While Leavy's point is well taken, his criticism is strong only to the degree that theorist-clinicians such as Bergin and Meissner intend to explain away the objective object behind god representations and religious belief with new, adaptive and creative, yet *ultimately* endopsychic factors or laws. It seems to me, however, as I elaborate in the text, that their intention is to offer a new interpretive template through which psychological and religious factors might be more productively correlated and not to argue for a specific causal relationship that moves necessarily and undirectionally from psyche to spirit.

2. Rabbi Joseph Dov Soloveitchik's reflections on the aesthetic aspects of sin and repentance, for example, would gain further illumination from the sort of observations made by Likierman. Compare Likierman's analysis with Soloveitchik's which follows and which must be cited at length (1974/1980, pp. 214–15, emphases added):

> The sinner, also, mourns. What does the sinner mourn? He mourns that which he has irretrievably lost. What has he lost? Everything.

The sinner has lost his purity, his holiness, his integrity, his spiritual wealth, the joy of life, the spirit of sanctity in man; all that gives meaning to life and content to human existence . . . Mourning inevitably contains a masochistic element. The mourner tortures and torments himself; he hates himself. In the bereavement of sin there is also a clear masochistic element. The sinner begins to sense a feeling of contempt and disgust toward himself. He experiences masochistic self-hatred. The sin is seen as an abomination, an object of revulsion, something utterly nauseating. The feeling generated by sin is not a moral sensation; the moral sense in man is not such a powerful force. *The feeling of sin which drags a man to repentance is an aesthetic sensation, or more correctly, a negative aesthetic reaction.* . . . The natural inclination or desire of man is for the beautiful, for the aesthetic; man despises the ugly—it is this which draws him away from the sin into which he has sunk, inasmuch as sin contains ugliness, disgust, and abomination which repel man's aesthetic consciousness. *Thus, when God seeks to draw man to repentance, He arouses not only his moral awareness, which is usually not sufficiently strong to awaken him from his sin, but, more so his aesthetic consciousness which has better chances of effecting the repulsion of the despised and loathsome sin.*

These aesthetic properties, one might restate following Likierman, are not merely valuational components of the *act* of sin, but rather belong to the conceptually and emotionally larger moment of devastated relationship between a human and God. Ultimately, they are properties of the devaluated self-representation itself. This is why merely *not sinning* is never satisfactory to modify fully the sense of guilt or shame. In addition, the "unaesthetic self-representation" must be modified, often in ways far more extensive than made possible by ritualistic flogging of the heart alone (*M.T., Hil. Teshuvah* 2). To my way of thinking, Rabbi Soloveitchik has given poetic form to what may be termed the schizoid aspects of sinfulness and the depressive-restorative potential of repentance. A sequel to the present text, my forthcoming analysis of repentance from a psychoanalytic and linguistic point of view (*The Well-House: Psychoanalytic and Object Relational Aspects of Repentance*) will describe this more fully.

   3. Wellisch (1954) spoke of the differences between the classical oedipal drama and the drama represented by the biblical *akedah* crisis (the so-called binding of Isaac). He posits that the successful resolution of the *akedah* is based on the introjection of not only parental images—the basis of the classical oedipal superego—but also of "the image of man's divine calling." Unfortunately, Wellisch does not specify by what mechanism this latter introjection comes about (nor would that be a pedestrian undertaking). According to the mode of thinking I am trying to develop here, one would, indeed, be interested in the way in which God-the-real-object was perceived by Abraham and Isaac and how such an object was differentiated from the then-prevalent infanticidal parental-god images.

4. I have discussed in detail elsewhere the powerful impact of psychotic religious processes and related states of mind upon the therapist, from a psychoanalytic object relations point of view (Spero and Mester 1988). See there, in particular, the case of S., the "Messiah" (Illustration 4) (cf. also Perez, 1977).

Chapter 4

1. The relationship between illness, or neurosis, and "sin" has tantalized many writers. This analogy has been of particular interest because the implications of any such analogy are not only philosophical or existential, but also practical; for example, to what degree can one be considered psychologically responsible for sinful behavior, given that sin may have unconscious determinants, or morally responsible for psychiatrically aberrant behavior, given that some forms of psychopathology are deemed sinful by religio-ethical standards? I have elsewhere reviewed the sources and formulated my own contribution to the topic (1980, chap. 4; see also Schimmel 1977).

I would here wish only to bring to light the following additional source which very clearly drives a wedge between illness and sin in that it contrasts the truly preemptory nature of mental illness *per se* (that is, owing to its unconscious determinedness) and the seemingly compulsory quality of acts that may be more properly deemed sinful. The citation further confirms the great care one must exercise in striking analogies across the two systems. I cite the comments of a Tosafist (thirteenth century glossator) to the following talmudic statement (Talmud, *Erub.* 41b): "Three things deprive a man of his right mind [*da'ato*] and from knowledge of his [God]: idolatry, mental illness [*ru'ah ra*], and the afflictions of poverty." To this, the Tosafist (s.v. *"mi she-hoẓi'u"*) remarks: "Now even though *witchcraft* also denies the [authority of the] Heavenly Court, this would appear to be included under the category of *ru'ah ra;* [yet regarding] the *yeẓer ha-ra* [the 'evil inclination' of human personality], although elsewhere [Talmud, *M.K.* 17a] it appears that man is sometimes overwhelmed by his *yeẓer* and cannot overcome it, nevertheless one can be cautious to not come to this." The Tosafist, in other words, differentiates between truly uncontrollable influences, such as mental illness—and magical spells!—and ultimately controllable influences, such as man's own inclinations or *yiẓrim* (see, recently, Bar-Ilan 1990).

2. The idea of *a priori* halakhic structures in the world is illustrated in a most poetic way in the following midrash (Lev. R. 27:2):

> Rabbi Tanḥuma introduced a teaching regarding the passage, "Who has preempted me, that I must repay him?" (Job 41:3) [i.e., who has preceded God in anything that he dare make demands of God?] . . .
> Said Rabbi Jeremiah, "The heavenly spirit declares: Who has preempted me, that I must repay him?—Who [could possibly] extol My praises before I had endowed him with a soul? Who praised My

Name before I gave him a son? Who constructed a [protective] fence [*in re* Deut. 22:8] before I gave him a roof? Who attached a *mezzuzah* [to his doorpost, Deut. 6:9] before I gave him a house? Who has built a *sukkah* [Lev. 23:42] before I gave him a place? Who [purchased] a *lulav* [Lev. 23:40] before I gave him money? Who has [place on his garments] *zizit* [fringes, Num. 15:38] before I gave him a shawl? Who has hallowed the corner of his field [Lev. 19:9] before I gave him fields? Who has hallowed a tithe [Ex. 22:28; Lev. 22:4–10] before I gave him a threshing floor? Who has hallowed his bread [Num. 15:20] before I gave him flour? And who has brought sacrifices before I gave him animals?

The principle teaching, simply understood, is that Halakhah sets greater store by religious observance which follows the expressed divine command than that which results from spontaneous intuition (Talmud, *Kid.* 31a; cf. Num. R. 14:2, regarding Abraham's intuitive knowledge of God). However, it also portrays the divine commandments, including their implicit applicanda, as somehow substantive prior to creation itself.

3. Oden's description reverberates in Rabbi Joseph B. Soloveitchik's independent existential analysis of sin:

> Man is surely aware of many needs, but the needs he is aware of are not always his own. At the very root of this failure to recognize one's truly worthwhile needs lies man's ability to misunderstand and misidentify himself; i.e., to lose himself. Quite often man loses himself by identifying himself with the wrong image. Because of this misidentification, man adopts the wrong table of needs which he feels he must gratify. Man responds quickly to the pressure of certain needs, not knowing *whose* needs he is out to gratify. At this juncture, sin is born. What is the cause of sin, if not the diabolical habit of man to be mistaken about his own self? Let me add that man fails to recognize himself because he is man . . . In other words, adoption of a wrong table of needs is part of the human tragic destiny. (1978, p. 62)

4. Compare Oden's use of Mark's testimony with these remarks made by Carl G. Jung in his essay, "Psychotherapists or the Clergy?"

> That I feed the beggar, that I forgive an insult, and I love my enemy in the name of Christ—all these are undoubtedly great virtues. What I do unto the least of my brethren, that I do unto Christ. But what if I should discover that the least amongst them all, the poorest of all beggars, the most impudent of all offenders, yea the very fiend himself—that these are within me, and that I myself stand in need of the alms of my own kindness, that I *myself* am the enemy who must be loved—what then? Then, as a rule, the whole truth of Christianity is reversed; there is then no more talk of love and long-suffering; we

say to the brother within us "Raca," and condemn and rage against ourselves. We hide him from the world, we deny ever having met this least among the lowly in ourselves, and had it been God himself who drew near to us in this despicable form, we should have denied him a thousand times before a single cock had crowed. (1932, p. 223)

For Jung, in general, God is the *self,* or a godself structure, such that whereas Oden conceives of the therapist as engaged in Christ-like behavior by virtue of helping a fellow human, for Jung his would mean, ultimately, that the therapist is also helping himself or herself, curing the needy or angry or self-ish god within.

5. The text in the Talmud, *Ber.* 3a, is:

> R. Yose said: Once I was walking on the road and I entered one of the ruined places in Jerusalem in order to pray. Elijah [the prophet] appeared to me . . . and he said to me, "Son, what sound do you hear in this ruin?" And I said to him, "I hear a heavenly voice [*bat kol*] shrieking like a dove and saying: 'Woe is to my children because of whose sins I destroyed my House and burned my Holy Place and exiled them among the heathens!'" Elijah said to me, "Son, by my life and yours, not just for an hour does this voice shriek, but three times each day. Moreover, whenever Israel enters their houses of prayer and academies of study and recites, "Amen, May His name be exalted and blessed," the Holy One nods His head and says: "Fortunate is the king who is so praised in his own home!"

6. The text in the Talmud, *Shab.* 89a, reads:

> R. Joshuah ben Levi said: When Moses ascended to the heavens, he found The Holy One attaching crowns to the letters [of the Torah]. Moses said: [Is it not customary to extend the greeting "Shalom!" in Your town?] The Holy One answered him: It is you who should offer to help me [i.e., you should greet me, "Success in Your endeavor!"]. Immediately, Moses recited [the passage]: "And now, I pray Thee, let the power of the Lord be great, in accordance with Your word!" (Num. 14:17)

7. The Talmud viewed the formal redaction of prayer as a replacement to the sacrificial order which ceased in the decades following the destruction of the Second Temple (Talmud, *Ber.* 26b). More specifically, the Talmud (*Ta'an.* 27b; *Meg.* 31a) states that studying the complicated laws of the sacrificial order or even reciting the relevant biblical passages describing the sacrificial service is deemed equivalent to actually offering sacrifices:

> Abraham asked, "It is well [that Israel can offer sacrifices] when the Temple exists [for they may thus supplicate You and be answered];

but when the Temple no longer exists, what shall become of them?"
The Lord answered: "I have already arranged for them the order of
the sacrifices [in the Bible]. When they read the order before me, I
consider it as if they brought sacrifices, and I will forgive them their
iniquities."

This notion is expressed in many different ways throughout rabbinic literature, sometimes emphasizing merely the reading of the relevant biblical
passages, as above, and other times stressing study, explication, and intellectual toil ("ha-osek") (Talmud, Men. 110a; Lev. R. 9; Num. R. 18; cf. Tanḥu-
mah ad loc):

> And so taught R. Samuel bar Abba: Said the Lord . . . There will be a
> time when the sacrifices will be abolished. Do not forget to arrange
> for yourselves the passages of the sacrificial order, but read them and
> remember them and delve in them.

The text in Ex. R. 38 reads:

> Israel beseeched the Lord and cried, "We are impoverished!" [since
> the abolishment of the sacrificial order] . . . The Lord answered, "I
> only desire words, as it is written, 'Take with you words and return to
> the Lord' [Hos. 14:3], and I will forgive all your transgressions; [And
> the meaning of "words" is] the words of the sacrificial order.

Even more evocative is the text in Songs. R. to Songs 4:3:

> "Your lips are like a crimson thread"—This refers to the crimson
> strand [tied during the order of the Yom Kippur service between the
> horns of the scapegoat, and which would turn white to indicate
> that God had forgiven Israel's transgressions]. "And your mouth is
> comely"—This refers to the scapegoat. Said Israel to the Lord, "Mas-
> ter of the Universe! We [no longer have] the crimson thread or the
> scapegoat!" The Lord said to them, "'Your lips are like a crimson
> thread'—the acquisitions of your lips [i.e., recitation of the sacrificial
> order] are precious to me like the crimson strand; 'And your mouth is
> comely'—your words are appealing."

This substitution of words for actual sacrifice was not intended as a search for
an incruente immolatur ("bloodless sacrifice") or as a mere consolation for the
termination of the sacrificial order. The references abundantly suggest a trans-
position of a verbal-representational structure for an act-representational
structure. In other words, there is here a recognition that verbally generated
concepts may create robust internal representations on a par with those
gleaned from direct behavior or action. It reflects an attempt to internalize a
specific component of the person-God relationship in the face of lack (the

absence of the Temple and the sacrificial order and the closeness to God these provided). And the test for identity is a pragmatic one: the verbally generated structures must evoke sufficient insight and self-change to warrant divine atonement.

8. See Shihor's (1978) trenchant critique of Rabbi Joseph Soloveitchik's panhalakhicism.

9. For a somewhat similar effort to propose analogies for the field of social work, such as between the social helping role and the Jewish ethos of *ḥesed* (charitableness), see Linzer (1979). Perhaps one might also link *ḥesed* with Jaspers's (1960) concept of the therapist's requisite *passion* for helping the other.

10. The psychotherapist's role may also be conceptualized via halakhic analogy to the halakhic concept of an *epitropos* (administrator, guardian) for the court. Although the Jewish *bet din* (court) does not typically appoint a guardian for sentient adults (Talmud, *B. M.* 39a, Rashi, s.v. "*epitropo*"; *M. T. Hil. Naḥalot* 7:5), the psychotherapy patient may be considered as lacking "*daʿat*" or insight in the domain of his or her psychological scotoma. This argument certainly applies for psychotic-level disturbance, or in the case of minors (*M.T., Hil. Naḥalot* 10:8, after Talmud *Ket.* 48a and *Yeb.* 113a). Finally, there is active here as well the principle of "*zokhin le-adam she'lo be-fanav*" (Talmud, *Kid.* 23, 42a to Num. 34:18)—one may possess or otherwise benefact for one's neighbor *in absentia*—which the law permits even against the beneficiary's will (see *Keẓot ha-Ḥoshen* 105:1; and *Ḥiddushei ha-Ritva* and *Rashba* to Talmud, *Kid.* 23a).

11. The idea of striking a balance between lending oneself *as person*, as a "good" object to the patient, on one hand, and the overall stance of neutrality (psychotherapist incognito), on the other hand, has an interesting halakhic analogy. The Bible instructs regarding ethical jurisprudence (Deut. 1:17): "You shall *not favor* persons in judgment [*Lo takiru panim ba-mishpat*]. The critical Hebrew phrase is *lo takiru*, whose cognate in Semitic morphology (*nkr*) implies both "stranger, strangeness" as well as "recognition, familiarity" (as in *agnoscere-noscere*). Hence, we find the following interpretation in the Talmud (*Sanh.* 7b): "R. Judah taught: *lo takiru*—[read:] *lo-takiruhu*, [instructing] do not be overly familiar [in judgment]. R. Elazar taught: *lo takiru*—[read:] *lo tenakaruhu*, [instructing] do not estrange yourself from him." Since, in fact, it is not forbidden to have *any* feelings toward the adjudged (see *Rama* to *Sh. A., Ḥ. M.* 7:7), the rabbis must plainly be seen as asking for balanced, professionally neutral perception. As above, if one views this exegesis as revealing the biblical word, one has here another element of divine participation in the structural form of reality—*a priori* in its pure halakhic state; empirical and *a posteriori* as implemented in the therapeutic moment.

12. This raises the complicated philosophical and theological problem of how such change might take place in God! Clearly, at some level it is important that the subject be able to feel that he or she has caused or evoked change in the other. To speak in terms of the halakhic metapsychology: If God has asked man to repent, and has indeed created an *a priori* structure

called *teshuvah* (repentance), does this mean that "repentance" of some kind and in some way applies to God as well? Is this conceptually acceptable from the point of view of Jewish philosophy and theology? (see Montefiore 1904). A complete answer is not possible here, but evidently the biblical text acknowledged the possibility. In Genesis 6:6, God "repents" (*va-yinahem*) or recants his decision to create Adam (cf. the interesting reversal in Gen. R. [Rashi, *loc. cit.*; cf. Talmud, *Sanh.* 108a, "R. Dimi taught . . ."]) and is implored to repent or change His plans in Exodus 32:12. The possibility of God's change of heart is held forth by the prophets Samuel (1, 15:11), Jeremiah (26:13), Joel (2:14), and Jonah (3:9). Most important, consider Isaiah's emphasis on the reciprocal nature of this repentance (43:25–26):

> I, even I, am He that blots out your transgressions for My own sake;
> And your sins I will not remember.

> Put Me in remembrance, *let us plead together;* Declare [your case], that you may be justified.

13. Rabbi Soloveitchik himself once put forth an apparent challenge to the panhalakhic perspective. In a highly poetic discussion of the relation between Halakah and spiritual consciousness (1979), Rabbi Soloveitchik tendered a lengthy footnote (pp. 209–12) in which he reconsidered a well-known halakhic question: Why does the intercession of the Sabbath during the *shivah* mourning period *not* cancel the obligation to complete the remaining days, whereas when *holidays* (*hagim*) intercede during the *shivah*, the obligation to complete the remainder of the *shivah* period is indeed fully obviated? The presumption of the question is the idea that a state of profound happiness is antithetical to mourning (Talmud, *M.K.* 10b). Indeed, Rabbi Soloveitchik first of all fortifies this very notion by indicating that if Halakhah were merely an act-technology, it *could* readily have required the simultaneous observance of holiday rituals as well as the rituals of mourning! One must conclude that Halakhah does attend to psychological states and considers the state of mourning counterposed to the requisite joy of holidays. Precisely, therefore, to return to our question, it is not at all clear why Halakhah does not decree similarly that the Sabbath also obviates the mourning period.

Rabbi Soloveitchik eventually responds, amplifying the view of the *Tosafot* (see Talmud, *M.K.*, 23b, Tos., s.v. *"man de'amar"*), by distinguishing between the unique happiness or *simhah* of the holidays—which inheres in no particular act but rather suffuses the day by virtue of the divine gift or the essence of the day itself—and the restful affective states of pleasure (*oneg*) and reserve (*kavod*) that permeate the Sabbath. The latter set of emotions are not "*mizvot* of the heart," but rather are directly tied to particular acts of commission or omission that characterize the Sabbath observance. The *oneg* of Sabbath, while sufficiently powerful to interdict public signs of mourning, simply does not infiltrate deeply enough into the spirit as to militate against *essential* "mourning of the heart." The *mizvah* of *simhah* on holidays, however, is itself an essential state and as such is sufficiently powerful to outweigh the pangs of loss and mourning. But, even if one should rush to conclude from Rabbi Soloveitchik's distinction that we have discovered a pocket of human nature to which Halakhah does not apply—that is, inasmuch as the formality of the Sabbath pleasure apparently cannot be imposed upon the psychological realities of mourning—this would be an error. For, in fact, the only structure which regulates whether or not, and under what conditions, *aveilut* (mourning) is superimposed upon or absorbed by other psychological-religious states is Halakhah itself, rather than idiosyncratic need or caprice (see also Feldman 1977; Spero 1977c).

Chapter 5

1. Freud introduces the term *archaische Erbschaft* ("archaic heritage") in a paragraph dated 1919 added to *The Interpretation of Dreams*, chap. VII (B) (1900, p. 700), and it appears to have been an idea that occurred to him during the course of composing the essay "A Child Is Being Beaten" (1919a) that same year, where the same term appears as well (p. 180). The concept was one of Freud's favorites, I believe, in that it was among those select, never completely clarified terms in which Freud kept alive a certain degree of that which mystified him, that which did not yet submit itself willingly and entirely to his intellectual or analytic insight (the concept of the "uncanny" [*das unheimliche*] [1919b] is another example of this). The concept of a transcultural, archaic memory trace, however, seems to have been percolating in Freud's mind even earlier, such as in the final paragraphs of *Totem and Taboo* (1913), and remains with him until the very last paragraph of *Moses and Monotheism* (1939). The concept was important for Freud because it was a potential link in the transmission of the bedrock cultural-religious experiences, including the preconfigurational outline of the oedipal dynamic.

2. Relevant to the notion of matching the patient's religious language artificially is the commonplace that religious patients fare better with therapists of matching belief. The usual rationale focuses upon the patient's purported need to be understood, to experience "syntonicity," to not experience "strangeness" in therapy (see Levitz 1979; Wikler 1979, 1982, 1986). These approaches, however, essentially legitimize the patient's early need to maintain narcissistic defenses against full engagement in therapy and to resist the therapist's analyzing instruments.

I recall one particular patient who spent the first two months in therapy covering me in a welter of complex rabbinic-type exegeses (*derashot*), intellectual discoveries, and Hasidic anecdotes. The trick was that, one, this material was of high caliber indeed and, hence, seductive, but, second, certainly always contained clinically relevant, if disguised, unconscious derivative material. That is, this material could be viewed as resistance, on one hand, but it was also eminently revealing, on the other hand. Happily, psychotherapists operate within a framework of guidelines which dictate that the focus at this early point in therapy ought to be the patient's use of such material as resistance above all else. I found it useful to demonstrate to this patient that he was searching for the "yeshivah boy" in me, attempting to collude on a no-interference pact between the therapeutic part of me and himself. This intervention was successful, but it did not remove all resistance in one fell swoop. Rather, it moved the patient to a new, adaptively regressive level of relationship where he dealt with deeper shame and self-consciousness by revelling us in all manner of witticism, jokes, and thinly veiled jibes. This offensive-defensive wave, too, required working-through, but was no longer covered by "religious" resistance. And when religious material did emerge at this stage, it now tended to be available for interpretation rather than merely as a block to therapeutic dialogue.

I concur with Pruyser (1971) and Sevensky (1984) that the search for "likeness" between therapist and patient tends to be an expression of conflict and ambivalence. The smattering of empirical evidence favoring this truism (Weisbord et al. 1988; Welkowitz et al. 1967) supports only the reported preferences of *nonclinical* subjects *contemplating* entering therapy or simply projecting their preferences through some artificial experimental task reasonably similar to the tasks of therapy. We also know that forced or overemphasized similarity, especially if it emerges through an overly self-disclosive style in therapy, eventually produces a ceiling effect whereby patients begin to reveal less and less clinically relevant material (see Heller 1972; Langs 1976, pp. 424–30; Weiner 1976, p. 43). Consider, as a final piece of support, the reports of Kahn (1985), rabbi and psychologist, and Kehoe (nun and psychologist) and Gutheil (1984), whose patients initially rejected precisely those aspects of their therapists' obvious characteristics which were apparently similar to the patients'.

Chapter 7

1. As humans exercise their psychic apparatus, flexing the range of their object-relational and psychodynamic potential for creating, destroying, and recreating images and inner worlds, they in this, too, reciprocate divine activity (Gen. R. 3:9): "In what was the Lord engaged [prior to the creation of the world]? He created worlds and destroyed them." In both instances, reference is probably to some kind of psycholinguistic endeavor (the Talmud generally emphasizes that God creates with the *word*).

2. The earliest impression of God, emerging as it does on the threshold of consciousness of self and psychic interiority, fits hand-in-glove with Daniel Stern's (1985) concept of the "evoked companion," one of the initial presences which accompany the child during early stages of self-other differentiation. The early perception of God, that is to say, could take the form of an evoked companion which, however, only represents a single affectively toned interaction. Following the myriad kinds of interactions outlined in the text, the representation of God would eventually take on increasingly greater de-

grees of generalizability, although the original "evoked companion" never disappears entirely from the panoply of mental contents. There is much to say about this last idea, as well as about the similarity between Stern's concept of an "evoked companion," the object relations school's concept of an introject, and the rabbinic concept of *de'mut de'yukon*, which appears in several places in the Talmud and Midrash. I discuss this relationship in detail in a forthcoming monograph *Identification, Internalization, and the Rabbinic Midrash* (Bar-Ilan University Press).

References

Adams, J. 1970. *Competent to counsel.* Phillipsburg, N. J.: Presbyterian & Reformed Publishing Co.

Ahlskog, G. 1985. Latent theology. In *Psychotherapy of the religiously oriented patient,* ed. E. Stern, pp. 63–70. New York: Haworth.

Ahren, Y. 1970. Review: *Judaism and psychology* by Abraham Amsel. *Tradition* 11:97–100.

————. 1980. Remarks on Freud's determinism. *Journal of Psychology and Judaism* 4:222–27.

Alexander, F. M., and T. French. 1946. *Psychoanalytic therapy.* New York: Ronald Press.

Allport, G. 1950. *The individual and his religion.* New York: Macmillan.

Almansi, R. 1983. On the persistence of very early memory traces in psychoanalysis, myth, and religion. *Journal of the American Psychoanalytic Association* 31:391–421.

Amsel, A. 1969. *Judaism and psychology.* New York: Feldheim.

————. 1976. *Rational irrational man.* New York: Feldheim.

Anthony, E. J. 1971. *Folie á deux:* A developmental failure of the process of separation-individuation. In *Separation-Individuation,* ed. by J. B. McDevitt and C. F. Settlage, pp. 234–61. New York: International Universities Press.

Appel, K., J. W. Higgins, M. Ostow, and E. Von Domarus. 1959. Religion. In *American handbook of psychiatry,* vol. 2, ed. S. Arieti. New York: Basic Books.

Arieti, S. 1975. Psychiatry controlling man's destiny. *American Journal of Psychiatry* 132:39–42.

————. 1981. *Abraham and the contemporary mind.* New York: Basic Books.

Arlow, J. 1961. Ego psychology and the study of mythology. *Journal of the American Psychoanalytic Association* 9:371–93.

Assagioli, R. 1956. Spiritual development and nervous disease. *Journal of Psychotherapy as a Religious Process* 3:30–40.

Attfield, D. 1975. The argument from religious experience. *Religious Studies* 11:335:42.

Atwood, G. E. 1978. On the origins and dynamics of messianic salvation fantasies. *International Review of Psycho-Analysis* 33:85–96.

Bakan, D. 1958. *Sigmund Freud and the Jewish mystical tradition.* New York: Schocken.

Bar-Ilan, N. 1990. The patient who is overcome by his impulses. [Hebrew]. *Assia* 49–50:35–42.

Becker, E. 1973. *The denial of death.* New York: Free Press.

Beit-Hallahmi, B. 1975. Encountering orthodox religion in psychotherapy. *Psychotherapy* 12:357–59.

———, and M. Argyle. 1975. God as a father projection. *British Journal of Medical Psychology* 48:71–75.

Berger, P. 1979. *The heretical imperative.* New York: Anchor.

Bergin, A. 1980. Psychotherapy and religious values. *Journal of Consulting and Clinical Psychology* 48:95–105.

———. 1983. Religiosity and mental health. *Professional Psychology* 14:170–84.

Bergman, P. 1953. A religious conversion in the course of psychotherapy. *American Journal of Psychotherapy* 12:41–51.

Bindler, P. 1976. A psychological analysis of kavannah in prayer. *Proceedings of the Associations of Orthodox Jewish Scientists* 3–4:133–44.

———. 1980. Meditative prayer and rabbinic perspectives on the psychology of consciousness. *Journal of Psychology and Judaism* 4:228–48.

———. 1983. Self-awareness (*ḥesbon ha-nefesh*) and self-analysis. *Proceedings of the Associations of the Orthodox Jewish Scientists* 7:123–52.

Bion, W. 1959. Attacks on linking. *International Journal of Psycho-Analysis* 40:308–15.

———. 1967. *Second thoughts.* London: Maresfield.

———. 1977. *Seven servants: Four works by Wilfred R. Bion.* New York: Aronson.

Bird, B. 1972. Notes on transference: Universal phenomenon and the hardest part of the analysis. *Journal of the American Psychoanalytic Association* 20:267–301.

Blanck, G., and R. Blanck. 1974. *Ego psychology: Theory and practice.* New York: Columbia University Press.

———. 1979. *Ego psychology II: Psychoanalytic developmental psychology.* New York: Columbia University Press.

———. 1986. *Beyond ego psychology: Developmental object relations theory.* New York: Columbia University Press.

Bleich, J. D. 1989. Faith and dogma in Judaism. In *Encounter: Torah and modern life,* ed. H. Schimmel and A. Carmel, 8–21. Jerusalem: Feldheim.

Boisen, A. 1952. *The exploration of the inner world.* New York: Harper & Row.

Bolgar, H. 1960. Values in therapy, in psychoanalysis, and human values. In *Science and psychoanalysis,* vol. 3, ed. J. H. Masserman. New York: Grune & Stratton.

Bollinger, R. 1985. Differences between pastoral counseling and psychotherapy. *Bulletin of the Menninger Clinic* 49 : 371 – 86.

Bonhoeffer, D. 1955. *Ethics.* N. H. Smith, trans. London: S. C. M. Press.

Boss, M. 1957. *Psychoanalyse und Daseinsanalytik.* Heidelberg: Bern Und Stuttgart.

Boss, M., and G. Condrau. 1967. Existential psychoanalysis. In *Psychoanalytic techniques,* ed. B. Wolman, pp. 443 – 69. New York: Basic.

Bradford, D. T. 1984. *The experience of God.* New York: Peter Lang.

Brayer, M. B. 1990. The concept of insanity in rabbinic law and in psychiatry. *Proceedings of the Associations of Orthodox Jewish Scientists* 10 : 15 – 66.

Breitman, B. 1983. Jewish identity and ethnic ambivalence in clinical practice. *Journal of Jewish Communal Service* 60 : 129 – 37.

Brierley, M. 1951. *Trends in psycho-analysis.* London: Hogarth.

Bronner, A. 1964. Psychotherapy with religious patients. *American Journal of Psychotherapy* 18 : 475 – 87.

Browning, D. 1966. *Psychotherapy and atonement.* Philadelphia: Westminster.

Buhler, C. 1962. *Values in psychotherapy.* New York: Free Press.

Bulka, R. P. 1976. Setting the tone: The psychology-Judaism dialogue. *Journal of Psychology and Judaism* 1 : 3 – 13.

―――, and M. H. Spero. 1983. Bibliography: Psychology and Judaism. *Proceedings of the Associations of Orthodox Jewish Scientists* 7 : 187 – 226.

Burnham, J. C. 1985. The encounter of Christianity, theology, and deterministic psychology and psychoanalysis. *Bulletin of the Menninger Clinic* 49 : 321 – 52.

Canda, E. R. 1988a. Spirituality, religious diversity, and social work practice. *Social Casework* 69 : 238 – 47.

―――. 1988b. Conceptualizing spirituality for social work. *Social Thought* 14 : 30 – 46.

―――. 1989. Religious content in social work education. *Journal of Social Work Education* 25 : 36 – 47.

Chajes, T. H. 1849. *The student's guide through the Talmud.* [Hebrew.] New York: Feldheim, reprint: 1960.

Chused, J. 1987. Idealization of the analyst by the young adult. *Journal of the American Psychoanalytic Association* 35 : 839 – 59.

Clark, J. 1979. Cults. *Journal of the American Medical Association* 242 : 279 – 81.

Clark, R. 1980. Religious delusions among Jews. *American Journal of Psychotherapy* 34 : 62 – 71.

Clark, W. H. 1958. *The psychology of religion.* New York: Macmillan.

Cohen, R. 1977. Socially reinforced obsessing: A reply. *Journal of Consulting and Clinical Psychology* 45 : 166 – 71.

―――, and F. Smith. 1976. Socially reinforced obsessing: Etiology of a disorder in a Christian Scientist. *Journal of Consulting and Clinical Psychology* 44 : 142 – 44.

Compton, A. 1987. Objects and attitudes. *Journal of the American Psychoanalytic Association* 35 : 609 – 28.

Dahl, H. 1965. Observations on a "natural experiment": Helen Keller. *Jour-*

nal of the American Psychoanalytic Association 13:533–50.

———, H. Küschale, H. Thöma. 1988. *Psychoanalytic process research strategies.* Heidelburg/New York: Springer-Verlag.

DeLuca, A. 1977. *Freud and future religious experience.* Totowa, N. J.: Littlefield, Adams.

Deutsch, H. 1951. *Psychoanalysis of the neuroses.* London: Hogarth.

Dewald, P. 1976. Transference regressions and the real experience in the psychoanalytic process. *Psychoanalytic Quarterly* 45:213–30.

———. 1983. Elements of change and cure in psychoanalysis. *Archives of General Psychiatry* 40:89–95.

DiCaprio, N. 1974. *Personality theories.* Philadelphia: W. B. Saunders.

Don, Y. 1975. *Musar and Derush literature.* [Hebrew.] Jerusalem: Keter.

———. 1985. On the history of the theory of repentance of the Askenazim. [Hebrew.] In *Orot Jubilee: The thought of Rabbi Abraham Issac ha-Cohen Kuk,* ed. B. Ish-Shalom and S. Rosenberg, pp. 62–93. Jerusalem: AviChai/World Zionist Federation.

Doniger, S., ed. 1962. *The nature of man in theological and psychological perspective.* New York: Harper & Row.

Ducker, E. N. 1964. *Psychotherapy: A Christian perspective.* London: George Allen & Unwin.

Duffy, A. 1979. Psychopathy and moral understanding. In *Biomedical ethics and the law,* eds. J. M. Humber and R. F. Almeder, pp. 165–83. New York: Plenum.

Eagel, M. 1983. Interests as object relations. In *Empirical studies of psychoanalytic theories,* ed. J. Masling, pp. 159–87. Hillsdale, N.J.: Analytic Press.

Edelson, M. 1975. *Language and interpretation in psychoanalysis.* New Haven: Yale University Press.

———. 1983a. Is testing psychoanalytic hypotheses in the psychoanalytic situation really impossible? *Psychoanalytic Study of the Child* 38:61–109.

———. 1983b. *Hypothesis and evidence in psychoanalysis.* Chicago: University of Chicago Press.

———. 1988. *Psychoanalysis.* Chicago: University of Chicago Press.

Edward, J., J. Ruskin, and P. Turrini. 1981. *Separation-Individuation.* New York: Gardner Press.

Eigen, M. 1975. Psychopathy and individualization. *Psychotherapy* 3:289–90.

———. 1986. *The psychotic core.* New York: Aronson.

Ekstein, R. 1956. A clinical note on the therapeutic use of a quasi-religious experience. *Journal of the American Psychoanalytic Association* 4:304–13.

Elkind, D. 1971. The origin of religion in the child. *Review of Religious Research* 12:35–40.

Epstein, I. 1954. *The faith of Judaism.* London: Soncino.

Epstein, L. and A. Feiner, eds. 1979. *Countertransference.* New York: Aronson.

Erikson, E. H. 1937. Configurations in play. *Psychoanalytic Quarterly* 6:139–54.

———. 1959. *Identity and the life cycle.* New York: W. W. Norton.

———. 1966. Ontogeny of ritualization. In *Psychoanalysis—A general science,* ed. R. Loewenstein, L. Newman, M. Schur, and A. Solnit, 601–21. New York: International Universities Press.

———. 1982. *The life cycle completed.* New York: W. W. Norton.

Fairbairn, W. R. D. 1927. Notes on the religious phantasies of a female patient. In *Psychoanalytic studies of the personality.* London: Routledge & Kegan Paul, 1952 reprint.

———. 1943. The repression and return of bad objects (with special reference to the "war neuroses"). In *Psychoanalytic studies of the personality.* London: Routledge & Kegan Paul, 1952 reprint.

———. 1952. *Psychoanalytic studies of the personality.* London: Routledge & Kegan Paul.

———. 1955. Observations in defence of the object-relations theory of the personality. *British Journal of Medical Psychology* 28 : 144–56.

———. 1958. On the nature and the aims of psychoanalytical treatment. *International Journal of Psycho-Analysis* 29 : 374–85.

Farrell, B. 1955. Psychological theory and the belief in God. *International Journal of Psycho-Analysis* 36 : 187–201.

Fauteux, A. 1982. "Good/bad" splitting in the religious experience. *American Journal of Psychoanalysis* 41 : 261–67.

Fayek, A. 1981. Narcissism and the death instinct. *International Journal of Psycho-Analysis* 62 : 309–22.

Feigl, H. 1967. *The mental and the physical.* Minneapolis, Minnesota: University of Minnesota Press.

Feldman, E. 1977. *Biblical and post-biblical defilement and mourning: Law as theology.* New York: Ktav/Yeshiva University Press.

Finkelstein, L. 1977. Judaism as a system of symbols. In *Conservative Judaism and Jewish law,* ed. S. Siegel, pp. 196–215. New York: Ktav.

Fisher, S., and R. Greenberg. 1977. *The scientific credibility of Freud's theories and therapy.* New York: Basic Books.

Fodor, J. 1968. *Psychological explanation.* New York: Random House.

Fowler, J. W. 1976a. Stages in faith: The structural-developmental approach. In *Values and moral development,* ed. T. C. Hennessy, pp. 186–97. New York: Paulist Press.

———. 1976b. Faith development and the aims of religious socialization. In *Emerging issues in religious education,* eds. G. Durka and J. Smith, pp. 29–42. Paramus, N.J.: Paulist Press.

———. 1981. *Stages of faith.* San Francisco, Ca.: Harper & Row.

Frankl, V. 1955. *The doctor and the soul.* New York: Knopf.

———. 1975. *The unconscious god.* New York: Simon & Schuster.

Freud, A. 1936. *The ego and the mechanisms of defense.* New York: International Universities Press.

Freud, S. 1895. Project for a scientific psychology. In vol. 1 of *The standard edition of the complete psychological works of Sigmund Freud,* ed. and trans. James Strachey. London: Hogarth.

———. 1900. *The interpretation of dreams*. In vols. 4–5 of *The standard edition of the complete psychological works of Sigmund Freud*, ed. and trans. James Strachey. London: Hogarth.

———. 1901. *The psychopathology of everyday life*. In vol. 6 of *The standard edition of the complete psychological works of Sigmund Freud*, ed. and trans. James Strachey. London: Hogarth.

———. 1905. *Three essays on the theory of sexuality*. In vol. 7 of *The standard edition of the complete psychological works of Sigmund Freud*, ed. and trans. James Strachey. London: Hogarth.

———. 1906. Leonardo da-Vinci and a memory of his childhood. In vol. 9 of *The standard edition of the complete psychological works of Sigmund Freud*, ed. and trans. James Strachey. London: Hogarth.

———. 1909a. Notes upon a case of obsessional neurosis. In vol. 10 of *The standard edition of the complete psychological works of Sigmund Freud*, ed. and trans. James Strachey. London: Hogarth.

———. 1909b. Analysis of a five-year-old boy. In vol. 10 of *The standard edition of the complete psychological works of Sigmund Freud*, ed. and trans. James Strachey. London: Hogarth.

———. 1910. A special type of choice of object made by men. In vol. 11 of *The standard edition of the complete psychological works of Sigmund Freud*, ed. and trans. James Strachey. London: Hogarth.

———. 1911. Psycho-analytical notes on an autobiographical account of a case of paranoia (Dementia Paranoides). In vol. 12 of *The standard edition of the complete psychological works of Sigmund Freud*, ed. and trans. James Strachey. London: Hogarth.

———. 1912. Recommendations to physicians practicing psycho-analysis. In vol. 12 of *The standard edition of the complete psychological works of Sigmund Freud*, ed. and trans. James Strachey. London: Hogarth.

———. 1913. *Totem and taboo*. In vol. 13 of *The standard edition of the complete psychological works of Sigmund Freud*, ed. and trans. James Strachey. London: Hogarth.

———. 1918. From the history of an infantile neurosis. In vol. 17 of *The standard edition of the complete psychological works of Sigmund Freud*, ed. and trans. James Strachey. London: Hogarth.

———. 1919a. "A child is being beaten": A contribution to the study of the origin of sexual perversions. In vol. 17 of *The standard edition of the complete psychological works of Sigmund Freud*, ed. and trans. James Strachey. London: Hogarth.

———. 1919b. The uncanny. In vol. 17 of *The standard edition of the complete psychological works of Sigmund Freud*, ed. and trans. James Strachey. London: Hogarth.

———. 1922. Dreams and telepathy. In vol. 18 of *The standard edition of the complete psychological works of Sigmund Freud*, ed. and trans. James Strachey. London: Hogarth.

———. 1923. A 17th-century demonological neurosis. In vol. 19 of *The stan-*

dard edition of the complete psychological works of Sigmund Freud, ed. and trans. James Strachey. London: Hogarth.

———. 1925. Negation. In vol. 19 of *The standard edition of the complete psychological works of Sigmund Freud*, ed. and trans. James Strachey. London: Hogarth.

———. 1927. *The future of an illusion*. In vol. 21 of *The standard edition of the complete psychological works of Sigmund Freud*, ed. and trans. James Strachey. London: Hogarth.

———. 1928a. A religious experience. In vol. 21 of *The standard edition of the complete psychological works of Sigmund Freud*, ed. and trans. James Strachey. London: Hogarth.

———. 1928b. Doestoevsky and parricide. In vol. 21 of *The standard edition of the complete psychological works of Sigmund Freud*, ed. and trans. James Strachey. London: Hogarth.

———. 1930. *Civilization and its discontents*. In vol. 21 of *The standard edition of the complete psychological works of Sigmund Freud*, ed. and trans. James Strachey. London: Hogarth.

———. 1933. New introductory lectures on psycho-analysis (Lectures XXIX– XXXV). In vol. 21 of *The standard edition of the complete psychological works of Sigmund Freud*, ed. and trans. James Strachey. London: Hogarth.

———. 1939. *Moses and monotheism*. In vol. 23 of *The standard edition of the complete psychological works of Sigmund Freud*, ed. and trans. James Strachey. London: Hogarth.

———. 1940. *An outline of Psycho-Analysis*. In vol. 23 of *The standard edition of the complete psychological works of Sigmund Freud*, ed. and trans. James Strachey. London: Hogarth.

Freud, S. 1954. *The origins of psychoanalysis: Letters to Wilhelm Fleiss, drafts and notes—1887–1902*, ed. M. Bonaparte, A. Freud, and E. Kris. New York: Basic.

Friedman, L. 1982. Sublimation. In *Introducing psychoanalytic theory*, ed. S. Gilman, pp. 68–76. New York: Brunner/Mazel.

Fromm, E. 1947. *Man for himself*. New York: Holt, Rinehart, & Winston.

———. 1950. *Psychoanalysis and religion*. New Haven: Yale University Press.

———. 1955. *The sane society*. New York: Fawcett.

———. 1963. *The dogma of Christ and other essays on religion, psychology, and culture*. New York: Holt, Rinehart, & Winston.

———. 1966. *You shall be as gods*. Greenwich, Conn.: Fawcett.

Fynn. 1974. *Mister God, this is Anna*. London: William Collins & Sons.

Galper, M. F. 1983. The atypical dissociative disorder. In *Psychodynamic perspectives on religion, sect, and cult*, ed. D. A. Halperin, pp. 353–62. Littleton, Mass.: John Wright/P.S.G.

Gartner, J., M. Harmatz, A. Hohmann, D. Larson, and A. Gartner-Fishman. 1990. The effect of patient and client ideology on clinical judgment. *Psychotherapy* 27:98–106.

Gay, P. 1987. *A godless Jew*. New Haven: Yale University Press.

Globus, G. 1973a. Consciousness and the brain. I: The identity thesis. *Archives of General Psychiatry* 29:153−60.

———. 1973b. Consciousness and the brain. II: Introspection, the qualia of experience, and the unconscious. *Archives of General Psychiatry* 29:167−73.

Glover, E. 1956. *Freud or Jung?* New York: Macmillan.

Gold, H. R. 1971. Judaism: A psychological approach. In *Judaism in a changing world*, ed. L. Jung, pp. 124−46. New York: Oxford University Press.

Goldberg, H. 1976. Toward an understanding of Rabbi Israel Salanter. *Tradition* 16:83−119.

———. 1982. *Israel Salanter: Text, structure, idea*. New York: Ktav.

Gorkin, M. 1986. Countertransference in cross-cultural psychotherapy. *Psychiatry* 49:69−79.

Gorlin, M. 1970. Mental illness in biblical literature. *Proceedings of the Associations of Orthodox Jewish Scientists* 2:43−62.

Gosse, E. 1909. *Father and son*. London: Heinemann.

Gottlieb, M. 1975. Rabbi Salanter and therapeutic values. *Tradition* 15:112−29.

Goz, R. 1975. On knowing the therapist "as a person." *International Journal of Psychoanalytic Psychotherapy* 4:437−58.

Green, A. 1978. Potential space in the psychoanalysis. In *Between reality and fantasy*, ed. S. Grolnick, L. Barkin, and W. Muensterberger, pp. 167−89. New York: Aronson.

Green, J. 1950. *If I were you*, trans. J. H. F. McEwen. London: Heinemann.

Greenberg, D. 1984. Are religious compulsions religious or compulsive? *American Journal of Psychotherapy* 38:524−32.

Greenberg, J. 1986. Theoretical models and the analyst's neutrality. *Contemporary Psychoanalysis* 22:87−106.

Greene, J. 1969. A "madman's" searches for a less divided self. *Contemporary Psychoanalysis* 6:58−75.

Gross, M. 1959. Jewish ethics and self-psychology. *Tradition* 1:185−92.

Grotstein, M. 1980. A proposed revision of the psychoanalytic concept of primitive mental states, I. *Contemporary Psychoanalysis* 16:479−546.

Grünbaum, A. 1979. Epistemological liabilities of the clinical appraisal of psychoanalysis. *Psychoanalysis and Contemporary Thought* 2:451−526.

Guntrip, H. 1949. *Psychology for ministers and social workers*. London: Independent Press.

———. 1957. *Psychotherapy and religion*. New York: Harper & Row.

———. 1961. *Personality structure and human interaction*. New York: International Universities Press.

———. 1969a. Religion in relation to personal integration. *British Journal of Medical Psychology* 42:323−33.

———. 1969b. *Schizoid phenomena, object relations, and the self*. New York: International Universities Press.

Halperin, D., ed. 1983. *Psychodynamic perspectives on religion, sect, and cult*. Littleton, Mass.: John Wright/P.S.G.

Hankoff, L. 1979. Psychotherapy and values. *Journal of Psychology and Judaism* 4:5–14.

Hartman, D. 1976. Halakhah as a ground for creating a shared spiritual language. *Tradition* 16:7–40.

Hartmann, E. 1966. The psychophysiology of free will. In *Psychoanalysis: A general psychology*, ed. R. M. Loewenstein, L. M. Newman, M. Schor, and A. J. Solnit, pp. 521–26. New York: International Universities Press.

Hartmann, H. 1960. *Psychoanalysis and moral values*. New York: International Universities Press.

———, E. Kris, and R. Loewenstein. 1946. Comments on the foundation of psychic structure. *Psychoanalytic Study of the Child* 2:11–38.

Havens, J. 1968. *Psychology and religion*. Princeton, N.J.: Van Nostrand.

Heinrichs, D. 1982. Our Father who art in heaven: Parataxic distortions of the image of God. *Journal of Psychology and Theology* 10:120–29.

Heller, K. 1972. Interview structure and interview style in initial interviews. In *Studies in dyadic communication*, ed. A. W. Siegman and B. Pope, pp. 264–72. New York: Pergamon.

Heller, P. 1990. *A child analysis with Anna Freud*. New York: International Universities Press.

Hendel, R. J. 1976. Toward a definition of Torah. *Proceedings of the Associations of Orthodox Jewish Scientists* 3–4:171–90.

Heschel, A. J. 1955. *God in search of man*. New York: Harper & Row.

———. 1977. Toward an understanding of Halachah. In *Conservative Judaism and Jewish law*, ed. S. Siegel, pp. 134–51. New York: Rabbinical Assembly of America.

Hirsch, W. 1947. *Rabbinic psychology*. London: Goldston.

Hodis, L. 1986. The effect of yerida (emigration) on the therapeutic relationship between Israeli psychotherapist and patient. *Israel Journal of Psychiatry and Related Sciences* 23:89–106.

Hoehn-Saric, R. 1974. Transcendence and psychotherapy. *American Journal of Psychotherapy* 28:252–68.

Hong, K. M. 1978. The transitional phenomena. *Psychoanalytic Study of the Child* 33:47–79.

Hook, S., ed. 1959. *Psychoanalysis, scientific method, and philosophy*. New York: New York University Press.

Horwitz, M. 1974. *Clinical prediction in psychotherapy*. New York: Aronson.

Ilan, E. 1977. The treatment of a refugee child in a home for disturbed children and a follow-up thirty years later. *Psychoanalytic Study of the Child* 32:453–78.

Ish-Shalom, B. 1985. Religion, repentance, and human freedom in the thought of Rabbi Kuk. [Hebrew.] In *Orot Jubilee: The thought of Rabbi Abraham Issac ha-Cohen Kuk*, ed. B. Ish-Shalom and S. Rosenberg, pp. 295–332. Jerusalem: AviChai/World Zionist Federation.

James, W. 1897. *Pragmatism and other essays*. New York: Washington Square Press.

————. 1902. *The varieties of religious experience.* New York: Philosophical Library.

Janet, P. 1890. *L'automatisme psychologique.* Paris: Alcan.

————. 1926. *De l'angoisse à l'extase.* 2 vols. Paris: Alcan.

Jaspers, K. 1960. *The nature of psychotherapy.* Chicago: University of Chicago Press.

————. 1963. *General psychopathology,* trans. J. Hoenig and M. Hamilton. Chicago: University of Chicago Press.

Jung, C. G. 1928. Relations between the ego and the unconscious. In vol. 7 of *The collected works of Carl Gustav Jung,* trans. R. F. Hull. London: Bollingen Press.

————. 1931. Analytical psychology and weltanschauung. In vol. 8 of *The collected works of Carl Gustav Jung,* trans. R. F. Hull. London: Bollingen Press.

————. 1932a. Psychology and religion: West and east. In vol. 11 of *The collected works of Carl Gustav Jung,* trans. R. F. Hull. London: Bollingen Press.

————. 1932b. Psychotherapists or the clergy? In vol. 11 of *The collected works of Carl Gustav Jung,* trans. R. F. Hull. London: Bollingen Press.

————. 1933. Brother Klaus. In vol. 11 of *The collected works of Carl Gustav Jung,* trans. R. F. Hull. London: Bollingen Press.

————. 1942. A psychological approach to the dogma of the trinity. In vol. 11 of *The collected works of Carl Gustav Jung,* trans. R. F. Hull. London: Bollingen Press.

————. 1952. Answer to Job. In vol. 11 of *The collected works of Carl Gustav Jung,* trans. R. F. Hull. London: Bollingen Press.

————. 1958. Flying saucers: A modern myth. In vol. 10 of *The collected works of Carl Gustav Jung,* trans. R. F. Hull. London: Bollingen Press.

————. 1976. Jung and religious belief. In vol. 18 of *The collected works of Carl Gustav Jung,* trans. R. F. Hull. London: Bollingen Press.

Kadushin, M. 1972. *The rabbinic mind.* New York: Bloch.

————. 1977. Halakhah and Haggadah. In *Conservative Judaism and Jewish Law,* ed. S. Siegel, pp. 218–36. New York: Rabbinical Assembly of America.

Kahn, P. 1985. Religious values and the therapeutic alliance. In *Psychotherapy of the religious patient,* ed. M. H. Spero, pp. 85–95. Springfield, Ill.: Charles C. Thomas.

Katz, D. 1974. *Tenuat ha-Musar.* 6 vols. Tel Aviv: Ruben Mass.

Katz, R. L. 1959. Empathy in modern psychology and in the aggada. *Hebrew Union College Annual* 30:191–211.

————. 1975. Martin Buber and psychotherapy. *Hebrew Union College Annual* 46:413–31.

Kauffman, G. 1981. *The theological imagination.* New York: Basic Books.

Kegan, R. 1982. *The evolving self.* Cambridge: Harvard University Press.

Kehoe, N., and T. Gutheil. 1984. Shared religious belief as resistance in psychotherapy. *American Journal of Psychotherapy* 38:579–85.

Khan, M. M. R. 1969. Vicissitudes of being, knowing, and experiencing in the analytic situation. *British Journal of Medical Psychology* 42:383–93.

———. 1972. Dread of surrender to resourceless dependence in the analytic situation. *International Journal of Psycho-Analysis* 53 : 234–41.

———. 1973. The role of illusion in the analytic space and process. *Annual of Psychoanalysis* 1 : 224–38.

Kirkpatrick, L. A., and P. Shauer. 1990. Attachment theory and religion. *Journal for the Scientific Study of Religion* 29 : 315–34.

Klahr, C. N. 1976. Science versus scientism. In *Challenge,* ed. A. Carmel and C. Domb, pp. 70–82. Jerusalem: Feldheim.

Klauber, J. 1972. On the relationship of transference and interpretation in psychoanalytic therapy. *International Journal of Psycho-Analysis* 53 : 385–91.

Klein, G. S. 1956. Perception, motives, and personality: A clinical perspective. In *Psychology of personality,* ed. J. L. McCary, pp. 121–99. New York: Logos Press.

———. 1967. Preemptory ideation. In *Motives and thought: Psychoanalytic essays in honor of David Rapaport,* ed. R. R. Holt, pp. 78–128. New York: International Universities Press.

Klein, J. 1979a. *Judaism encounters psychology.* Philadelphia: Philosophical Library.

———. 1979b. On the conflict between applied psychology and Judaism. *Journal of Psychology and Judaism* 4 : 15–31.

Klein, M. 1942. Some psychological considerations: A comment. In *Envy and gratitude and other works (1946–1963).* London: Virago.

———. 1955. On identification. In *New directions in psycho-analysis,* ed. M. Klein, P. Heimann, H. Segal, and J. Riviere, pp. 106–24. London: Hogarth.

———. 1975. *Love, guilt, and respiration, and other works (1921–1945).* London: Virago, reprint.

Knight, R. 1937. Practical and theoretical considerations in the analysis of a minister. *Psychoanalytic Review* 24 : 350–64.

Kobler, F., ed. 1964. *Casebook in psychopathology.* New York: Alba House.

Koltko, M. 1990. How religious beliefs affect psychotherapy. *Psychotherapy* 27 : 132–41.

Krasner, B. 1981–82. Religious loyalties in clinical work. *Journal of Jewish Communal Service* 58 : 108–14.

Krill, D. F. 1974. Existential social work. In *Social work treatment,* ed. F. Turner, pp. 83–92. New York: Free Press.

Kris, A. 1982. *Free association.* New Haven: Yale University Press.

Kris, E. 1952. *Psychoanalytic explorations in art.* New York: International Universities Press.

———. 1956. On some vicissitudes of insight in psychoanalysis. *International Journal of Psycho-Analysis* 37 : 445–55.

Kuk, A. I. 1930. *Orot ha-teshuvah,* Y. H. Pilver (ed. and annotated). Jerusalem: Gal-Or, 1977 reprint.

Küng, H. 1979. *Freud and the problem of God.* New Haven: Yale University Press.

Lacan, J. 1964. *The four fundamental concepts of psycho-analysis,* ed. J.-A. Miller, trans. A. Sheridan. New York: Norton, 1978, reprint.

————. 1977. *Écrits: A general selection*, trans. A. Sheridan. New York: Norton.

Langs, R. 1976. *Resistances and interventions*. New York: Aronson.

————. 1981. *The therapeutic interaction*, 2 vols. New York: Aronson.

Laor, N. 1989. Psychoanalytic neutrality and religious experience. *Psychoanalytic Study of the Child* 44:211–30.

Laplanche, J., and J.-B. Pontalis. 1973. *The language of psycho-analysis*. New York: Norton.

Leavy, S. 1986. A Pascalian meditation on psychoanalysis and religious experience. *Cross Currents* 36:147–55.

————. 1988. *In the image of God*. New Haven: Yale University Press.

————. 1990. Reality in religion and psychoanalysis. In *Psychoanalysis and the humanities*, ed. J. Smith, pp. 43–59. New Haven: Yale University Press.

Leibowitz, Y. 1975. *Judaism, the Jewish nation, and the State of Israel* [Hebrew.] Jerusalem: Shocken.

Leitman, L. 1982. Liberalism, perspectivism, chaotic fragmentalism, and psychotherapeutic technique. *British Journal of Medical Psychology* 55:307–17.

Levi, L. 1970. Toward a Torah-based psychology. *Proceedings of the Associations of Orthodox Jewish Scientists* 2:81–114.

————. 1979. Torah and secular studies: The humanities. *Proceedings of the Associations of Orthodox Jewish Scientists* 5:153–67.

————. 1981. *Sha'arei talmud Torah*. Jerusalem: Feldheim.

Levitz, I. 1979. Orthodoxy and mental health. *Journal of Psychology and Judaism* 4:87–99.

Levine, H. I. 1987. On the relation between law and exegesis. In *Studies in talmudic law and halakhic midrashim* [Hebrew], pp. 27–59. Ramat-Gan: Bar-Ilan University Press.

Lèvi-Strauss, C. 1949. The effectiveness of symbols. In *Structural anthropology*, trans. C. Jacobson and B. Schoepf, pp. 186–205. New York: Basic, 1963.

Levy, C. M. 1976. Personal values versus professional values. *Clinical Social Work* 4:110–20.

Lewis, H. B. 1971. *Shame and guilt in the neuroses*. New York: International Universities Press.

Lewis, H., and J. Brooks. 1975. Infants' social perception. In *Infant perception from sensation to cognition*, vol. 2, ed. L. B. Cohen and R. Salapatek, 362–70. New York: Academic.

Lichtenstein, A. 1963. Rabbi Joseph Soloveitchik. In *Great Jewish thinkers of the twentieth century*, ed. S. Noveck, pp. 281–97. New York: Bnai Brith.

————. 1975. Does Jewish tradition recognize an ethic independent of Halachah? In *Modern Jewish ethics*, ed. M. Fox, pp. 163–79. Columbus: Ohio State University.

Likierman, M. 1989. Clinical significance of aesthetic experience. *International Review of Psycho-Analysis* 16:133–50.

Linzer, N. 1979. A Jewish philosophy of social work practice. *Journal of Jewish Communal Service* 55:309–17.

Loewald, H. W. 1953. Psychoanalysis and modern views on human existence and religious experience. *Journal of Pastoral Care* 7:1–15.

————. 1988. *Sublimation*. New Haven: Yale University Press.

Loewenberg, F. M. 1988. *Religion and social work practice in contemporary American society*. New York: Columbia University Press.

London, P. 1964. *The modes and morals of psychotherapy*. New York: Holt, Rinehart, & Winston.

————. 1976. Psychotherapy for religious neuroses? *Journal of Consulting and Clinical Psychology* 44: 145–47.

Lovinger, R. 1984. *Working with religious issues in psychotherapy*. New York: Aronson.

Lytton, S. 1984. Values judgments in psychoanalytic thought and theory. *Journal of the American Psychoanalytic Association* 32: 147–56.

Maeder, A. 1955. A new concept of the psychotherapist's role. *Journal of Psychotherapy as a Religious Process* 2: 38–46.

Mahler, M. S. 1971. A study of the separation-individuation process and its possible application to borderline phenomena in the psychoanalytic situation. *Psychoanalytic Study of the Child* 26: 403–24.

————, F. Pine, and A. Bergman. 1975. *The psychological birth of the human infant*. New York: Basic Books.

Marmor, J. 1960. The reintegration of psychoanalysis into psychiatric practice. *Archives of General Psychiatry* 3: 569–74.

Masling, J., ed. 1983. *Empirical studies of psychoanalytic theories*, vol. 1. Hillsdale, N.J.: Analytic Press.

————. 1986. *Empirical studies of psychoanalytic theories*, vol. 2. Hillsdale, N.J.: Analytic Press.

Maslow, A. 1954. *Toward a psychology of being*. New York: Van Nostrand.

Masson, J. M., ed. 1985. *The complete letters of Sigmund Freud to Wilhelm Fliess, 1887–1904*. Cambridge: Harvard University Press.

May, R. 1953. *Man's search for himself*. New York: W. W. Norton.

————. 1961. The emergence of existential psychology. In *Existential psychology*, ed. R. May, pp. 10–24. New York: Random House.

————, A. Angel, and H. Ellenberger. 1958. *Existential psychiatry*. New York: Random House.

————, and A. van Kamm. 1963. Existential theory and therapy. In *Current psychiatric therapies*, vol. 3, ed. J. Masserman, pp. 74–81. New York: Grune & Stratton.

McDargh, J. 1983. *Psychoanalytic object relations theory and the study of religion*. Lanham, Md.: University Press of America.

————. 1991. Concluding clinical postscript: On developing a psychotheological perspective. In *A clinical case approach to religious experience in psychotherapy*, ed. M. L. Randour, pp. 243–60. New York: Columbia University Press.

McKeowan, B. F. 1976. Identification and projection in religious belief. In *Psychoanalysis and contemporary science*, vol. 5, ed. T. Shapiro, pp. 479–510. New York: International Universities Press.

Meehl, P. 1959. Some technological and axiological problems in the therapeutic handling of religious and valuational material. *Journal of Consulting Psychology* 6:254–59.

Meier, L. 1988. *Jewish values in psychotherapy.* New York: University Press of America.

Meissner, W. W. 1978. Psychoanalytic aspects of religious experience. *The Annual of Psychoanalysis* 6:103–41.

———. 1981. *Internalization in psychoanalysis.* New York: International Universities Press.

———. 1984. *Psychoanalysis and religious experience.* New Haven: Yale University Press.

Mendez, A., and H. Fine. 1976. A short history of the British school of object relations and ego psychology. *Bulletin of the Menninger Clinic* 40:357–82.

Meng, H., and E. L. Freud. 1963. *Psychoanalysis and faith: The letters of Sigmund Freud and Oskar Pfister.* New York: Basic Books.

Mermelstein, J. 1976. Halachic values and the clinical practice of psychotherapy. *Intercom* 16:4–9.

Mester, R., and H. Klein. 1981. The young Jewish revivalist. *British Journal of Medical Psychology* 54:299–306.

Milner, M. 1969. *The hands of the living God.* London: Hogarth.

Modell, A. 1963. The concept of psychic energy. *Journal of the American Psychoanalytic Association* 11:605–18.

Montefiore, C. 1904. The rabbinic conception of repentance. *Jewish Quarterly Review* 16:209–57.

Moore, B., and B. Fine. 1968. *A glossary of psychoanalytic terms and concepts.* New York: American Psychoanalytic Association.

Moxon, C. 1931. Freud's denial of religion. *British Journal of Medical Psychology* 11:152–58.

Noveck, S. 1956. *Judaism and psychiatry.* New York: Basic Books.

Novey, S. 1957. Utilization of social institutions as a defense in the neuroses. *International Journal of Psycho-Analysis* 38:82–91.

———. 1960. Considerations on religion in relation to psychoanalysis and psychotherapy. *Journal of Nervous and Mental Disease* 130:315–24.

Nuttin, J. 1962. *Psychoanalysis and personality.* Chicago: Mentor.

Oden, T. 1967. *Contemporary theology and psychotherapy.* Philadelphia: Westminster Press.

Ogden, T. 1984. Instinct, phantasy, and psychological deep structure: A reinterpretation of aspects of the work of Melanie Klein. *Contemporary Psychoanalysis* 20:500–25.

Olinick, S. L. 1959. The analytic paradox. *Psychiatry* 22:333–39.

Ostow, M. 1977. The psychologic determinants of Jewish identity. *Israel Annals of Psychiatry and Related Disciplines* 15:313–35.

———. 1982. *Judaism and psychoanalysis.* New York: Ktav.

———. 1986. Archetypes of apocalypse in dreams and fantasies, and in religious scripture. *Israeli Journal of Psychiatry and Related Sciences* 23:107–22.

———, and B.-A. Scharfstein. 1954. *The need to believe.* New York: International Universities Press.

Ostrov, S. 1976. A family therapist's approach to working with orthodox Jewish clientele. *Journal of Jewish Communal Service* 53 : 147–54.

Otto, R. 1917. *The idea of the holy,* trans. J. Harvey. New York: Oxford University Press.

Outler, A. 1954. *Psychotherapy and the Christian message.* New York: Harper.

Pachter, M. 1972. *The writings of Rabbi Israel Salanter* [Hebrew.] Jerusalem: Olamot.

————. 1985. The conception of repentance in the thought of Rabbi Yisrael Salanter and the Musar movement. [Hebrew.] In *Orot Jubilee: The thought of Rabbi Abraham Issac ha-Cohen Kuk,* ed. B. Ish-Shalom and S. Rosenberg, pp. 257–76. Jerusalem: AviChai/World Zionist Federation.

Patai, R. 1977. *The Jewish mind.* New York: Scribner's.

Pattison, E. M. 1978a. Psychiatry and religion circa 1978: Part I. *Pastoral Psychology* 27 : 8–25.

————. 1978b. Psychiatry and religion circa 1978: Part II. *Pastoral Psychology* 27 : 119–41.

————, ed. 1969. *Clinical psychiatry and religion.* Boston: Little, Brown.

Penfield, W. 1974. The mind and the highest brain mechanism. *American Scholar* 43 : 237–46.

Perez, L. 1977. The messianic psychotic patient. *Israel Annals of Psychiatry and Related Disciplines* 15 : 364–74.

Peteet, J. 1981. Issues in the treatment of religious patients. *American Journal of Psychotherapy* 35 : 559–64.

————. 1985. Clinical intersections between the religion of the psychiatrist and his patients. In *Psychotherapy of the religious patient,* ed. M. H. Spero, pp. 63–84. Springfield, Ill.: Charles C. Thomas.

Philp, H. L. 1958. *Jung and the problem of evil.* New York: Longman, Green.

Piaget, J. 1937. *The construction of reality in the child.* New York: Basic, 1954.

————. 1945. *Play, dreams, and imitation in childhood.* New York: Norton, 1951.

————, and B. Inhelder. 1948. *The child's conception of space.* New York: W. W. Norton, 1967 reprint.

Plaut, E. A. 1986. Quality of object relations: The psychoanalytic value system. *Annual of Psychoanalysis* 14 : 207–19.

Post, S. C., ed. 1972. *Moral values and the superego concept in psychoanalysis.* New York: International Universities Press.

Progoff, I. 1956. *The death and rebirth of psychology.* New York: Julian Press.

Propst, L. R. 1987. *Psychotherapy in a religious framework.* New York: Human Sciences Press.

Pruyser, P. 1960. Some trends in the psychology of religion. *Journal of Religion* 40 : 113–29.

————. 1971. Assessment of the psychiatric patient's religious attitudes in the psychiatric case study. *Bulletin of the Menninger Clinic* 35 : 272–91.

————. 1974. *Between belief and unbelief.* New York: Harper & Row.

————. 1977. The seamy side of current religious beliefs. *Bulletin of the Menninger Clinic* 41 : 329–40.

————. 1983. *The play of the imagination: Toward a psychoanalysis of culture.* New York: International Universities Press.

————. 1985. Forms and functions of the imagination in religion. *Bulletin of the Menninger Clinic* 49:353–70.

Rabinowitz, N. E. 1991. All of Israel are responsible [*ar'eivim*] one for the other [Hebrew]. *Tehumin* 11:41–72.

Rachlis, A. 1974. The mussar movement and psychotherapy. *Judaism* 23: 337–45.

Rachman, S, ed. 1963. *Critical essays on psychoanalysis.* New York: Macmillan.

Ragland-Sullivan, E. 1986. *Jacques Lacan and the philosophy of psychoanalysis.* Chicago: University of Illinois.

Randour, M. L., and J. Bondanza. 1987. The concept of God in the psychological formation of females. *Psychoanalytic Psychology* 4:301–13.

Rank, O. 1941. *Beyond psychology.* Camden: Hadden Craftsmen.

————. 1950. *Psychology and the soul.* Philadelphia: University of Pennsylvania Press.

Rapaport, D. 1951. *The organization and pathology of thought.* New York: Columbia University Press.

————. 1967. *The collected papers of David Rapaport,* ed. M. Gill. New York: Basic.

Reik, T. 1951. *Dogma and compulsion.* New York: International Universities Press.

Richards, G. 1989. *On psychological language.* London: Routledge.

Ricoeur, P. 1970. *Freud and philosophy: An essay on interpretation.* New Haven: Yale University Press.

Rieff, P. 1966. *The triumph of the therapeutic: Uses of faith after Freud.* New York: Harper & Row.

Rizzuto, A.-M. 1974. Object relations and the formation of the image of God. *British Journal of Medical Psychology* 47:83–99.

————. 1976. Freud, God, and the devil and the theory of object representations. *International Review of Psycho-Analysis* 31:165–70.

————. 1979. *The birth of the living God.* Chicago: University of Chicago Press.

————. 1982. The father and the child's representations of God. In *Father and child,* ed. S. Cath, A. Gurwitt, and J. Munder Ross, pp. 357–82. Boston: Little, Brown.

Roberts, C. W. 1989. Imagining God: Who is created in whose image? *Review of Religious Research* 30:375–86.

Rockowitz, R., J. Korpela, and K. Hunter. 1981. Social work dilemma—When religion and medicine clash. *Health and Social Work* 6:5–11.

Rogers, C. R., and R. Dymond. 1954. *Psychology and personality change.* Chicago: University of Chicago Press.

Rosenfeld, H. 1987. *Impasse and interpretation.* London: Routledge.

Rosenthal, G. S. 1990. Omnipotence, omniscience, and the finite God. *Judaism* 39:54–72.

Rubenstein, B. 1967. Explanation and mere description: A metascientific examination of certain aspects of psychoanalytic theory of motivation. In *Motives and thought*, ed. R. Holt, pp. 18–77. New York: International Universities Press.

Rubins, J. 1955. Neurotic attitudes toward religion. *American Journal of Psychoanalysis* 5:71–81.

Rubinstein, R. 1968. *The religious imagination*. New York: Bobbs-Merrill.

Rudnytsky, P. 1989. Winnicott and Freud. *Psychoanalytic Study of the Child* 44:331–50.

Rychlak, J. 1977. *The psychology of rigorous humanism*. New York: Wiley.

Saari, C. 1986. *Clinical social work treatment*. New York: Gardner.

Salzman, L. 1953. The psychology of religious and ideological conversion. *Psychiatry* 16:177–87.

Samuelson, N. 1969. On knowing God: Maimonides, Gersonides, and the philosophy of religion. *Judaism* 18:64–77.

Sand, G. 1854. The history of my life, trans. M. Joel. In *Studies of childhood*, ed. J. Sully, pp. 46–59. New York: Longmans, Green.

Sandler, J. 1960. The background of safety. *International Journal of Psychoanalysis* 41:352–56.

———, and B. Rosenblatt. 1962. The concept of the representational world. *Psychoanalytic Study of the Child* 17:128–58.

Saussure, F. de 1916. *Course in general linguistics*, ed. C. Bally and A. Sechehaye, trans. W. Baskin. New York: McGraw-Hill, 1966, reprint.

Schafer, R. 1968. *Aspects of internalization*. New York: International Universities Press.

———. 1983. *The analytic alliance*. New York: Basic Books.

Schechter, S. 1909. *Aspects of rabbinic theology*. New York: Macmillan.

Schimmel, H., and A. Carmel. 1989. *Encounter: Essays on Torah and modern life*. Jerusalem: Feldheim.

Schimmel, S. 1977. Free-will, guilt, and self-control. *Judaism* 26:418–29.

Schindler, R. 1987. Intergenerational theories in social work intervention with religious Jewish families. *Journal of Social Work and Policy in Israel* 1:99–114.

Schleiermacher, F. D. E. 1830. *The Christian faith*, trans. H. R. Mackintosh and J. S. Stewart. Edinburgh: T. & T. Clark, 1928, reprint.

Searles, H. 1979. *Countertransference and related subjects*. New York: International Universities Press.

Sevensky, R. 1984. Religion, psychology, and mental health. *American Journal of Psychotherapy* 38:73–86.

Shaffir, W. 1983. The recruitment of baʿalei teshuvah in a Jerusalem yeshiva. *Jewish Journal of Sociology* 25:33–46.

———, and R. Rockaway. 1987. Leaving the ultraorthodox fold: Haredi Jews who defected. *Jewish Journal of Sociology* 24:97–114.

Schafranske, E., and H. N. Malony. 1990. Clinical psychologists' religious and spiritual orientations and their practice of psychotherapy. *Psychotherapy* 27:72–78.

Shands, H. 1970. Momentary deity and personal myth. *Semiotica* 2:1–34.

Shihor, R. 1978. On the problem of Halacha's status in Judaism. *Forum* 30–31:146–54.

Shokek, S. 1985. "In the place where *ba'alei teshuvah* stand." [Hebrew.] In *Orot Jubilee: The thought of Rabbi Abraham Issac ha-Cohen Kuk*, ed. B. Ish-Shalom and S. Rosenberg, pp. 245–56. Jerusalem: AviChai/World Zionist Federation.

Siegel, S. 1977. Jewish law and Jewish ethics. In *Conservative Judaism and Jewish law*, pp. 124–32. New York: Ktav.

Silberer, H. 1912. On symbol formation. In *Organization and pathology of thought*, ed. D. Rapaport, pp. 208–33. New York: Columbia University Press, 1951.

———. 1914. *Problems of mysticism and its symbolism*. New York: Macmillan, 1917.

Singer, E. 1979. The function of analytic anonymity. In *The human dimension in psychoanalytic practice*, ed. K. Frank, pp. 36–46. New York: Grune & Stratton.

Singer, M. T. 1979. Coming out of cults. *Psychology Today* 12:79–81.

Sinsheimer, R. 1969. The existential casework relationship. *Social Casework* 50:67–73.

Slawson, P. 1973. Treatment of a clergyman: Anxiety neurosis in a celibate. *American Journal of Psychotherapy* 27:52–60.

Smart, N. 1962. *Historical selections in the philosophy of religion*. New York: Harper & Row.

Smith, J. 1978. The psychoanalytic understanding of freedom. *Journal of the American Psychoanalytic Association* 26:87–107.

Solomon, A. 1973. Eros-Thanatos: A modification of Freudian instinct theory in the light of Torah teachings. *Tradition* 14:90–102.

Solomon, R. C. 1974. Freud's neurological theory of mind. In *Freud*, ed. R. Wollheim, pp. 25–52. New York: Anchor.

Soloveitchik, J. B. 1944a. *The halakhic mind*. New York: Free Press/Seth, 1986 reprint.

———. 1944b. *Ish ha-Halakhah: Galui va-Nistar* ["Halakhic man"], *Talpiot*, 1:651–735.

———. 1965. The lonely man of faith. *Tradition* 7:5–67.

———. 1971. Imitating God—The basis of Jewish morality [Reconstructed by A. R. Besdin]. In *Reflections of the Rav*, ed. A. R. Besdin, pp. 23–30. New York: World Zionist Association, 1981 reprint.

———. 1976. *Be-sod ha-yaḥid ve'ha-yiḥud*. ["In aloneness, in togetherness".] Jerusalem: Orot.

———. 1978. Redemption, prayer, talmud Torah. *Tradition* 17:55–72.

———. 1979. *U-bikashtem misham*. In *Ish ha-Halakhah: Galu'ui ve-nistar*, pp. 117–235. Jerusalem: World Zionist Organization.

———. 1980. *On repentance*, ed. P. Peli. Jerusalem: Orot.

Sosevsky, M. 1976. The lonely man of faith confronts the *Ish ha-Halakhah*. *Tradition* 16:73–89.

Spence, D. 1982. *Narrative truth and historical truth*. New York: Norton.

Spero, M. H. 1976. The critical review in psychology and Judaism. *Journal of Psychology and Judaism* 1:79–97.

———. 1977a. The critical review in psychology and Judaism. *Journal of Psychology and Judaism* 1:83–102.

———. 1977b. The critical review in psychology and Judaism. *Journal of Psychology and Judaism* 2:73–92.

———. 1977c. Halakhah as psychology: Explicating the laws of mourning. *Tradition* 16:172–84.

———. 1978. The critical review in psychology and Judaism. *Journal of Psychology and Judaism* 2:62–68.

———. 1980. *Judaism and psychology: Halakhic perspectives*. New York: Ktav/Yeshivah University.

———. 1982a. Psychotherapeutic procedure with religious cult devotees. *Journal of Nervous and Mental Disease* 170:332–44.

———. 1982b. The use of folklore as a developmental phenomenon among nouveaux-orthodox religionists. *American Journal of Psychoanalysis* 42:149–58.

———. 1983. Modern psychotherapy and Halakhic values. *Journal of Medicine and Philosophy* 8:287–316.

———. 1984. Shame. *Psychoanalytic Study of the Child* 39:259–82.

———. 1985. The reality and the image of God in psychotherapy. *American Journal of Psychotherapy* 39:75–85.

———. 1986. *Handbook of psychotherapy and Jewish ethics*. Jerusalem: Feldheim.

———. 1987a. The didactic-psychological function of three rabbinic blessings. *Proceedings of the Associations of Orthodox Jewish Scientists* 8–9:111–46.

———. 1987b. Identity and individuality in the nouveau-religious patient. *Psychiatry* 50:55–71.

———. 1989. Current trends in psychotherapy, clinical social work, and religious values. *Journal of Social Work and Policy in Israel* 2:81–110.

———. 1990a. Parallel dimensions of experience in psychoanalytic psychotherapy of the religious patient. *Psychotherapy* 27:53–71.

———. 1990b. Identification between the religious patient and therapist in social work and psychoanalytic psychotherapy. *Journal of Social Work and Policy in Israel* 3:83–98.

———, and R. Mester. 1988. Countertransference envy toward the religious patient. *American Journal of Psychotherapy* 48:43–55.

Spero, S. 1965. Judaism and the ontological argument. *Judaism* 14:44–56.

———. 1973. Is the God of Maimonides truly unknowable? *Judaism* 22:66–78.

———. 1980. Selfhood and godhood in Jewish thought and modern philosophy. *Tradition* 18:160–71.

———. 1983. *Morality, Halakha, and the Jewish tradition*. New York: Ktav/Yeshiva University Press.

Spiro, M. 1966. Religion: Problems of definition and explanation. In *Anthropological approaches to the study of religion*, ed. M. Banton, pp. 104–26. London: Tavistock.

Stamey, H. 1971. The "mad at God" syndrome. *American Journal of Psychotherapy* 25:93–103.

Stapleton, R. C. 1977. *The experience of inner healing*. Boston: G. K. Hale.

Stern, D. 1985. *The interpersonal world of the infant*. New York: Basic Books.

Stern, E. M., and B. Marino. 1970. *Psychotheology*. Paramus, N.J.: Paulist Press.

Stern, E. M. 1985. *Psychotherapy of the religiously committed patient*. New York: Haworth.

Stolorow, R. and G. Atwood. 1973. Messianic projects and early object relationships. *American Journal of Psychoanalysis* 33:213–15.

Stone, L. 1981. Some thoughts on the "here and now" in psychoanalytic technique and practice. *Psychoanalytic Quarterly* 50:709–31.

Strupp, H. 1968. Psychoanalytic therapy of the individual. In *Modern psychoanalysis*, ed. J. Marmor, pp. 293–342. New York: Basic Books.

———. 1983. Psychoanalytic psychotherapy. In *The clinical psychology handbook*, ed. M. Hersen, A. Kazdin, and A. Bellak, pp. 471–88. New York: Pergamon.

Tarachow, S. 1963. *An introduction to psychotherapy*. New York: International Universities Press.

Taylor, G. R. 1979. *The natural history of the mind*. New York: Dutton.

Tendler, M. 1969. Halachic and scientific categories. *Gesher* 4:83–95.

Tillich, P. 1953. *Systematic theology*. London: James Nisbet & Co.

———. 1958. Psychoanalysis, existentialism, and theology. In *Theology of culture*, ed. R. Kimball, pp. 112–27. Oxford: Oxford University Press, 1959, reprint.

Tolpin, M. 1971. On the beginnings of a cohesive self. *Psychoanalytic Study of the Child* 26:316–52.

Tustin, F. 1981. *Autistic states in children*. Boston: Routledge & Kegan Paul.

Tyrrell, B. 1975. *Christo-therapy*. New York: Paulist Press.

Urbach, E. A. 1984. *The Halakhah: Its sources and development*. Jerusalem: Massadah.

Vande Kemp, H. 1985. Psychotherapy as a religious process. In *Psychotherapy and the religiously committed patient*, ed. M. Stern, pp. 135–46. New York: Haworth Press.

Van Kamm, A. 1985. Formation counseling. In *Psychotherapy of the religiously committed patient*, ed. E. M. Stern, pp. 89–106. New York: Haworth Press.

van der Leeuw, G. 1963. *Sacred and profane beauty*, trans. D. Green. New York: Holt, Rinehart, & Winston.

Vergote, A. 1988. *Guilt and desire: Religious attitudes and their pathological derivations*, trans. M. Wood. New Haven: Yale University Press.

Vogel, L. 1975. Freud and Judaism: An analysis in the light of his correspondence. *Judaism* 24:181–94.

Von Eckardt, E. 1982. The scientific status of psychoanalysis. In *Introducing psychoanalytic theory*, ed. S. Gilman, pp. 139–80. New York: Brunner/Mazel.

Waelder, R. 1936. The problem of freedom in psychoanalysis and the problem of reality-testing. *International Journal of Psycho-Analysis* 17:89–108.

Wallerstein, R. 1989. The psychotherapy research project of the Menninger Foundation. *Journal of Consulting and Clinical Psychology* 57:197–205.

Wangh, M. 1962. The "evocation of a proxy": A psychological maneuver, its uses as a defense, its purposes and its genesis. *Psychoanalytic Study of the Child* 17:451–69.

———. 1988. The genetic sources of Freud's difference with Romain Rolland on the matter of religious feelings. In *Fantasy, myth, and reality*, ed. H. Blum, Y. Kramer, A. K. Richards, and A. D. Richards, pp. 259–86. Madison, CT.: International Universities Press.

Wapnick, K. 1985. Forgiveness: A spiritual psychotherapy. In *Psychotherapy and the religiously committed patient*, ed. E. M. Stern, pp. 47–54. New York: Haworth Press.

Weiner, I. B., ed. 1976. *Clinical methods in psychology.* New York: John Wiley.

Weisbord, A., M. Sherman, and B. A. Hodinko. 1988. Impact on precounseling information. *Journal of Psychology and Judaism* 12:60–78.

Welkowitz, J., J. Cohen, and D. Ortmeyer. 1967. Value system similarity. *Journal of Consulting Psychology* 31:48–55.

Wellisch, E. 1954. *Isaac and Oedipus.* London: Routledge & Kegan Paul.

Wikler, M. 1979. Fine-tuning: Diagnostic techniques used by orthodox Jewish patients. *Journal of Psychology and Judaism* 3:184–94.

———. 1982. Another look at the diagnosis and treatment of orthodox Jewish family problems. *Journal of Psychology and Judaism* 7:42–53.

———. 1986. Pathways to treatment: How orthodox Jews enter therapy. *Social Casework* 67:113–18.

Wilden, A. 1981. *Speech, language, and psychoanalysis.* Baltimore: Johns Hopkins.

Wile, P. 1977. Ideological conflicts between psychotherapist and patient. *American Journal of Psychotherapy* 31:437–41.

Will, Jr., O. A. 1979. Comment on the professional life of the psychotherapist. *Contemporary Psychoanalysis* 15:560–76.

Williams, D. D. 1961. *The minister and the care of souls.* New York: Harper & Row.

Winnicott, D. W. 1953. Transitional objects and transitional phenomena. *International Journal of Psycho-Analysis* 34:89–97.

———. 1958. *Collected papers: Through paediatrics to psycho-analysis.* London: Tavistock.

———. 1963. Morals and education. In *The maturational processes and the facilitating environment.* Madison, Conn.: International Universities Press, 1965 reprint.

———. 1971. *Playing and reality.* London: Tavistock.

Witztum, E., D. Greenberg, and J. T. Buchbinder. 1990. "A very narrow bridge": Diagnosis and management of mental illness among Bratslav hasidim. *Psychotherapy* 27:124–31.

Witztum, E., D. Greenberg, and H. Dasberg. 1990. Mental illness and religious change. *British Journal of Medical Psychology* 63:33–43.

Wolberg, L. 1977. *The technique of psychotherapy.* New York: Grune & Stratton.

Wulff, J. A. 1971. *Torat ha-nefesh be-aspaklariah Toratit.* (The theory of the soul in a Torah perspective.) [Hebrew.] Bnai Brak: Eshel.

Wurzburger, W. 1962. Metahalakhic propositions. In *The Leo Jung jubilee volume,* ed. M. M. Kasher, N. Lamm, and L. Rosenfeld, pp. 211–22. New York: Shulsinger Bros.

Yogev, A., and J. El-Dor. 1987. Attitudes and tendencies toward return to Judaism among Israeli adolescents. *Jewish Journal of Sociology* 29 : 5–17.

Zilboorg, G. 1967. *Psychoanalysis and religion.* London: George Allen & Unwin.

Index